# LANGUAGE

# AND

# MEANING

**Robert C. O'Hara**
*University of South Florida*

KENDALL/HUNT PUBLISHING COMPANY
2460 Kerper Boulevard  P.O. Box 539  Dubuque, Iowa 52004-0539

Copyright© 1993 by Kendall/Hunt Publishing Company

ISBN 0-8403-8600-1

Library of Congress Number: 93-78412

Printed in the United States of America
10 9 8 7 6 5 4 3 2 1

# CONTENTS

# INTRODUCTION

A student assigned to write a report on the book, *The Care and Feeding of Minks*, ended by saying: "This book told me more about minks than I would really care to know." The purpose of this book is not to tell you more than you would care to know about the subject of language and meaning. Rather, its intent is to open up this complex subject.

Also, the material is not developed following one particular school of either linguistics or semantics. Rather, it will examine aspects of the subject in a general manner [which will not be pleasing to either the linguist or the semanticist] in the belief that you will be stimulated to think, discuss, and perhaps read further on the subject.

The materials began in a sophomore-junior level course designed to meet the interests of those who wished to know more about language and meaning but did not want to explore the topic in the detail that would be necessary in a course in linguistics or semantics. It evolved into its present form over a period of fifteen years. The pattern of organization also evolved through the process of trial and error. It became evident that there were many misconceptions about language and meaning. The logical place to begin was with a look at statements about language and meaning which are accepted as having validity, but which, in reality, are wrong headed.

Having looked at what language and meaning isn't, the next task was to look at what language is. That is, to examine some of the finding of neurolinguistics. Here the verdict is still out on how the brain processes language. The generalizations made, while sometimes stated as fact, are in reality educated guesses. As more is learned about how the brain processes language, revisions will of necessity have to be made. Indeed, there is disagreement among neurolinguists about some of the present findings.

With this as a base, the discussion moves to the functions of language in two areas: perception and social. Are we prisoners of our language or does it simply habituate us to perceive the world and those around us in certain terms? To what extent does society and the various social groups we interact with influence our language behavior? And, conversely, to what degree does this influence our view of ourselves and those around us?

The discussion of language as a sign and symbol system is admittedly an oversimplification but if one is to reach an operational definition of language, the topic must be opened up because language is both a sign and a symbol system. Obviously, books have been written on the nature of signs and symbols. The justification for using a simplistic approach is that this is a means to an end, not an end in itself.

From here it is then possible to move to a consideration of the metaphor as a means of communicating the unknown or unfamiliar through a comparison with the known or the familiar. It follows that some metaphors are "dominant" in a language. That is, they influence our perception of the world in subtle ways primarily because they contain secondary metaphors which are implied rather than explicitly stated.

Some consideration is given to how words are formed, not in the morphological sense but the various ways they are created. This leads to discussion of how past events and changes in our society have influenced both the meanings of words as well as the ways in which they reflect our society.

While it may appear to be a subject that should have been taken up earlier, meaning follows more naturally at this point. First, an examination of the problem of trying to define meaning and then a look at both how meanings change and why they do.

Taboos influence not only the choice of language but the attitudes of people about the appropriateness, or inappropriateness, of that choice. Here two areas dominate. The first is the "grammatical" taboos generated as a result of the eighteenth century attempts to "fix" and "ascertain" the language. The second is cultural. Society's attitudes toward certain subjects such as sex and body functions which limits one's choice of words in certain social situations.

Because of taboos, we must euphemize. When we euphemize, we raise the level of abstraction. The higher the level of abstraction the greater the likelihood of obscuring, perhaps even obliterating, meaning. We "label" things and this leads to distortion. The discussion here centers on Gordon Alport's "Basic Pattern of Distortion" and what he calls "labels of primarily potency."

While it may appear to be "wedged" at this point, some consideration of standards, styles, and keys of discourse fits. There must be "rules" which govern the choice of words as well as sentences in given social situations.

Thus far, the discussion has examined language and meaning without a proper consideration of the fact that they are communicated primary through speaking. Three factors must be looked at: the intonation of the voice, kinesics or the use of facial expressions as well as body movement to influence meaning, and finally, proxemics or space and distance as a factors in controlling meaning.

This exploration of the aspects of language and meaning concludes with first examining the question of the racist and sexist potential of language and some of its implications. Finally, a consideration of the implications of manipulating language and meaning for various purposes.

Most of the sources cited are "dated" in the sense that some of them are several decades old. For the benefit of those who believe that currency of publication is a necessary criterion for the citation of authority, let me assure them that the literature in these areas has been reviewed. It is sometimes the case that little of substance has been added to earlier discussions. For example, Paul Lazersfeld and Thomas Merton's "Mass Communication, Popular Taste, and Organization," although now some forty years old, has not been superseded in its conclusions, merely elaborated on. Unless there was something substantive, I opted to go with the earlier works.

While I alone am responsible for both the organization of the material as well as its presentation, others have contributed in ways even they may not be aware. I am indebted to Roger Cole, a colleague for many years, who encouraged me to develop these materials. To John Broderick of Old Dominion for critiquing my presentation and organization. To Tom Wilson, Director of the Open University at the University of South Florida, who smoothed the transition from notes to television scripts. Posthumous recognition must be made of Thomas Dilkes who argued with me and set my head straight on issues involved both with symbols as well as metaphors and to John Camp, a true eccentric, who added much to my appreciation of a number of subjects. Both left us far too soon.

*Robert C. O'Hara*

# MISCONCEPTIONS ABOUT LANGUAGE AND MEANING

*"The next time someone calls you that, tell them: 'Sticks and stones may break my bones but words will never hurt me.'"*

*"I don't care what anyone says about me as long as they spell my name correctly."*

Both speakers have one thing in common. Neither, apparently, fears language and what language can do. Others believe the opposite. In his article, "The Nemesis of Authority," Robert Nisbitt writes:

> *Nothing so aids the advance and corruption of authority as does the prior degradation of not merely the ideas but also the words and phrases making up a language. . . . A generation that has formed itself linguistically around the primitivism of "like," "cool," "man," "feel," and above all "you know" will not be a difficult generation to enslave politically, socially, and culturally. Weaken, corrupt, dissolve the authority of language and the rest follows rather easily.*

So, we have contrasting views about the power of language. But before discussing "language" and the power it may or may not have, there must be some understanding of the nature of the beast. We will begin by looking at some of the things we do know and don't know about language.

To do this, we must examine bits and pieces and try to fit them into a picture, almost like working a jigsaw puzzle. The important thing to remember is that these pieces are parts of a whole and it is only as they are assembled that the picture emerges. Further, no one piece is more significant than another. Unlike mathematics where the whole is equal to the sum of its parts, with language, the whole is always more important. Why? **Language MEANS in a way quite different from the way mathematics MEANS.**

Because language is so much a part of our daily routine, we take it for granted. Most of the time we don't even stop to think about it. Or, if we do, we frequently think about it in a superficial way. When this happens, "misconceptions" about language and meaning take root. Misconceptions are popularly held beliefs incapable of verification but which seem to have validity. Here are just a few which surround language and meaning.

## Language means exactly what is said or written.

How wrong this is can be easily shown. Have you ever had someone misinterpret something you said? Your reply is, "But that's not what I meant to say." One reply to this might be, "If that's not what you meant to say, why did you say it?" We are all familiar with a politician who after making a speech must either interpret what he said or have someone else attempt to do it for him.

*"Have you got the time?"*

What does this mean? In one context, it might be telling someone to quit stalling and attend to business. If addressed to a person of the opposite sex, it could be taken as a proposition. This apparently simple question can mean many different things depending on the context.

Anyone who believes that language means exactly what is said (or written) is one of those types referred to by Nisbitt. If language meant exactly what was said, then there would be very little confusion; everyone would understand. But language is no more perfect than the world within which it operates.

## There is a single source for the origin of language.

We do not know where, when, or how language evolved although *Genesis 11:1* tells us, "And the whole world was of one language and one speech." Later, in *Genesis 11:7*, God says, observing the construction of the Tower of Babel, "Go to, let us go down, and there confound their language that they may not understand one another's speech."

But this is a parable and parables are not meant to be taken literally. Rather, they are intended to convey in a brief form something complex and, therefore, not easily understood. The story of the Tower of Babel is a "theory" which is intended to explain how the diversity of languages we find in the world came about.

There are any number of ingenious theories purporting to explain the origins of language. One of the more persistent is commonly called "The Bow-Wow Theory." According to it, humans were first set on the path of language by imitating the sounds of animals — all creatures great and small. IF this theory were true, then we might reasonably expect the sounds believed to be characteristic of a given animal to be the same or very similar in languages around the world.

English speakers hear their dogs as making the sounds, "bow-wow." But the Chinese hear their dogs as "wang-wang." English sheep go "baa" but the Chinese hear this as "meih" in contrast to German sheep and goats who utter "meck-meck." Our insects "buzz" but the Chinese hear "weng-weng."

There are other theories about the origins of human language: "The Ding-Dong Theory" is essentially the same as "The Bow-Wow" but incorporates other "natural" sounds such as those made when the wind blows or the waves hit the shore. There is also "The Yo-He-Ho" and its variant, "The Whistle and Grunt." Both attribute language to the sounds of exertion made while either working or trying to get attention.

The names are an indication of what serious students of language origins think about them. All theories of language, and some are deceptively clever, are equally suspect. First, they account only for single words. And, as shown, words for the same thing vary from one language to another. One of the requirements of a workable theory is that it enables you to account for examples not considered when the theory was formed. If it can't, then the theory has a rather large hole. So you had best modify your theory or search for a new one that leaks less.

There is another problem with these theories. They do not explain how humans moved from single words into more complex levels such as the phrase, the clause, and the sentence. Since these are not equivalent in all languages then offering something as simplistic as "The Bow-Wow Theory" tries to explain too much with too little.

Will we ever be able to determine the origins of human language? Probably not. But the attempts continue. For a number of years the French Academy of Sciences refused to publish papers dealing with this subject. Only recently have they started to accept them. So the arguments are once again flying.

There are two camps. One is usually referred to as the "monogenesis" or "monogenetic" and the other as the "polygenesis" or the "polygenetic." The former argues for the single source while the latter holds for multiple origins.

Look at the following words for male and female parents:

| English | father | mother |
|---------|--------|--------|
| German | Vater | Mutter |
| Dutch | vader | moeder |
| Swedish | fader | moder |
| French | pere | mere |
| Spanish | padre | madre |
| Italian | padre | madre |
| Portuguese | pai | mae |

The similarities would seem to argue for a monogenetic theory. But these similarities are deceiving. When there are systematic similarities in sounds, vocabulary, and grammar, we say that such languages are members of a "family." So the examples listed indicate they are related. There are many "families" of languages in the world. While the members of a family will have similarities, there are few, sometimes none, between families. And the few similarities that one may find are the result of accident and not part of some grand design. The examples listed are representative of the Indo-European family: English, German, Dutch, and

Swedish are members of the Germanic (or Teutonic) branch while French, Spanish, Italian, and Portuguese belong to the Italic (or Romance).

There are languages which have little or no systematic resemblance in sounds, vocabulary, and grammar to those classified as Indo-European. If at one time in the past there had been a common parent from which all languages evolved, we should be able to demonstrate it. But we cannot! So we do not know when, where, or how human language evolved. Anyone, therefore, is free to develop a theory. All they have to do is provide sound evidence for its acceptance and convince skeptics to accept it.

## Language doesn't change.

Some believe that language is, or should be, a fixed thing. Further, when a change occurs that change is "bad"—if not subversive. This attitude is seen in some critics' reaction to Webster's *Third International Dictionary*, better known as the "Unabridged," when it was published September 28, 1951.

"The Death of Meaning" was the opinion of the Toronto *Globe and Mail*. *Life* magazine termed it "A Non-Word Deluge." So did the American Bar Association *Journal* as well as terming it "Logomacy - Debased Verbal Currency." The Washington *Post* advised readers to "Keep Your Old Websters." The Richmond *News Leader* believed "Webster's Lays an Egg." While the *Atlantic Monthly* viewed the publication as "Sabotage in Springfield." *Time-Life* publications banned the new edition from its offices and reportedly bought a quantity of the second edition for future use.

What had Dr. Philip Gove, the senior editor of Webster's 3, and his colleagues, done to create such a furor? First, they dropped a number of words from the third edition; they were accused of throwing the words out of the language. But with what frequency are words such as "dethronize," "disagreeance," "ridiculize," and "subsign" used either when speaking or writing? The words were not "thrown out" by the editors but by the users of the language simply because people stopped using them. One has only to look at Joseph T. Shipley's *Dictionary of Early English* to appreciate how many words have drifted from the language over the centuries.

A second fault found with Webster 3 was the failure to apply "restrictive labels" such as "non-standard" or "slang" to certain word usages. "Wise up" should be labeled "slang" along with "dig" as in "I don't dig classical music." Or because "countdown" wasn't labeled "non-standard," a judgment that would be considered as peculiar today.

A third area the critics found wanting was the citation of contemporary persons as authorities on usage. It graveled them that in some instances entertainers, athletes, and politicians were given preference over Milton, Shakespeare, Shelley, and Wordsworth. Actually, these people were quoted to illustrate current practice not because they were "authorities" and knew more about language. Rather, they are prominent persons who are likely to have their use of the language attended to because it is reported through the various media.

Finally, many critics objected to the inclusion of a large number of words not found in Webster 2. Some felt that the new entries were either too scientific and specialized for inclusion or they were too colloquial or so current they had not stood the proverbial test of time. Among those objected to were "astronaut," "beatnik," and "sputnik."

Arguing whether Webster 3 is a "good" or a "bad" dictionary is a pointless exercise and about as productive as the critic who objected to the dictionary because its illustration of a "piggy bank" did not have a slot in which to drop coins. An overview of the "pro" and "con" positions can be found in James Sledd's *Dictionaries and THAT Dictionary.*

The question is, "Has the language been 'debased' by the changes printed in Webster 3?

One cannot usefully or rationally argue if change in a language is synonymous with "debasement." Change is an inevitable fact of life. And language is just as organic as the people who use it. Society changes and the language must change to reflect this. What functioned well in one time will not necessarily function in another. Look at a scholarly edition of Shakespeare and see the number of words that are "glossed." There is a note at the bottom of the page telling, approximately, what the word meant in Shakespeare's time. If this were not done, the present day reader would have great difficulty in understanding what is going on. Hamlet speaks of bearing "fardels" and making a "quietus" with a "bare bodkin." Today we would be at a loss to know what these meant unless the end notes told us they were a bundle of sticks, a leave-taking, and a dagger.

"Modernized" translations of the Bible are appearing. One reason is to bring the book more in line with current biblical scholarship. But another is to make it more assessable to the modern reader who does not always understand what some of the words mean, especially in the 1611 King James Version.

Grammatical and sound changes in a language take place slowly. Words and their meanings can change rapidly. English has changed so dramatically since 1000 A.D. that we must now study Old English (Anglo-Saxon) as though it were a foreign language. Today there are a number of forces which make change more difficult than in the past. Public education is no small factor in this. And to a degree, books and magazines preserve words and grammatical forms.

Despite this, change continues. This was evident some years ago when cigarette advertising was permitted on television and one brand stated that it "tasted good like a cigarette should." The objection was to the use of "like" as a conjunction. The grammar sharps said it should be "as." Such a protest ignores the evidence that "like" as a conjunction can be documented before Shakespeare. Similar battles are joined over the grammaticality of such words as "irregardless" and "hopefully." And don't forget those two suffixes "-ize" and "-wise" in words such as "finalize" and "weatherwise." Earlier, these suffixes were frequently used for deriving adverbs: "otherwise," "lengthwise." For some reason they fell into disfavor during the eighteenth century but are again becoming popular despite strenuous efforts of some to suppress them.

Language change cannot be stopped; it can only be slowed. Further, it is difficult to evaluate whether a change is "good" or "bad." These are value judgments. One, however, should not argue against setting standards for language use in given situations. In this sense, a word may be either appropriate or inappropriate to the occasion. But this has little to do with change.

To the degree that a change enables us to make more precise distinctions and think more clearly, then that change is desirable. To the degree that a change muddles precision and clouds thinking it is undesirable.

## One language is better than another.

Prior to and shortly after World War II, chemistry and physics majors were required to take courses in German. They did so because they were told, "German is the language of science." All this really meant was, at that time, most of the significant writing in those areas was in German and very little of it had been translated into English.

Similarly, at one time, diplomats were expected to be fluent in French because "French is the language of diplomacy." In the reign of Catherine the Great of Russia, French was the official court language. This, of course, was true prior to World War I because France had for some years been the major political force in Europe. This didn't mean that French was any better than another language. It was simply a matter of politics.

Today in chemistry, physics, and politics most of the significant work is published either in English or in Russian. These languages have not in some mysterious way become "better" for science and diplomacy. Their dominance is simply a reflection of scientific, political, and economic reality. They are "better" only in the sense they are the ones one must attend to.

**Each language, within the context of the culture using it, is a perfectly adequate vehicle for communication.** There is no recorded instance of a people giving up their language because they believed another was "better." A language which may be classified as "deficient" in one area will in all likelihood be more precise in another when comparisons are made.

Cultural anthropologists have demonstrated that our English kinship vocabulary (and that of the other members of the Indo-European family) is both inadequate and imprecise when compared to those found in some other languages. Once we get past "mother," "father," "son," "daughter," "brother," and "sister" you must start specifying which side of the family a kinship term refers to. Is your "aunt" your mother's or your father's sister? This also applies to grandparents, uncles, and cousins. Once we go back a generation, we have to append "great" to the designation.

Thus your father's father's father is your "great" grandfather. Your mother's father's father is also your "great" grandfather but on your mother's side. If we wish to go back generation after generation the "greats" start stacking up. The only conclusion we can reach from these examples is that we do not place a very high value on kinship beyond the third generation. By comparison with the kinship vocabularies of some other languages, English is not only primitive, it is practically in the Stone Age when it comes to kinship designations.

Whatever is important in a culture will be reflected in the language the culture uses. Will Rogers once observed, "We're all ignorant, just on different subjects." We can paraphrase this: "All languages are deficient but just in different areas." English is a better language for science and technology than that used by the Trobriand islanders simply because the Trobriand islanders have little need for a complex scientific and technological vocabulary. If they develop the need, they will acquire the vocabulary. Conversely, the Trobriand islanders have a very elaborate vocabulary for discussing yams and is, therefore, "better" for that subject. Should yams become vital to us, we will develop an elaborate yam vocabulary.

## Some languages are more "beautiful" than others.

A poet observed that beauty is in the eye of the beholder. This also holds true for languages. Some people will try to argue that French, Spanish, Italian, Greek, or even Urdu is more "beautiful" than English. A professor of Middle English told his classes that Chaucerian English was infinitely more beautiful during the thirteenth and fourteenth centuries than its modern form. For him the language had become "uglified" over the centuries.

Beauty is an esthetic concept. There is no objective way to prove, for example, that French is in any way more "beautiful" than English. You might just as profitably argue the reverse for all the good it will do. When you get into value judgments of this sort there is very little to recommend either side of the argument. If you wish to believe that one language is more beautiful than another then by all means do so. Just don't try to prove it.

## Some languages are more logical than others.

A Russian student constantly complained that English was an "illogical" language. He based his conclusion on the fact that English has articles (a, an, the) and Russian does not. Since he was constantly at a loss as to which one to select, and invariably it was not the appropriate one, he reasoned that any language which compelled its users to make such a choice was illogical.

In 1956 a group of Korean public officials came to the University of Minnesota to do graduate work in political science. This was the year of the second Eisenhower-Stevenson presidential campaign. They were convinced that Stevenson could never be elected but their reasoning had nothing to do with Eisenhower's great popularity. They argued that before a man can be head of his country, he must be head of his "canton." Stevenson qualified because he had been governor of Illinois. But before he can be head of his canton, he must be head of his village. They were willing to waive this criterion. But before a man can be head of his village, he must be head of his family. Stevenson was divorced, therefore, he was not the head of his family. Since he was not the head of his family there was no way he could be head of the nation.

The reasoning in both of these cases may strike us as "illogical." But within the contexts of Russian and Korean, these are perfectly "logical" conclusions. Before arguing if one language is more logical than another, give some thought to the fact that "logic" may be relative. What is apparently inconsistent from the perspective of one language may be perfectly consistent from the perspective of another.

## There is a relation between language and the national spirit of the people using it.

At one time it was popular to try and explain the military aggressiveness of the Germans in terms of the "harshness" of their language. Even the distinguished linguist Otto Jespersen in *The Growth and Structure of the English Language* contended that the speakers of French, Spanish, and Italian lack "vigor and energy" because of the nature of their languages. He also characterizes the natives of the South Pacific as "childlike" because of the number of vowel sounds in their language. Then in a burst of Teutonic chauvinism he concluded, "But how different are our Northern tongues. . . . Thus we may perhaps characterize English . . . as possessing male energy, but not brutal force . . . English is more masculine than other languages."

Dr. Jespersen, despite his undoubted expertise in other aspects of language studies, would have an impossible task trying to prove his case—especially to speakers of French, Spanish, and Italian. Just as in the argument that one language is more "beautiful" than another so it is with the contention that there is a correlation between language and national spirit. How does one define "harsh" sounds? Where is there proof that because a language has a large number of vowel sounds, when compared with another, that it then makes the speakers more "childlike?" There is no way to demonstrate objectively any correlation between language and the "national spirit" of a people.

## There is a correlation between race and language.

Some people believe there is a connection between the physical characteristics of a race and the ability (or inability) to use language in a given way. This usually centers on pronunciation. There is no difference between this argument and the one offered decades ago that whites are superior to blacks in intelligence because of brain size. A white pathologist of some note carefully weighed and measured the brains of deceased whites and blacks and on the basis of his data came to this conclusion. But it wasn't until years later that another pathologist discovered the data were deliberately manipulated to prove a preconceived theory. The truth, is you cannot tell one race from another simply by looking at the brain.

Similarly, you can arrange the vocal apparatus of a number of human beings and close inspection will reveal no racial differences among them. This fact has not prevented those who choose to believe what they wish to contend that blacks cannot pronounce certain sounds because of the size of their lips. This is the reason, they argue, that blacks will say "dat" instead of "that," "dere" instead of "there" and so on.

First, large lips are not a racial characteristic of blacks providing, of course, you can define what is meant by "large lips." Depending on the standards used, as many whites as blacks could be said to have "large" lips, not to mention American Indians, South Africans, Aborigines, and even the Lapps.

Second, there are just as many whites as blacks who say "dat," "dere," "dese," "dem," and "dose" if we discount entirely the silliness of lip size. Race has nothing to do with it. **Where you learn your language determines how you speak it**! If you grew up hearing "dese," "dem," and "dose" that is the way you are going to pronounce these words.

## SOME MISCONCEPTIONS ABOUT MEANING

A prominent television evangelist said in one of his sermons:

> *I have heard young people say they want to "live." And I have heard others boast they have "lived." I would just like to remind them that "live" spelled backwards is EVIL and that "lived" spelled backwards is DEVIL.*

The following letter was written to the editor of a Florida newspaper:

> *I recently read an article in your paper about how dogs are used for experimenting with the effects of drugs as well as different types of surgery. As a result these noble animals are either maimed or die.*
>
> *I want to express my public outrage at this. Remember that God loves the dog because He gave them His name spelled backward.*

## The Flip-Flop or the Universal Reversal Fallacy.

The two examples above illustrate this misconception. It claims that by reversing the letters in a word you will come up with another word whose meaning will reveal something about the nature of the first word.

This can be a rather fun game to play. If we reverse "nap" we'll get "pan," "tap" yields "pat" and "rat" gives "tar." If there is a meaning tie in these, and a number of other reversals that are possible in English, **you** must be the one who supplies it. The correspondences are more a testimony to the ingenuity of the person finding them then they are for supplying penetrating insights about language.

Just for the devil of it, assume there is some sort of meaningful tie in the reversals cited in the quotes. Consult a dictionary for the etymologies of "live," "evil," and "devil."

| | | |
|---|---|---|
| Live | O.E. "livian" | Ger. "leben" |
| Evil | O.E. "yfel" | Ger. "ubel" |
| Devil | O.E. "deofel" | Lat. "diabolus" |

If, indeed, there is some grand semantic scheme afoot, then it is one of modern origin. When we examine the historical roots we find that no reversal is possible prior to about 1500 A.D. and then only in English. But to be fair and open-minded in the matter, let's run another type of check. This time using the "God"—"dog" reversal.

| | | |
|---|---|---|
| English | dog | God |
| German | Hund | Gott |
| Dutch | hond | God |
| French | chien | Dieu |
| Spanish | perro | Dios |
| Italian | cane | Dio |

Obviously no "flip-flop" is possible except in English. What is illustrated is something discussed earlier namely, that English, German, and Dutch belong to one branch of the Indo-European family and French, Spanish, and Italian to another. It is not possible to go beyond this.

## There is a correlation between the name of a thing and the name itself.

There is a story that may help illustrate this. It stems from *Genesis 2:19*:

> *And out of the ground the Lord God formed every beast of the field, and every fowl of the air; and brought them unto Adam to see what he could call them; and whatsoever Adam called every living creature, that was the name thereof.*

When this story begins, Adam has been at the task of creature-naming for hours and is starting to weary. He turns to Eve, and says:

*"I've been at this for over eight hours. I'm bushed. You name the next one."*
*"All right," says Eve, "We'll call this one a rhinoceros."*
*"Why," asked Adam, a little startled, "do you want to call it a rhinoceros?"*
*"Because," Eve replied, "it looks more like a rhinoceros than anything else we've seen today."* What, one might legitimately ask, should a rhinoceros look like? Eve's explanation will serve as well as any other off-the-cuff one you may wish to opt for. If, however, the dictionary is again consulted for etymology, you find that the word derives from the Greek: "rhino" = nose; "keros" = horn. Hence a horned nosed animal. This is why when you have what is inelegantly called a "nose job," the surgeon refers to it as "rhinoplasty."

There is a section in Aldous Huxley's *Chrome Yellow* where the country squire and his manager tour the estate. When they arrive at the swine yard, the manager says, "Look at 'em, sir, rollin' in the slop and mud. Rightly is they called pigs." The squire replies, with a touch of cynicism, "Rightly is we called man."

There is no connection between the habits of the creature called "pig" and the name assigned to it. Similarly, there is no connection between the creature we call "man" and the word itself. As Juliet observed, "What's in a name? That which we call a rose by any other name would smell as sweet."

## Words have meaning.

This misconception should not be confused with the one just mentioned. The argument now is: **words in and of themselves have NO meaning.** Rather, the speakers of a language determine what a word means both in terms of its reference as well as the emotional reactions it may call forth. Here's a brief illustration. This is a list of familiar words but following each is an earlier definition.

| | |
|---|---|
| **argue** | to make clear |
| **cunning** | knowledge or skill |
| **doom** | to judge |
| **fame** | a rumor |
| **immoral** | not customary |
| **smug** | neat |

Since language changes, then the meanings of words will also change. There is no evidence that a collection of sounds (which is what a word really is) has any meaning until enough people agree that it does. And if they wish to change the meaning, they can! These changes, however, are not sudden. People just don't get together and say, "Hey, let's change the meaning of . . ." Meaning changes are gradual.

While it is sometimes possible to trace the historical process of a meaning change we can only make a few generalizations about the reasons for it. In many instances, however, the question of "why" the meaning of a word will change cannot be discovered. But change they will!

## There is a relationship between sound and meaning.

From time to time for reasons difficult to comprehend, polls will be taken to determine what people believe to the "ugliest" and "prettiest" words in the language. Some results gleaned from various surveys seem to agree on these.

**Ugliest**
1. A "four-letter word" referring to sex
2. Snot
3. vomit
4. Another "four-letter word" clinically called "feces"
5. Slime

**Prettiest**
1. lullaby
2. diaper
3. cinnamon
4. lilac
5. swish

Any attempt to find a logic in this list, or any of the others, is a bootless task. Such surveys are highly subjective and unscientific. Anyone is free to make a list. What you discover is not insights into meaning in an objective sense but a reflection of personal attitudes and values.

Nevertheless, a number of careful studies have been made to determine if there is a relationship between sound and meaning. Ronald Langacker, in *Language and Its Structure*, points out that the sound phonetically represented by the symbol [^] seems to have negative reactions for the speakers of English. Among the words having this sound are "bulge," "bug," "clumsy," "bulk," "mud," "dumb," "hulk," "rubble," "numb," "pudgy," "slug," "rut," "rump," "puss," and "sullen."

He then breaks these into three semantic categories:

| Heaviness | Filth | Dullness |
|-----------|-------|----------|
| bulge | bug | clumsy |
| bulk | mud | dumb |
| hulk | rubble | numb |
| pudgy | slug | rut |
| rump | puss | sullen |

But as Langacker points out, two of the titles he gives to these categories ("heaviness" and "filth") do not contain the [^] sound.

Similarly, Langacker and others seeking relationships between sound and meaning note that in English the [I] as in "hit," is frequently found in words indicating either quickness or slightness.

| Quickness | Slightness |
|-----------|-----------|
| zip | whim |
| flicker | zip |
| flip | whisper |
| sizzle | frill |
| swish | little |

You should, however, be cautious about claiming too much from this evidence. There are a number of words containing the [I] sound which will not fit either of these semantic categories. If there is a connection between sound and meaning it is not a strong one. Nor should we try to generalize from what we find in English to what may be found in other languages.

But hope springs eternal. Someone noted the following informal words for "father" and "mother" in various languages.

| | | |
|---------|------|------|
| **English** | papa | mama |
| **Swahili** | baba | mama |
| **Turkish** | baba | ana |
| **Aztec** | ta | nan |

Aha!, they thought. Here we have examples from an Indo-European language (English), the Chari-Nile family (Swahili), the Turcic (Turkish), and the Central American Indian or Macro-Penutian (Aztec). Further, there is a connection between **sound** and **meaning**. Might this not serve to prove that there is a common origin to the world's languages?

Unfortunately, this is not the case. We know from studies of child language acquisition that the first sounds an infant masters, regardless of the language family into which they're born, are ones such as [p] in "pup," [b] in "bum," [m] in "may," [n] in "now," and [a] in "ah." These are simple sounds to form. So an infant, experimenting with the vocal apparatus, is always going to start by making sounds much like "mamamamama," or "nanananana," or "papapapa," or "bababababa." Since parents do like their children to recognize them, when the mother hears the infant babbling "mamamama" she will immediately reinforce the repetition by saying, "That's right, darling, 'mama,' 'mama,' 'mama.'" And the father, not wishing to be left out will encourage "papa" when he hears the child babbling "papapapa."

So there it goes! Another beautiful theory down the tubes. Intriguing as the thought may be, we have no evidence to argue for a relationship between sound and meaning either within a language or among languages.

## There are "good" words and "bad" words.

At one time it was a cliche that parents would threaten to wash a child's mouth out with soap if they ever heard them using a "dirty" word. While beauty may be in the eye of the beholder, a "dirty" word exists in the mind of the hearer.

Words do not have meaning. They have meaning assigned to them. Therefore, saying a word is "bad" or "good" is also something we assign and **does not** exist within the word itself. Rather, it exists in the attitudes of society. Since language changes to reflect the needs of society, the attitudes towards certain words will also change. What was once socially acceptable may become unacceptable, and vice versa.

The subject of language taboos will be looked at later. But saying words may be "good" or "bad" implies taboos so a brief look is in order. Here is another list of words. Are they "dirty" or "bad" words?

❏ swive
❏ sard
❏ know
❏ occupy
❏ fizzle

The first two words may be unfamiliar since "swive" and "sard" dropped out of general usage several centuries ago. Only "swive" is defined in *The American Heritage Dictionary*. *The Random House Dictionary* lists neither. Yet, at one time, the first four words meant to have sexual intercourse. Only "know" is heard today. "He knew her but not in the biblical sense." Of course, if you don't know the "biblical sense" the point is missed. There is still an echo of that earlier meaning in the phrase "carnal knowledge." "Fizzle" was equivalent to what we sometimes today will call "breaking wind."

As evidence of how a general attitude shift in what constitutes "good" and "bad" affects words, look at "hell" and "damn." These were once regarded as "bad" words and their use was strictly forbidden in movies and on television. This was done, one presumes, to protect us from any possible corrupting influence—although most people had them as part of their active vocabulary and not always in the biblical sense. There are still people who scrupulously avoid their use and are offended on hearing or reading them.

Their use was legitimized in literature long before they could be heard in movies or on television. But it was not uncommon in the nineteenth and early twentieth centuries to find in British and American literature such oddities as

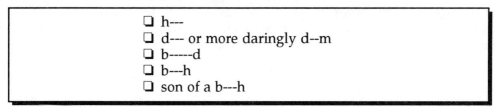

❏ h---
❏ d--- or more daringly d--m
❏ b-----d
❏ b---h
❏ son of a b---h

All of the "bad" words, and a number of others, are now not only in literature but also in movies and on television—though the latter is still a more conservative medium and will frequently "bleep" out words and phrases felt to be objectionable. And in the process, television added a new word to the language, "bleep."

Our general acceptance of these words is an indication that our attitudes have changed. Regardless of what one may feel subjectively about them, they are neither "good" nor "bad." The labeling is a result of our attitudes. There is nothing to argue against the possibility that words which we find perfectly acceptable today will be regarded as "bad" or "dirty" by future users of the language. Words which we now find offensive may not be to future generations.

## The meaning of a word should not vary.

This is the attitude of the "semantic purist." But meanings **do** change and a word may develop two or more meanings over the years. In some cases the earlier meaning will disappear. In others it will coexist with the new meaning or meanings.

The "semantic purist" insists, usually in a contradictory fashion, that some words should **always** be used in a given sense. One critic took an author to task for saying a character had a "dilapidated" appearance. The reason the critic objected to the use of "dilapidated" was that it means to take apart stone by stone and was, therefore, inappropriate in describing a person. If he objected to "dilapidated" then he should have also been consistent and objected to the author's reference to another character: "The candidate wore his best blue suit to meet the workers." Etymologically, if the critic had bothered to check a dictionary, "candidate" means to be "dressed in white." Therefore, he could not possibly have been a candidate dressed in a blue suit. But as Emerson observed: "A foolish consistency is the hobgoblin of little minds."

There is nothing wrong with insisting that words be used with precision in order that the meaning intended comes through. For example the words "informer" and "informant," while they occupy roughly the same semantic space (someone who supplies information), will lose precision if used as synonyms. These two sentences signal different meanings

> He was an informant.
> He was an informer.

In the first instance, "informant" refers simply to one who supplies information about a subject. But "informer" also carries with it the implication that this information will in some way be detrimental to someone. When the distinction isn't made, the communication loses a degree of precision.

To insist on retaining earlier meanings for some words but not for others flies in the face of reason. There is also the question of who is to judge. When compiling *The American Heritage Dictionary*, the editors selected 100 people from various areas to act as "experts" in cases of divided usage and meanings. In very few cases were they in total agreement.

These misconceptions about language and meaning do not exhaust the various wrong-headed views some people have about language and meaning in general. Perhaps we hold them because language is so intimately bound up in everything we do that we cannot look at it objectively. But when a view of language behavior is obviously in conflict with what we know to be true, then it should be either modified or discarded. The aim is to become open minded without becoming vacant minded.

# 2

# FUNCTIONS OF LANGUAGE

When you look at a normal human brain the surface features of race, ethnicity, and social distinctions are meaningless. The brain gives the appearance of being a unitary whole. There are two hemispheres, the left and the right. The left controls functions on the right side of the body, and the right hemisphere controls the left. We are, in a very real sense, cross wired. What is heard in the left ear is registered on the right; what is heard in the right ear is registered on the left. Both hemispheres are wired into the eyes.

Connecting the hemispheres is a mass of neural fibers called the **corpus callosum**. These are "circuits" which enable the two hemispheres to transfer different types of messages and coordinate them.

Shortly after birth the hemispheres begin to specialize, a process known as lateralization. In more than 90 percent of all humans, the left hemisphere becomes the dominant one for language (both speech and writing) as well as for mathematics. The right hemisphere, while capable of some language functions, primarily controls our spatial concepts, presuppositions, and some of the major aspects of musical ability. Also, we apparently dream in the right hemisphere.

Various metaphors have been used to explain how the brain functions. One that was quite popular for years compared it to a telephone switchboard, complete with operators who pulled and put in plugs to make connections. In recent years the one most used is the computer. The left hemisphere is not unlike a digital computer in that it processes information sequentially. The right is an analog computer where several sources of information are drawn together for comparison, contrast, and synthesis.

Should a person, at an early age, suffer a severe injury to the left hemisphere, the right will assume the language functions. One dramatic case concerned a teenage boy injured in a high school football game. He was taken to a hospital as a precautionary measure and in the process of the examination no activity was found in the left hemisphere. A brain scan revealed that the hemisphere was atrophied, withered, and had apparently been for some years. When doctors questioned the parents, they were told he had fallen off a swing when he was about two and suffered a severe concussion on the left side of his head. But he recovered and nothing more was thought of the incident. Yet all of the young man's language functions were unimpaired. The right hemisphere took over the process of language learning when the left failed.

Human language, then, is something genetically coded into the neocortex and initially resides in both hemispheres. It is almost as though we are provided during our early years with a back-up system to take over should one fail. But the older we become, the greater the risk of permanent language impairment should the left hemisphere sustain a severe injury.

Once lateralization is completed, and evidence indicates this is shortly after puberty, various parts of the left hemisphere will assume particular language functions. These are conventionally named after the men who first isolated them.

The location of these will vary slightly from one individual to another. That is why a neurosurgeon will carefully map the left hemisphere when performing an operation involving that area.

Three of the major areas are:

> ❏ Broca's Point (or Area)
> ❏ Wernicke's Center
> ❏ Exner's Center

A massive disruption of one of these areas, either through injury or a stroke, will, in addition to varying degrees of right-side paralysis, also lead to language disruption ranging from partial to total loss. The technical term for this is aphasia.

## Broca's Point.

This area controls the ability to form words into sentences (our syntax). If it sustains an injury we cannot utter coherent sentences even though the words are there. Since Broca's Point is approximately in the area where prefrontal lobotomies are performed to relieve extreme anxiety and aggressiveness, patients undergoing this operation are at risk and may suffer degrees of language disorientation.

## Wernicke's Center.

Here is where we "store" the names of things. An injury here leads to "anomia," the inability to give the names of objects. You might be able to recognize it, even a face you've been familiar with for years, but you cannot supply the name.

## Exner's Center.

This governs our ability to read and write. A disruption here does not affect our ability to speak or to understand when spoken to. Writer, critic, and lexicographer H.L. Mencken suffered a stroke in this area late in life. He could dictate his articles and understand them when they were read back to him but he could neither read nor write himself.

There are various types of therapy for aphasia and if the damage is not too severe a person may regain the full range of language ability. Others attain only partial restoration. In some cases, unfortunately, the damage is so severe that no rehabilitation takes place.

So, we are genetically programmed for language. But we are not born with language, only the capacity to learn one.

> ## The brain doesn't care what language it learns.

Say you were to take a black, white, chicano, or any infant born of American parents and send it to be reared in Japan. At the same time you bring a Japanese infant to the United States. Both children are then permitted to be reared without interference from their respective places of birth. The American child will mature speaking fluent Japanese and the Japanese child will speak fluent American English. Your language and the way you speak it are the result of the place where you are reared. The brain will accept any language as its model to be learned.

Nor does the brain care if the centers necessary for the functioning of the other senses are impaired. Although we associate sight and hearing with language ability, one or both may be nonfunctional and the individual can still learn language. As a child, Helen Keller lost both sight and hearing.

Yet, through the efforts of Annie Sullivan, she was taught language. She also learned to speak even though she never heard the sound of her own voice. There are any number of equally dramatic cases of persons born without sight and hearing who have learned to use language.

We have few examples of humans who for one reason or another were deprived of language stimulation. The reports on feral children, those found like Kipling's "Jungle Boy" wandering in the wilds, tell us very little. The reports are usually received second- or thirdhand and are neither systematic nor scientific. Eric Lenneberg noted in this regard:

> The only safe conclusions to be drawn from the multitude of reports is that life in dark closets, wolves' dens, forests, or sadistic parents' backyards is not conducive to good health and normal development.

As we near puberty, if only one language is learned, the ability to learn a second language will decrease. Once we are in our mid-teens, the acquisition of a second language becomes increasingly difficult if not impossible for some people.

Americans are notoriously poor second language learners. Perhaps one of the reasons for this, aside from our belief that everyone should speak English, is that we do not start teaching second languages until that time when the brain resists the acquisition of another.

Research indicates that a child raised in a home where a second language is spoken and used regularly into the critical period of the teens will have comparatively little difficulty acquiring other languages. The key here is the continued use of both languages! Americans who take their young children abroad for extended periods discover very shortly that the child will develop a mastery of that country's language. Indeed, service families and business executives report that their children will shortly act as their translators. But when the child returns to the United States and has little or no opportunity to use the second language with any regularity, it will gradually slip away.

Henry Lee Smith once observed that until the age of six we are all geniuses. When you stop to consider that during those years we learn to distinguish most of the sounds of our language, its basic grammar, and a good part of our vocabulary, the statement is not too far off the mark.

We now know, thanks to the work of linguists and psychologists interested in the process of language acquisition, that learning a language is not a haphazard process. For a number of years it was thought we acquired language by babbling away until we got it right. But the left hemisphere processes information sequentially and to have sequencing you must have order. There are, therefore, "stages" in the acquisition of language.

## Babbling.

We go through this stage quite early as we learn to control the vocal apparatus. Studies of newborns in England indicate this begins as early as the second week following birth. We soon learn that some sounds are easier to articulate than others. As noted in the previous chapter, these are [m], [n], [p], [b], [a]. The more difficult sounds such as [f], [v], [s] are added until by the age of five or six most of the sounds we need for speaking our language are in place.

## Holophrastic.

Even as we are mastering the sounds of our language we move from "babbling" to what is called "holophrastic." Here a single word is equivalent to an entire communication. "Go" = "I want to go." "Eat" = "I'm hungry." "Cat" = "That's a cat." "Potty" = "Somebody had better get me to the facility."

## Two Word Stage.

This could be regarded as the suburbs of grammar. One word will serve as a "pivot" around which other words, sometime called "open classes," will move.

| Pivot | Open Class |
|-------|-----------|
|       | food |
|       | coat |
| my    | milk |
|       | mommy |
|       | daddy |

Or the pivot may appear in second rather than initial position.

| Open Class | Pivot |
|-----------|-------|
| food      |       |
| rain      |       |
| mommy     | go    |
| daddy     |       |
| man       |       |

Very shortly after this, pivots will begin to serve as open classes and open classes as pivots. When this happens we are well on the way to acquiring the basic grammar of our language.

The brain first sequences sounds into words and words into larger units. We discover by trial and error that some combinations work and others don't. We discard those that don't and keep those that do. At the same time we are receiving verbal stimulation from adults who have mastered, to varying degrees, the possibilities. We use them as models as well as other forms of verbal stimulation which are available. In the United States the child has access at infancy to television, radio, and recordings.

The degree to which these other forms of verbal stimulation will have an affect on the child's language learning ability is as yet unexplored.

Some years ago a preliminary study was made of the impact of television on child language acquisition. Pre-school children from families with and without access to television were tested for verbal ability as well as other skills. Regardless of socioeconomic group, children with access to television exhibited higher verbal skills than those without television. But by the time they had entered the second grade this advantage had disappeared for some children. It may be that the commencement of formal training in language has a dampening effect on the informal. Or perhaps something happens to our language learning abilities even in the initial stages of acquisition. Regardless, while the process of language acquisition may on one level be trial and error, it is an orderly trial and error. That is why by the age of five or six we have acquired the basic grammar of our language. Grammar not in the sense of "correct" and "incorrect," but grammar in the sense of being able to sequence sounds into words and words into sentences. Anything that happens after the age of six is merely a refinement, sort of "fine tuning" of this basic grammar. And how "fine" it is tuned is a function of social factors rather than biological ones.

What is the relationship of the brain to that thing we call the "mind?" There are some, such as the psychologist B.F. Skinner (see his book, *Verbal Behavior*), who deny there is such a thing as the "mind." They argue that what we call "thinking" is a chained process of conditioned responses which we acquire through a process of trial and error, reward and punishment called "operant learning."

If this were true, and the position has many supporters, then it should be the case that we are limited in both our verbal and non-verbal responses to what we have "learned." But the fact that we can utter, hear, read, and understand sentences we have never uttered, heard, or read raises a serious question about the validity of Skinner's assertion.

A child may initially have difficulty reading sentences such as: "I have a dog. His name is Wag. He goes bow-wow." But the child will have little difficulty understanding, when spoken, the sentence:

> "I have a dog named Wag that goes bow-wow."

This is not "learned" behavior. It is the brain processing language. And the operant learning theory does not explain how it is possible to combine words into sentences and larger blocks of thought. An in-depth discussion and criticism of Skinner is found in Noam Chomsky's *Language and Mind*.

Without becoming overly involved, we can say that the brain is an electrochemical organ (the most important and complex in the body) and the activity it performs is what we call "thinking." The sum total of this process is called the "mind."

"The degree to which we think is regarded as a measure of our intelligence." In our culture, this almost always is measured through language performance. There are seemingly countless tests to evaluate our verbal skills directly or to use them as an indirect means of quantifying our other skills and aptitudes. Just how accurate an index these provide is a subject of much debate.

There are proponents and opponents of all of our testing procedures. One point, however, needs to be made about the brain and language. If this has implications for testing and testing procedures they must be debated in another forum. We know that the brain stores a great deal of language information which we will rarely if ever use. This information enables us to read, hear, and more importantly understand sentences which we would never, ourselves, utter or write. This is what we call our language competence. There is as yet no way we can usefully measure an individual's language competence. What we produce is called our performance. Here we have a number of tests with varying degrees of validity to test performance. One of the axioms in linguistic studies of verbal behavior is: **Competence always exceeds performance**.

This is, of course, largely assumption. But there is a growing body of evidence to support the generalization. We have all met individuals where we would swear that competence and performance are matched with both on a low level. As an instructor once commented on a student's paper, "Your expression is cramped and your vocabulary impoverished. Both, however, are adequate for the expression of your thoughts."

Conversely, we sometimes encounter individuals with a very high degree of verbal facility (performance). We therefore assume they must be quite intelligent. There is no necessary correlation between the lack of language performance and intelligence. Nor is there any necessary correlation between verbal facility and intelligence.

The state of our knowledge about the interrelationships of language, brain, and mind is at best imperfect. But new studies continue to supply us with more insights. There is, for example, evidence to indicate that people who are bilingual store the native language in the right hemisphere when they are compelled to speak the second language. If that second language is English and the native language Spanish, and the individual suffers a stroke that wipes out their English ability, they can frequently be approached through Spanish.

Another interesting finding is that women apparently have more language aptitude in the right hemisphere than do men. Also left-handed people apparently suffer less language impairment from a stroke of comparatively equal severity than do right-handed people. These findings, at this time, are tentative but they provide insights into the functions of the brain.

A great deal of this discussion is theoretical. But since language and brain are inseparable, it is well to have some general understanding of the organ where the phenomenon of language resides even though some of these generalizations may have to be modified or discarded as we learn more about the way the brain functions.

# THE NATURE OF LANGUAGE

## The Linguist's Perspective

What do we mean by "Language?" The *American College Dictionary* defines it as:

> 1. *communication by voice in the distinctively human manner, using arbitrary, auditory symbols in conventional ways with conventional meanings. 2. any set or system of such symbols as used in a more or less uniform fashion by a number of people who are thus enabled to communicate intelligibly with one another.*

*The American Heritage Dictionary* says:

> *1. the aspect of human behavior that involves the use of vocal sounds in meaningful patterns and, when they exist, corresponding written symbols to form, express, and communicate thought and feelings. 2. A historically established pattern of such behavior . . . in the culture it defines: (the English Language)*

Here is the one we will use. Notice it contains some of the elements in the two above but also has some other things added:

## Language.

An arbitrary learned system of vocal symbols used by human beings for communicating their culture - past, present, and future.

This is an "operational definition," which simply means we are defining it this way for the purposes of our discussion. There is nothing wrong with setting up operational definitions so long as you do not go beyond their limits or try and make them do more than you intended. Electricity, for example, is defined in the sciences as both a "particle" and a "wave." In the first, electricity flows along in discreet units one behind the other. As a "wave," electricity is viewed, as the name implies, as having peaks and valleys. If you apply the particle definition you can write one set of formulas; with the wave you can write another. Both sets will obtain results.

On the basis of our operational definition, what can we say about language? We'll begin by examining the last part of the definition first: ". . . used by human beings for communicating their culture—past, present, and future."

By limiting language to humans, we rule out the rest of the animal kingdom from further consideration. Dr. Doolittle wished for the ability to talk to the animals. Had his wish been granted he would have found the conversation limited.

Animals have **primary signaling systems** which enable them to communicate a single piece of information about a limited event. Some of these primary signaling systems are quite elaborate and complex. Dr. Karl von Frisch has done extensive work with the "dance" of bees. He learned to "read" these signals and found that the movements, accompanied by the frequency of the beating of the wings, indicated the direction and approximate distance for the location of food to be converted into honey.

Some people believe their pets can practically talk. Further, they "understand every word you say to them." You may be among these. At the risk of disillusioning you, the animal is responding to the tone of your voice and perhaps a limited number of conditioned reflexes to a limited set of sounds. They are also capable of reading facial expressions as well as various postures (see Thomas Sebeok, ed., *The Sign and Its Masters*). If you have a dog, try this. Say to it: "You're the most worthless beast God ever permitted to walk the earth. It would be a mercy to mankind if I had you put out of your misery." But do this in a soothing, calm tone of voice. You will find the dog will wag its tail and generally disport itself in a very friendly manner. All it heard was the tone of voice. You may reverse the experiment and say something very complimentary but in an angry tone. You will get the same reaction as when you reprimand the animal.

But what about the work done with chimpanzees such as Washoe, Lana, and Nim Chimsky to determine if they are capable of acquiring "language?" Since chimps do not have the vocal apparatus to articulate sounds, they have been taught sign languages of various sorts, sometimes with the aid of a computer. While some of them have become quite adept at manipulating these signs, they cannot go beyond the limits of what they're taught. That is, they cannot come up with original sequences of signs. Further, they are incapable of transmitting these to their offspring.

It is true that on one level human language operates as a primary signaling system. When we say things like "Good morning," "How are you?" "Help!" "Look out!" "Duck!" "Ouch!" the communication is immediate and one-subject oriented. These are all features of a primary signaling system. Here, human language and animal communication cannot be distinguished one from the other. Among the features of a primary signaling system are:

> The communication is about the immediate environment and does not extend beyond it.
> There is a one-to-one relation between a sound and its meaning.
> The number of utterances is limited.
> The signals are acquired through genetic inheritance rather than learned.
> Despite variations in intensity, the meanings of the sounds are the same.

As a closing note on the differences between the primary signaling systems of animals and human language, we should note a significant difference between the two. With human language we can not only talk about the present but reflect on both the past and the future. Primary signaling systems do not permit this.

But how do we know that animals are incapable of discussing the past and the present as well as speculating on what the future may hold? Where is the evidence? In formal logic this is called the "argumentum ad ignorantum," an argument based on ignorance or one incapable of proof. The only thing a rational person can do when one of these is posed is not take the bait.

A better understanding of human language can be obtained if we now return to the first part of the operational definition and examine the key terms: "arbitrary," "learned," "system," "vocal," and "symbols."

## Language is arbitrary.

The first definition of "arbitrary" in the *American College Dictionary* is: "determined by whim or caprice." The second is: "based on or subject to individual judgment or discretion." Both may be said to be true of language. Another aspect of arbitrariness is found in situations where there are several ways to resolve a particular problem, in this case communication. One will work just as well as another. With nothing in particular to recommend it, one of these will be selected and the others rejected. Such a choice is arbitrary.

Arbitrariness is characteristic of many aspects of our daily life. In an American car, the steering wheel is located on the left side and we drive on the right side of the road. In England, the steering wheel is on the right side and they drive on the left. What is there to recommend one as opposed to the other? The choice is purely arbitrary. Both solve the problem just as having the steering wheel on the left and driving on the left, or having it on the right and driving on the right would have worked.

As with cars and driving, so with sports. Comedian Bob Newhart has a routine in which Abner Doubleday is trying to sell a very skeptical manufacturer on marketing a new game called "baseball." Doubleday is asked such questions as: "Why three strikes?" "Why four balls?" "Why three outs?" "Why nine innings?" There is no logical answer to these questions. The choice of the numbers is purely arbitrary. Had other numbers been selected they would have worked just as well.

**How is language arbitrary**? To answer this question we must begin by noting that language is composed of three interlocking systems.

> The Phonological System
> The Syntactic System
> The Semantic System

**The Phonological System.** This is made up of those sounds which the speakers of a language recognize as signaling meaning. The human vocal apparatus is a very flexible instrument and apparently capable of producing an infinite variety of sounds. From this reservoir, any language will use only a few to signal meaning and the choice is purely arbitrary.

The speakers of English have accepted the distinction between the sounds [l] and [r] as significant. It makes a great deal of difference in meaning whether we say "lot" or "rot," "fly" or "fry," "tar" or "tall." But in many Oriental languages, this distinction is not significant. These sounds are used interchangeably and have no affect on meaning. When teaching English as a second language to groups of Koreans some years ago I never knew if my name would be pronounced "O'Hara" or "O'Hala." And sometimes it would be pronounced both ways in a single conversation. I could hear the difference because English has required that I hear it. But for my Korean students, the distinction was meaningless. Some learned to make it, others didn't think it worth the trouble.

Similarly, English makes a distinction between the [v] and [b] sounds as in "van" and "ban." The distinction between [y] as in "yellow" and [j] in "jello." Spanish speaking peoples do not. The capital of Cuba is pronounced as either "HaVana" or "HaBana." A Spanish entertainer made a television commercial extolling the quality of a particular brand of "green oliBes." And I was a little puzzled when a native Spanish speaker asked me to comment on his "Bowel" sounds. When I asked him to repeat the question, he carefully said: "V-O-W-E-L, Bowel." He could articulate the sound in isolation but not in combination with other sounds.

English speakers will also do the same thing with some sounds but since meaning is not affected by the substitution of one for the other and largely goes unnoticed. The sounds [b] and [p] can be substituted in medial position with some words. Listen carefully the next time you hear someone pronounce "aspirin" or "Baptist." You may even make the substitution yourself.

Therefore, the selection of sounds which make up the phonological system of any language is arbitrary. Some will have more sounds than English; some will have fewer. Georgian, spoken in Russia, has seventy-five sounds while Hawaiian has twelve.

**The Syntactic System.** This is the means by which a language combines the sounds in the phonological system into larger units of meaning roughly equivalent to words, the words into phrases and clauses, and these into sentences.

The options here are not nearly as great as they are for combining in the phonological system. If you wish to explore this further read Winfred P. Lehmann's *Historical Linguistics: an Introduction*. This is not a book to be approached lightly but well worth the effort. There are three large syntactic groups into which it is customary to group the world's languages. To further complicate matters, no language is all one or the other. English is primarily what is called an "inflecting" language. The various syntactic relationships are signaled by the endings we place on words. Thus,

> The boy is running.    The boys are running.

The {-s} attached to "boy" indicates more than one and this then means that we must change "is" to "are."

English syntax has adopted a system of NOUN + VERB +/- OBJECT.

| N + V | The man ran. |
|-------|--------------|
| N + V + O | The man ran a race. |

In addition there are various types of verbs in English: the linking, the transitive, the intransitive. There are also different types of objects: the indirect, the direct, and the object complement. Why did English settle on this syntactic system? As with the selection of sounds, the choice (if that is the appropriate word) was arbitrary. Another system could just have well been used. And we would be none the wiser.

**The Semantic System.** This refers to the meanings of words first as they exist in isolation and as they operate within the syntactic system. This ability of words to have more than one meaning is called **polysemy**. We will examine some of the whys and wherefores of this later. But for now, we will concentrate on the word "runs." In isolation you might say that the word indicates an activity of some sort. Now, we will place it in various contexts in the syntactic system and notice how the meaning changes.

> ❏ The man (runs).
> ❏ The watch (runs).
> ❏ He scored three (runs).
> ❏ She has (runs) in her stockings.
> ❏ My nose (runs) when I have a cold.
> ❏ In Mexico he drank the water and got the (runs).

You can undoubtedly think of other contexts which will give different meanings to "runs." Dictionaries will seldom list a single meaning for a word. Unless your dictionary is built on historical principles (the earliest recorded usage is listed first) you will find the various meanings listed in a descending order of frequency.

We noted in Chapter 1 that words themselves do not have meaning, but have meaning assigned to them. The semantic system, therefore, is just as arbitrary in what words mean as the phonological and syntactic systems. Consider the object at the end of your wrist. We call it a "hand." The object at the end of your ankle is a "foot." If at some time in the past the speakers of English had decided that the object at the end of the wrist would be called a "foot" and that at the end of the ankle a "hand" we would be none the wiser. For that matter they could have been called just about anything. There is nothing in the four sounds making up "hand" or the three of "foot" that makes them in some way uniquely suited for naming these parts of the body.

Language, therefore, is arbitrary in its three subsystems: Phonological, Syntactic, and Semantic. **Because it is arbitrary, a language CANNOT be analyzed by any system of external logic.** There is, as we shall see, an internal logic in language that can be understood only by analyzing how these three subsystems interact with one another.

## Language is learned.

This was discussed while looking at language and brain. To restate: we are born with the capacity to learn a language. But we must learn whatever language it is we will use. No one has as yet isolated one or more human infants and reared them in an environment where they are compelled to invent their own communication system. There is a story of a king who wished to find out what was the first language and isolated two infants in the care of a mute nurse. One version of this story ends with the discovery that the first language was Hebrew. Another that it was Greek, another Phrygian, and so on. The odds are that they would have emerged with a sophisticated primary signaling system but not human language.

## Language is a system.

In its simplest form a "system" is a group of related parts that work together to form a unitary whole. Each part will have a function which it must perform in relation to the other parts. If not then the system either operates ineffectively or it may not function at all.

Anyone who has a stereo system (tuner, preamplifier, amplifier, speakers, turntable, tape deck) has experienced the agony of what can happen if one of these components either doesn't function properly or stops functioning altogether. The automobile is an even more vexing system at times. The motorist sitting by the side of the road with the hood raised and peering at the engine is mute testimony to how a system must have its parts in the proper working order.

While the system of language is unitary, it permits its users a degree of flexibility in its subsystems, a luxury not always afforded by electrical and mechanical systems. But there are limits beyond which you cannot go because if you do, the system functions erratically or it may cease to function, i.e., communicate.

You may, for example, play all sorts of games with the phonological system. You can mispronounce words either deliberately or accidentally: "corpsucle" for "corpuscle," "insinuator" for "incinerator," "hypodemic nerdle" for "hypodermic needle." A good deal of American humor is grounded in just this type of phonological foul-up. These are sometimes called "Malapropisms," after the character Mrs. Malaprop in Sheridan's play "The Rivals." They are also called "Bunkerisms," after the tv character Archie Bunker who, after attending the funeral of a friend, reported that a lodge brother had performed the "urology" over the corpse and that the priest preceded the coffin from the church swinging "incest."

But if you go too far in twisting the phonological system there will be no referent in the semantic. Take a combination of sounds like "iffinthiggle." This doesn't quite cut it semantically. Sometimes, however, a sufficient number of speakers will become intrigued with a phonological invention and it becomes part of the language. "Gizmo" means anything you can't name and "glitch" refers to a malfunction of undetermined origin. These are but two such words that have carved out vague referents in our semantic system.

The systematic nature of language can be best seen in capsule form by examining the major way in which English indicates the difference between one and more than one. What we call "plurality." If someone were to ask you how to form a plural in English you might tell them, "Just add an {-s} to most words and you'll be safe."

Here are three columns of nouns:

| 1 | 2 | 3 |
|------|--------|--------|
| tub | map | gas |
| fad | mat | face |
| tag | tack | dish |
| fan | laugh | match |
| log | minute | garage |

These examples do not exhaust the possibilities but all we wish to do is illustrate the system. While you can add the letter "-s," or "-es" in some cases in Column #3, notice what happens when you pronounce these words. In Column #1 the sound is /-z/, what is called a "voiced" sound. In Column #2 the sound is /-s/, a "voiceless" sound. But in Column #3 you must add two sounds, /-ez/.

So when we speak, we do not add "-s," we must use one of these sounds. But which one? There is no mystery here. The last sound of the word in its singular form determines the sound that must be used to indicate plurality. In linguistics this is called "phonological conditioning." One sound will determine (condition) how another sound is articulated. Thus in Column #1 all of the words end in a "voiced" sound so to indicate plurality we must use another "voiced" sound. In Column #2 the end sound is "voiceless" so it is followed by a "voiceless" sound. In Column #3, the end sounds belong to special categories which require the addition of another sound before the /-ez/.

We, of course, have other ways of expressing plurality in English such as internal changes in some words, "woman - women," "mouse - mice," "tooth - teeth." We can indicate plurality by adding "-n" but only in three words, "children," "oxen," and "brethern." We even indicate plurality in some words by not adding a sound as with "moose," "deer," and "fish" in many contexts. (Note that all of the members of this group refer to animals.) And there a few Latin and Greek plurals, "criterion - criteria," "phenomenon - phenomena," "medium - media," and so on. But many of these are being adopted into the {-s} pattern. Few people today will use "formulae," they'll opt for "formulas." And the plural of "stadium" is almost always "stadiums" not "stadia."

This example of plurality also illustrates another statement made earlier. **Language cannot be examined by any external system of logic. The logic described here is internal and stems from the system.** If there is an external logic that applies to language in general, it has not yet been demonstrated.

Similarly, the syntactic and the semantic systems permit us a certain amount of latitude before the over all system breaks down or functions improperly. But there are limits beyond which you cannot go without meaning being either misdirected or disappearing completely. You have more latitude in speech than you do in writing, however, because you can always stop and restate—if you are lucky.

But, in writing, you don't have this luxury. Unless you're very careful the meaning that comes through may be entirely different from the one you intended.

> ❑ Dante wrote with one foot in the Middle Ages and with the other saluted the dawn of the Renaissance.
> ❑ After eating our breakfast, our bus departed for Atlanta.
> ❑ I wrote with one hand and talked on the telephone with the other.

These examples also illustrate another rule to keep in mind when writing English. **If the syntactic system and the semantic system conflict, the semantic system always wins.** The writers of these sentences obviously wished to communicate one thing but the syntax signals something quite different. In some cases you end up communicating no meaning at all.

## Language is vocal.

With the spread of printing after the fifteenth century, and what today passes as literacy, the tendency is for many to put the proverbial cart before the horse and view speaking as some sort of unfortunate offshoot of writing. But people spoke for a considerable time before writing systems were invented. Indeed, anything that happened before the advent of writing is usually referred to as "prehistory."

Even today, people speak far more than they write though with the increased consumption of TV, movies, radio, and popular music we seem to be doing less of both. More to the point, we must keep in mind that the great majority of languages spoken in the world have no written forms. Therefore, when linguists think about the nature of language they think of it as primarily a vocal phenomenon.

## Language is symbolic.

In another chapter we will examine in some detail signs and symbols. At that time a more precise definition will be needed. But for now we will work with an uncomplicated one.

**Symbol**: something that stands for something else.

We stated earlier that there is no necessary correlation between the name of a thing and the thing itself. Looked at in the light of this definition of symbol, we can say that a word stands for, or symbolizes, something else. Thus in English the word "cat" is a symbol for a particular type of animal. In other languages the animal is symbolized as:

| | |
|---|---|
| French | chat |
| Spanish | gato |
| Hungarian | macska |
| Japanese | neko |
| Swahili | paka |

Language has been examined from the standpoint of how it operates in the brain and how the linguist describes and analyzes it. Some of the generalizations made in regard to language and brain are based on the current state of our knowledge. But each year reveals new insights which frequently compel us to revise our earlier assumptions while verifying others. Our knowledge in this area is increasing. While we know agreat deal, we do not always understand what we know.

Linguists are also uncertain about some of their assumptions. For example, we can describe the basic English sentence pattern as N + V +/- O. But there is controversy as to which is the more important in English, the noun or the verb. Even the excellent studies on child language acquisition do not provide us with much information by way of resolving this question.

But our interest in examining the broad sweep of this topic is not to become involved in the theoretical questions, as intriguing as they may be. Our purpose is to have some understanding of language as a uniquely human activity. We know that while we are born with the ability to learn a language, it is the accident of birth which determines the language we speak. We also know that the process of learning a language is not a hit or miss operation. It is an orderly process. The linguist strives to examine this uniquely human trait in a systematic manner. But, they do not attempt to impose some sort of preconceived logical pattern on the subject. Rather, they analyze the data and describe what is there, not what they may privately feel should be there.

# 3

# THE FUNCTIONS OF LANGUAGE: Perception

"Purple," "blue," "green," "yellow," "orange," and "red" are six words used in English to express a portion of the color spectrum. In Shona, a language spoken in Zimbawa-Rhodesia only four words are needed. The speakers of Bassa in Liberia use two. Do the speakers of Shona and Bassa have visual defects which do not permit them to see these colors as precisely as we do?

NO! Their languages simply segment the color spectrum differently. Their physiological perception of color is unimpared. They see the differences in shades but find it unnecessary to designate them the way we do in English. Their ability to express differences in shades is not as lexically precise as in English. But this is a judgment from the perspective of English. If looked at from that of Shona or Bassa, one might argue the contrary; English has a unnecessarily complex color vocabulary expressing shades that are not that relevant.

What is meant by "perception?" We can define it as the ability to obtain information from the senses which is then translated into understanding.

Our understanding of perception, however, is about on the same level as our understanding of how the brain operates. We "know" a great deal but do not in many cases understand what it is that we know.

We do know it is primarily through language that humans orient themselves to the world and those around them. As we acquire our language we also acquire a large part of our attitudes and values.

We are told that we shouldn't do certain things because they are "bad." Some words are also classified "bad" as are people, ideas, and actions. Similarly, we learn that other things are "good" and we are told that we should be "good."

The linguistic anthropologist, Benjamin Lee Whorf, theorized that we are "prisoners" of our language and the only way we can perceive external reality is in the terms laid down by it. Whorf arrived at this conclusion after studying American Indian languages. He noted that where English was structured in a N + V +/- O, Hopi and several other American Indian languages apparently center on the verb. From this he argued that as speakers of English we see the world as comprised of objects (nouns) doing things (verbs) to other objects. The Hopi will see the world primarily in terms of actions in which the noun is in some way incidental. Thus he found a number of verbs to indicate specialized forms of movement such as a man moving, a woman moving, a fabric moving, a horse moving. There were special verbs to be used if you were turning over a round object as opposed to a square or an oblong one. Whorf's view is frequently referred to as "linguistic determinism."

Whorf's theories set off controversies that continue today about the role of language in perception. Numerous studies were made to see if they could be verified. The bulk of the evidence indicates Whorf was wrong. There is no evidence to support the idea that we are at the mercy of our language in quite the way he believed. The verb, which he found so significant, operates much the same way in English as in Hopi. Each of the following verbs must carry with it a particular movement.

| | |
|---|---|
| shrug | shoulders |
| blink | eyes |
| stub | toe |
| twiddle | thumbs |
| crack | knuckles |
| grit | teeth |
| bat | eyes |
| purse | lip |

Also, if language is as confining as Whorf's theories contend, then the act of translating from one language to another would be all but impossible. The old saying about losing something in translation has at best marginal validity. It is true that the task of accurate translation requires extensive knowledge on the part of the translator of the options available in both languages. If this is lacking, the results may range from humorous to disasterous. This was evident when former President Carter visited Poland. Since he did not speak the language, he used an American translator. In his initial speech, he spoke of the "desire" of the Polish people for peace. His translator, however, used the Polish word whose closest English equivalent is "lust" in the sexual sense. Fortunately, this mistranslation aroused only mild resentment but considerable amusement.

Sometimes, however, inaccurate translation can lead to disaster. Following the surrender of Germany in World War II, the heads of state for the Allies held a conference in Potsdam in late July of 1945. The result was a position paper, "The Potsdam Proclamation," which called for the unconditional surrender of Japan. When asked for his reaction, Japanese Prime Minister Suzuki said he would "mokusatsu" it. This word was literally translated as "to kill with silence" or its English equivalent "ignore" or "treat with silent contempt." As a consequence, the first atomic bomb was dropped on Hiroshima August 6th. The Prime Minister later said he had meant his use of the word to stand for the English equivalent of "no comment."

While most concepts and ideas can be translated from one language to another with varying degrees of ease, there are a few which resist all attempts. In the 1950s an Egyptian government official was sent to the University of Minnesota to obtain another Ph.D. He already had one from a British university. Part of his assignment was to translate into Egyptian Arabic certain materials published by the University. One of these was a small weekly magazine of essays on culture, politics, criticism, and poetry called "The Ivory Tower," a popular metaphor for the academic life. While he could translate the title it made no sense because there was no equivalent metaphor in Egyptian Arabic to convey the idea. He was never able to resolve his problem.

The significance of Whorf's hypothesis lies not in what it tells us about the relation of language to perception. It lies, rather, in the number of studies attempting to prove and disprove it. As the sociolinguist Joshua Fishman notes, the fact that the hypothesis has been shown to be wrong in no way detracts from the fact that Whorf asked a good question. What is the relationship between language and perception? If there is any weight to linguistic determinism, it is slight. While it might please some of the "determinist" persuasion to think we are prisoners of our language, the evidence is not there.

What role, if any, does language play in perception? The answer lies not in linguistic determinism but in "linguistic relativity." This is the term applied to the theories of Whorf's teacher, Edward Sapir. Unfortunately, discussions of the role of language in perception are frequently called the "Sapir-Whorf Hypothesis" ignoring the fact that the student carried the teacher's theories beyond where they were intended to travel. Sapir felt that we are not prisoners of our language in the sense that Whorf believed. Rather, our language predisposes us to perceive external events in what he calls "habitual" ways.

> *Human beings do not live in the objective world alone, nor alone in the world of social activity, but are very much at the mercy of the particular language which has become the medium of expression for their society. . . . The fact of the matter is that the "real world" is to a large extent unconsciously built up on the language habits of the group. . . . The worlds in which different societies live are distinct worlds, not merely the same world with different labels attached.*

-Edward Sapir, *Culture, Language and Personality*, p. 69.

In other words, you become a "prisoner" of your language only if **you** permit it. You can always break free but this is up to you! This is not always the easy thing to do; one must make a conscious effort. In the introduction to his book, *A Theory of Semiotics*, the Italian humanist Umberto Eco relates why he decided to write in English rather than in his native language and then having it translated. He concludes by saying that the experience gave him new insights into the soundness of the Sapir-Whorf Hypothesis. But the problems he discusses are primarily ones of semantics rather than syntax and while there were undeniable difficulties, he did perform the task.

How are we habituated by our language? In English, as well as some of the other members of the Indo-European family, we will more often than not divide people, actions, ideas, and even language use into opposites: good-bad, desirable-undesirable, favorable-unfavorable. A good portion of what we read in popular literature as well as see on TV and in movies reinforces this split. Once the categorization is made we feel we "perceive" the person, action, or idea. So deeply rooted is this that many people become acutely uncomfortable when confronted with situations which do not lend themselves to such an easy split. We are habituated!

Within a culture, males and females may be habituated to perceiving matters differently. For example, in American culture, colors (and color vocabulary) are largely regarded as the province of the female.

When confronted with the generic term "red," males will overwhelmingly opt for such imprecise variants as "dark red," "light red," and "pink." But most females will distinguish among "cardinal," "dubonnet," crimson," "scarlet," and "shocking pink" to list but a few. A male who complimented a young woman on her "green" sweater was told pointedly that it was not "green" but "aquamarine." This was then defined as a light blue with an undertone of green. When told, he could perceive there was indeed some green there.

This does not mean American males suffer varying degrees of color blindness. They have been habituated to perceiving colors in broad, general categories. If the situation demands, males can acquire a more precise color vocabulary. A fabric salesman or a male artist must by the very nature of their professions acquire and use the required terminology. If the need for greater precision arises it must be acquired and this is done through vocabulary.

Occupations as well as sex require vocabularies of varying degrees of complexity if you're going to express yourself with precision. The person who wishes to analyze literature is compelled to make distinctions between metaphor and simile, to recognize such literary devices as synecdoche, personification, alliteration, spondees, tropes, and so on through a long list. Once habituated to expressing analysis in these terms communication can take place with a greater degree of precision providing, of course, that others are equally familiar with them.

There is another aspect to the relation of language to perception. English, like any language, is rich in synonyms to express an idea. Thus if you wish to communicate that a person has little or no money we find, among other possibilities, the following synonyms:

| | |
|---|---|
| 1. busted | 5. penniless |
| 2. flat | 6. bankrupt |
| 3. broke | 7. insolvent |
| 4. poor | 8. indigent |

If you examine this list carefully you will notice that #1 through #4 are used more frequently than #5 through #8. We can classify the first four as high frequency words simply on the basis of their being used more often, while the last four are said to be low frequency words because we don't encounter them that much. These terms are borrowed from Henry Kucera and W. Nelson Francis, *Computational Analysis of Present Day English.*

Another item to note is that the first four words may be used more-or-less interchangeably. But you cannot do so with the second four. Thus a person may be "penniless" but not "bankrupt," "insolvent," or "indigent." A person who is "insolvent" is not of necessity either "bankrupt" or "indigent." So while the four carry the idea of having little or no money, they cannot be used interchangeably without doing damage to the meaning you wish to communicate.

How does this relate to language and perception? Research indicates that people who are able to use low frequency words with precision are more likely to make other types of distinctions with greater precision. Students with a command of low frequency words tend to do significantly better in tasks such as map reading, making analogies, and weighing options.

Whether this is a case of cause and effect or a statistical fluke controlled by some independent variable is not certain. So do not rush out and purchase a thesaurus to cram yourself with low frequency words. There is no guarantee that this will in some way make you a better thinker or a more perceptive person. Since the meanings of low frequency words shade off and demand greater precision in their use, you just might find yourself in water too deep to tread.

Although there is no absolute guarantee, there is an apparent correlation between a person's command of the semantic system and the ability to develop certain cognitive habits and skills.

There is also the question of whether you would be able to think and perceive without language. The answers here are about as polarized as they are on the Whorf hypothesis. We do know that human language is inadequate for the expression of certain types of thought especially in the hard sciences such as mathematics, physics, and chemistry. But the "languages" developed for this type of expression are quite different from human language. One could make a case for human language giving rise to the need to develop these other "languages."

# THE FUNCTIONS OF LANGUAGE
## Geographical and SocialDimensions

Henry Higgins says of Eliza Doolittle in the Lerner and Lowe musical "My Fair Lady":

> *Look at her a prisoner of the gutters.*
> *Condemned by every syllable she utters.*
> *By rights she should be taken out and hung,*
> *For the cold blooded murder of the English tongue.*
>     *It's "aow" and "garn" that keep her in her place,*
>     *Not her wretched clothes and dirty face.*

Language reflects culture. Whatever is important in the culture will be reflected in the language. Further, language changes to reflect the changing needs of the culture. But within a culture there are variations in the language, its phonology, syntax, and semantics, which further serve to mark the social boundaries of the groups speaking the language. This is what Henry Higgins was referring to when he said: "It's 'aow' and 'garn' that keep her in her place."

**Geographical Variations.** Anyone who has traveled about the country is aware that people will pronounce words differently from the way they do. The phonological system is where we are most aware of geographical differences. As a man in the Air Force from Wyoming remarked to another from Kentucky, "You sure talk funny!" The reply was, "So do you!" Dialectologists, linguists who study the differences in language on the basis of geographical location, have mapped out the major dialect areas in the United States. A detailed look at these can be obtained by glancing through *A Linguistic Atlas of the United States and Canada*. For a dated but excellent condensation see the chapter on American dialects by Raven I. McDavid III in W. Nelson Francis, *The Structure of American English*.

In some parts of the country "route" is pronounced so it rhymes with "shout," in others it rhymes "shoot." How would you pronounce "hoof," "roof," "garage," "about," "ambulance," "police," and "legislator?" For some, the vowel sound in the first two will sound the same as in "who," for others it will more closely match that in "but" or "cut." "About" may rhyme with "out" or with "boot." In some areas "ambulance" sounds as though it were spelled "ambYOUlance," "police" as "POElice," and "legislator" as "legislaTOR."

Geographical variations are also found in the syntactic and semantic systems. For example, depending on the area you come from, you will indicate a time reference by one or more of the following prepositions:

It's fifteen minutes  (till) nine.
                    (of)
                    (to)
                    (before)
If someone feels ill are they:
                Sick (to)
                    (at)
                    (of)
                    (on)    their stomach?
                    (in)
                    (with)

Depending on the geographical location the past tense of "dive" may be either "dived" or "dove," "shine" either "shined" or "shone," "dig" either "digged" or "dug" and "wake" as either "waked" or "woke." These are just a few of the syntactic variants found in different parts of the country.

In the semantic system, you will find that the same object will be referred to by different terms. Thus an iron, steel, or aluminum utensil with a handle in which grease is heated to cook foods may be a "skillet." "fry pan," frying pan," or "spider." Running and jumping on a sled can be a "belly flop," "belly bump," or "belly gut" among others. The object you turn on to get water may be a "faucet," "tap," "spiggot," or "spicket." Carbonated drinks are called "sodas" in some areas while in others the term is reserved for a drink concocted from ice cream, syrup, and soda water.

Geographical variations in the three subsystems are not as evident today as they were prior to the end of World War II. There are several reasons for this leveling of distinctions. One is mobility. Someone described Americans as a nation of nomads. While this is an overly dramatic way of putting it, Americans, as a society, tend to be less rooted to one geographical area. The odds are very good that if a person is reared in one area and goes to college, he or she will not return to that area.

Another factor to be considered is the impact of World War II, the Korean, and the Vietnam Wars. During World War II, especially, large numbers of servicemen and -women moved from one camp to another. Industries built plants which brought in workers from other parts of the country. These are just a few of the contributing factors. What resulted was a mixture of geographical dialects so that certain features of pronunciation, syntax, and semantics were eroded.

Nor should we forget the impact of the mass media, especially radio and television. Announcers tend to use an unaccented type of speech devoid of any regional identifying marks, a type of speech usually called "mid-western." For a number of years it was customary for potential candidates being sent to speech classes where most vestiges of regional dialect were carefully eradicated. There can be little doubt that this had some impact on the pronunciation, syntactic, and semantic systems of listeners and viewers.

Another problem in the semantic system is that words which in one part of the country may have a favorable referent will have an unfavorable one in another. The word "jazz" can refer both to a form of music as well as intercourse. Similarly, "hockey" may be either a sport or a euphemism for excrement. The names of male animals can develop unfavorable referents. The British will refer to a male chicken as a "cock" but in America we must now use "rooster," and in some rural areas even this is too specific for good taste; the creature is a "he-biddy." In others the bull is either a "he-cow" or a "cow critter."

We all carry with us varying aspects of our geographical origins. It is the rare person who can mask these completely because in times of stress the suppressed form, pronunciation, syntactic, or semantic, will assert itself. While regional differences in these three areas are not nearly so evident as they once were, they are still a part of our linguistic baggage. Indeed, in some areas, the geographical features are reasserting themselves as local radio and television stations employ persons with distinct regional features in their speech.

**The Social Dimension.** John Donne wrote that "no man is an island." Unless we become hermits living in a cave or recluses hiding in the attic of a house, we are members of various social groups. The degree of our identity with these groups will influence not only our language but also the meaning which we communicate to others as well as the meaning they communicate to us.

Earlier we noted that the acquisition of language is an orderly process. So is the "social" acquisition. William Labov, in his article, "Stages in the Acquisition of Standard English," says there are six of these but we will consider only the first three: "The Basic Grammar," "The Vernacular," and "Social Perception." Remember that these are "stages" and have no precise cut-off points for all people. You may enter the second stage while still in the first, and so on.

**The Basic Grammar.** This is the nuts-and-bolts stage as we move from babbling through holophrastic and into the two-word. Here we acquire our basic sentence patterns. Although some of these may never manifest themselves in our performance they become a part of our competence. There is general agreement among those who study language acquisition that we have this under control by the time we are five or six years old. Anything that takes place after that is a refinement and expansion of the basic grammar.

**The Vernacular.** Here we learn the dialect of our language consistent first with that spoken by our parents and relatives. We are also influenced by the children we may play with in our neighborhood and later by groups of friends at school. While the basic form of our dialect is likely to remain similar to that of our parents these other groups will bring about degrees of modification.

**Social Perception.** During this stage we begin to make judgments, either favorable or unfavorable, about the language habits of others who are outside our groups. Labov believes this begins during adolescence but recent studies indicate it may begin as we begin to get control of our basic grammar when parents or friends call to our attention that other people from other groups talk "funny." This can then be reinforced, either positively or negatively, by what happens in the classroom when formal training in the use of our language begins.

Each of the other three stages moves us toward what Labov calls a "consistent standard," one that conforms more and more to the pronunciations, syntax, and semantics of our groups of primary identification. While we may both exercise and tolerate degrees of language flexibility within those groups with which we identify, we become less tolerant of variants in the dialects of other groups. This means that each of us carries around in our head some "rules" which tell us how language should and should not be used. These "rules" usually reflect the variety of the language we have come to accept. All variations are evaluated and judged by these rules. Such evaluations and judgments are almost always unfavorable.

What is your reaction to the following sentences?

> ❑ It's me!
> ❑ The data shows that he will lose the election.
> ❑ The reason he did it is because he's stupid.
> ❑ The media is a powerful force in American life.
> ❑ He centered his argument around two points.

You may find all of these sentences perfectly acceptable. You may have objected to some but accepted others. Or you may have rejected all and labeled the user as either illiterate or at best semi-literate. Let's assume that you rejected all of these sentences. What are the "rules" that led you to do so?

> ❑ "It's me!" If you rejected this, you have a "rule" which says that when there is a linking verb followed by a pronoun, the pronoun is in the subject form: "I" = subject; "me" = object. Similarly, "It's he" not "It's him" and "It's she" not "It's her."
> ❑ "The data show that he will lose the election." Here you would argue that "data" is plural and the appropriate form of the verb should be "are" not "is." The singular of "data" is "datum."
> ❑ "The reason he did it is because he's stupid." "The reason" and "because" mean the same thing. Therefore the sentence is redundant and should be recast to read: "The reason is that."
> ❑ "The media is a powerful force in American life." The reasoning here is the same as with "data" "Media" is a plural form therefore the plural "are" should be used. "Medium" is the singular form.

❏ "He centered his argument around a number of points." Objection? The word "center" indicates a specific point. Therefore it is impossible to "center around" anything. You must center "on." The "rules" cited for the rejection of all five examples are made from the standpoint of the linguistic "purist" or the "strict constructionist's" perspective. Your acceptance or rejection of any or all of these forms is a matter of social dialect and the "rules" imbedded in it.

There is an interesting aspect of our reactions to the language forms of others. Research by Labov and others shows that in many instances we will make social judgments about those who violate one of our "rules" but we will have this same feature in our own speech. Thus we may stigmatize someone who says "It's me" but we will also use the same form. It's a case of don't do as I do but do as I say. Incidentally the five examples cited were all taken from the speech of composition teachers. Another illustration of what can happen when you drop your linguistic guard.

The study of the interrelationship of language and society is called "sociolinguistics." The sociolinguist seeks correlations between variations in the phonological, syntactic, and semantic systems with such factors as age, education, occupation, income, place of residence, race, religion, and sex. Because the subject ranges over such a broad area it is not the sole property of those in linguistics. Anthropologists, psychologists, political scientists, and sociologists also seek to understand this interrelationship. On the basis of the work from various disciplines we can now make some generalizations about the interaction of language and the social groups who use it.

Language gives you a sense of social identity. We must all function within social groups, some of which we will identify with more strongly than others. In the process of identification we accept the language norms of the groups. Conversely, we will reject the language norms that the groups reject. In some cases this may cause problems. For example, educators are constantly vexed with the question of why the children from some social groups will have more difficulty in school than children from other social groups.

There are any number of studies investigating this. Basil Bernstein, in studies of British school children, arrived at the conclusion that schools operate by a set of language criteria. All students, regardless of social group are expected to conform to these criteria. They include standards of pronunciation, syntax, and vocabulary. The performance of children from some social groups matches these criteria but others do not.

Students whose performance matches or closely approximates these criteria are rewarded with good grades. Students whose performance does not are given lower ones. Further, evidence indicates this also carries with it the implication that their form of the language is inferior. It follows that if their language is inferior then their social group must also be. One consequence of this is that students from these groups "turn off" the educational process. Another is they develop a hostile attitude not only toward the educational system but also toward those political and social institutions which support it.

Unfortunately, some educators totally misread Bernstein's work and developed what is called the "verbal deficit" theory to explain why students from some social groups did poorly in school. One even went so far as to claim that students from these groups were almost "totally devoid of language" and advocated teaching these children English as though it were a foreign language. Another suggested that such students were lacking in logic and the ability to make logical connections between or among things. For a refutation of both positions see William Labov's *The Logic of Non-Standard English.*

If there is a "deficit," it is one that results from different norms of language performance. Further, if this deficit does exist how do you account for the fact that students so classified can understand what is being said? They simply do not have these criteria as part of their performance. An ingenious method of showing that "deficiency" is relative to social group is sometimes called the "Cornbread and Chittlins Test." There are numerous versions of this. Basically what these tests do is take vocabulary items from the dialect of a stigmatized social group and ask those from other groups to define the words. Define these words:

> hog
> hammer
> shucking
> do

In some social groups a "hog" is a Cadillac, not an animal. A "hammer" is a pretty girl, not an implement for driving nails. "Shucking" has nothing to do with corn but refers to putting some one on, fooling them. An "do" is not the present tense of a verb, it is the hair style.

If you didn't answer these correctly does this not mean that you suffer from a verbal deficit? Obviously you need remedial work so your language performance conforms to the norms of the group. While useful for illustrating a point, such tests also create problems. Most of them are built on the vocabulary items of a particular group of blacks. As a consequence, they can give the impression that all blacks possess these terms and are able to define them. When this happens we run the risk of categorizing an entire racial group on the basis of the language performance of just a few subgroups within the larger group.

But such concerns would carry us far beyond the opening statement that language gives us a sense of social identity. It is sufficient to note that we do identify with groups through language. Further, while there is nothing wrong with establishing norms for language performance this carries cautions that should observed. When you criticize a person's language you are also attacking their sense of group identity.

Language gives us status within our social groups. "Gives" is used in the sense of enabling us to attain higher or lower status within the group depending on our verbal facility or the lack of it.

This is best illustrated by the "verbal duels" which we sometimes get into with one another. One way to do this is play the "insult" game. The object is to put down the other person harder than you're put down. If successful, you gain status. If not, you lose it. Here is such an exchange.

> Got a match?
> Yeah. My ass and your face.
> If your ass is so good looking, why do you keep it covered?

Unless the second speaker has a suitable comeback, the game is lost. This example is a mild form of the insult game. In some groups it is called "playing the dozens." Nor should this game be considered solely a male diversion. Women play it as well! If you examine your own social situations you will discover that in many instances you will play the game yourself. Perhaps it will not be like the example cited but regardless of the subject, the purpose is the same. Using language to gain status is not the exclusive property of certain socioeconomic or racial groups.

Language functions as a means of social advancement or repression. This, in part, is what the quote from "My Fair Lady" illustrates. When Eliza Doolittle learns to "speak properly," she is accepted as a "lady." She uses the language forms identified as being characteristic of a "lady" within the social groups where she must function. Later in the play Eliza complains that her new way of speaking makes it impossible for her to return to her former occupation.

If you consult the yellow pages in any large metropolitan phone book you will see listed not only speech pathologists, who are trained to handle pathological problems such as stuttering, lisping, and aphasia, but also voice training specialists (sometimes called "elocutionists"). They will train you to "speak properly" in much the same way Henry Higgins trained Eliza. That is, they will aid you in ridding your voice of geographical and social features which might call attention to themselves.

Studies by Joan Baratz, Barbara Love, M.A.K. Halliday and others indicate that doors are opened or closed depending on how well your language performance conforms with the expectations of either a teacher or a prospective employer. The linguist James Sledd charges that language instruction in the public schools is a not too heavily camouflaged device to keep minorities in their place and deny them the opportunity for social advancement. The title of his article is "Dialectology: Doublespeak in the Service of Big Brother." We cannot productively argue the merits of Sledd's position here. Read the article and make your own decision.

Those who interview prospective employees have been found to carry their own language prejudices into their evaluations and recommendations of whether or not to hire. In such situations the interviewees are at an obvious disadvantage because they are unaware that they are being evaluated by whatever norms the interviewer may possess. This is like trying to play a game when the rules are never given. So we are confronted with the uncomfortable reality that the way you use the language can either make you money or cost you money.

Language functions as a means of social group solidarity. You will find this in social groups which share not only such quantifiable features as economic, educational, and occupational similarities but also share a similarity in beliefs, attitudes, and values. The accepted language patterns are reinforced through such formal groups as political organizations, religious denominations, and social clubs. Nor should one forget the informal groups such as those that get together to play cards, tennis, or golf, go fishing, and so on. The old saying, "He speaks my language," can be interpreted quite literally here. "Speaking the language" both indicates that you are a member of the group and that you share certain attitudes, beliefs, and values.

An excellent illustration of how language functions as a means of group solidarity is found in what the late D.W. Maurer first labeled "criminal argots." Suppose you heard the following. What would it mean?

> We were operating four-handed. I was working in front of the gun. The frame gives me the office. I make the stall. The gun scores the mark, passes off to the backstop, and we're home free.

There isn't a word here you are unfamiliar with. But since you are not a member of this group the meaning of the communication is at best vague, at worst incomprehensible. What you overheard was one pickpocket talking to another. The passage may be translated as follows:

> 1. There are four people in this group.
> 2. The "frame" locates the wallet ("gives the office"); the "stall" brushes against the victim to prevent his being aware his pocket is being picked; the "gun" takes the wallet; the "back-stop" receives it. "Home free" means they escaped undetected.

This language is rarely if ever used around persons who are not members of this group. The terminology facilitates communication and provides a sense of solidarity for the members of the group. Although one could argue the example is overly dramatic it is not too different from what happens in other less controversial groups. There is hardly an occupation that does not have its special vocabulary, sometimes referred to as "shoptalk." Just as with the illustration of pickpocket argot, these vocabularies serve the dual function of facilitating communication and signaling group solidarity. Political and religious groups may also be studied in a similar fashion with the same conclusions.

Language functions to give you a sense of identity as an individual. This operates on two levels. We have already discussed how language serves to give you sense of identity within a social group. The other level on which language functions is to help you define yourself as an individual regardless of the social groups to which you belong.

The social psychologist George Herbert Meade said we are all really two people. The first is the "I" or the social self. This is what we present publicly. Here the various things discussed under social group identification play a role. Our language forms will approximate those of the groups we belong to. Then there is the "me." This is the private self or how we view ourselves apart from our social connections. Several years ago a popular song proclaimed, "I Gotta be Me!" And how many times have you heard, or even said yourself, that a type of clothing or hairstyle, or whatever is either "me" or "not me"?

When we begin to consider this function of language, we move into that gray area that separates sociolinguistics from psycholinguistics. The fact is that we will use certain forms of language not because of social perceptions but because we, as individuals apart from our groups, feel that this language is appropriate for us. Or we may reject certain forms on the same grounds. They do not conform, as Meade would put it, to our "me."

The five areas discussed do not constitute all of the social dimensions of language. While we have evidence which tends to support them we must explore this further. Also, there is a great deal about this function we do not know. At the present these can only be posed as questions. Is a person's ability to make decisions and choices from among a range of possibilities in any way limited by the language of social groups? If they are limited, to what extent is the person limited in being aware that there are alternate courses of actions?

We know that language influences our perception. We are not the prisoners that Whorf posited but rather our perceptions are habituated in ways suggested by Sapir. We become prisoners only if we permit it to happen. Aside from language **per se**, the ways it is used and viewed in various social situations influence our perceptions. What things "mean" in both an objective and subjective sense is controlled by these factors.

# 4

# SIGNS AND SYMBOLS

You are about to go out for a walk. As you leave you notice dark clouds on the horizon. Then there is a flash of lightning followed by thunder. You change your mind and come back in. When asked why, you reply, "It looks like rain." The clouds, the flash of lightning, and the thunder have served as a "sign" that it is about to rain. Or at least on the basis of your past experience, you assume it will.

Now, suppose you notice smoke rising in the distance. What would this be a "sign" of? Or there is someone across the street who sees you, raises their right arm, and waves the hand back and forth, horizontally. Does the gesture meaning something? You repeat the gesture and say, "Come on over." The person shakes their head from left to right several times, repeats the gesture with the hand and walks away. You do the same. You have communicated through "signs" that the two of you recognize as having "meaning."

What then is a sign? As with language, we will set up an operational definition.

> **Sign:** Anything that suggests the existence of a fact, condition, or quality and **controls** behavior.

If our behavior is not controlled, then whatever we are dealing with is not a sign. We have all, at one time or another, had the experience of observing the cloud, lightening, thunder combination and chose not to regard it as a sign only to find ourselves soaked to the skin and looking frantically for shelter. The sign is composed of two elements:

$$Si \longleftrightarrow R$$

The "Si" stands for the sign and the "R" is the referent—what the sign is supposed to mean. The solid line with the arrow at either end indicates that the sign and its referent are tied together.

You meet a friend. The eyes are slightly swollen, the skin around the eyes is pinkish, the whites are bloodshot and watery. What is this a sign of? Here are some possibilities. The person

❑ has been crying.
❑ has an eye infection which produces this condition.
❑ has been in the presence of something irritating to the eyes.
❑ is taking drugs of some sort.
❑ is suffering from a hangover.

There are, of course, a number of other possibilities. Regardless, we'll limit the list to these five. Which of the five possible explanations is the correct one? Since we have no additional information other than the condition of the face, any of the five possibilities could serve. What you are faced with is a situation where

$$Si \longleftrightarrow ?$$

You are left to determine which is the "right" one. The possible explanations are called "contexts" and help to supply us with the "referent" and, subsequently, the meaning. Therefore, we have to say: **Signs are context sensitive.** That is, the same sign may have multiple referents and can "mean" different things in different circumstances and situations.

So we must now modify the diagram like this:

$$Si \longleftrightarrow R$$

The purpose of enclosing the diagram in a box is to indicate there must be a context; the context enables us to select from a number of possible meanings the one that is accurate.

Suppose there is no context? What we do is generalize! That is, we will search our memory for real, or perhaps even imagined, contexts from our past experiences. On the basis of these, we assume the condition of the red and watery eyes "means" whichever of the five contexts appear to offer an explanation.

Here is another situation. The person doesn't have red and watery eyes. However, the skin around one of the eyes is purple and black—a classic shiner. We know that this condition is a sign that the person was struck in the eye. But what context supplies the meaning?

❑ Someone struck the person in the eye.
❑ The person walked into a door.
❑ The person was struck by an object other than a fist or a door.

With no further information than we have for these two examples, we may conclude in the first instance that the person has a hangover. In the second, someone hit the person in the eye. We later discover that the first person was crying because of some bad news. In the second, the person had, indeed, walked into a door.

Our past experiences, real or imagined, have betrayed us in both cases. Because they are context sensitive, and because the same sign can be interpreted differently in situations where there is no context, **the misinterpretation of signs is both the simplest and most frequent way to make mistakes.**

Under certain circumstances, we will create signs with the deliberate intent of having them misinterpreted. This is a form of lying. False signs are an integral part of most sports. In baseball, a pitcher will act as though he is about to throw to first base to keep the runner close. He may have done this because the runner led him to believe he was about to steal second base. Both men are offering signs for misinterpretation. And who is controlling the behavior of the other is an open question.

In football, the quarterback will look in one direction and throw the ball in another. Sports announcers call this "looking off the defenses." Similarly, a pass receiver will run in one direction and suddenly cut in another. Defenses will give the appearance of rushing the quarterback, "blitzing," and then fall back into a pass defense. All of these signs are meant to be misinterpreted and to lure the other side into making a mistake because they provided the wrong context.

This type of activity is not exclusively human. Some animals will roll over and play dead if they feel danger is at hand. A dog may bark loudly when you are at a distance but turn and run when you approach. A man approached a dog that was sitting calmly and vigorously wagging its tail. When he reached out to pat it on the head, the dog bit him. He had generalized that all dogs that wag their tails are friendly and wish to be patted. His past experience with similar situation provided his context and he acted upon it. His comment after being nipped, "That damn dog lied to me."

The poet A.E. Houseman observed, "Things are never what they seem." This could well serve as a motto whenever you encounter a sign in a context free situation and feel you must interpret it. Our past experiences are not always the best index for supplying meaning. Besides, there is always the possibility that the creator of the sign may have done so with the deliberate intent of having us misinterpret it.

There are many ways to classify signs. Some of these are quite complex and involved. But since our interest in the sign is as means to an end rather than an end in itself, we will break them into two major categories: Natural and Conventional Signs.

## Natural Signs.

These are, as the name implies, ones that occur in nature. The clouds, lightning, and thunder were natural signs which combined to control our behavior. So was the smoke. We do not know how severe the storm will be. It may be a gullywasher, only a sprinkle, or there may be no rain at all. In a similar manner, the smoke may indicate a fire about to start, one actually in progress, or one about to burn out.

We are surrounded by natural signs and given the appropriate context they can mean various things. There is the intensity of the wind from a breeze to a full gale. One can be restful, the other frightening. Motion pictures and TV programs frequently use various natural signs to add suspense and heighten our sense of apprehension or expectation.

Even silence can become a sign if we so choose to interpret it that way. A parent may become aware that a child is too quiet. This is usually interpreted to mean the child is doing something it shouldn't.

Natural signs can be misinterpreted. There is always the person who carries an umbrella and then complains, "It looked like rain. So I took my umbrella and nothing happened." Or the opposite, "It looked so nice out when I left and here I am soaked." This also implies a cause and effect relationship between our actions and those of nature. It may be flattering to believe that nature responds to our actions but such is not the case. The connection between washing the car and the coming of rain is a popular cliche.

Natural signs have the same meaning regardless of the language or cultural context in which they operate. The dark clouds, lightning, thunder, and column of smoke will "mean" essentially the same thing whether you are in the United States, New Zealand, or Japan. There may be some natural phenomena which are signs in one culture and not in another but that is a matter for the cultural anthropologist to explore.

## Conventional Signs.

Something that is the result of general agreement and acceptance is said to be a "convention." Therefore, conventional signs are ones we have arrived at through general agreement and have come to accept. They are created by humans for specific purposes. Because of this they are arbitrary in the same sense that the word was used in the definition of language. That is, there is nothing in the real world that says they must be this rather than that.

Further, there is no necessary correlation between the conventional sign and its referent. You will sometimes find conventional signs referred to as "artificial" perhaps to contrast them more specifically with natural signs.

We live in a world of conventional signs. Most of our everyday activity is to a large degree controlled by them. On a purely statistical basis, they far outnumber natural signs. And they can multiply, mutate, or disappear as we feel the necessity for increasing, changing, or dispensing with them. But they are always a matter of convention. Consider these signs.

```
          "S"              "c"
```

Using our past experience, we can say the first is a capital letter called "S." The second is a lower case "c", both of which exist in the English alphabet. If, however, I take this same sign "S" and place a single or double vertical line through it, "$" we call this a dollar sign. If a vertical line is placed through the "c," "¢" this is a cent sign. Our context must, of course, be American monetary notation. Other currency systems will use different signs to represent their monetary values.

There is nothing in nature which says that the sign "S" is a capital letter representing the final sound in "hiss" or the initial sound in "sister." This arbitrariness becomes even more apparent when you consider that the "c" is pronounced [s] in "cent" and also represents [k] in "can." We could well drop the "c" from our alphabet but it is now so much a part of our spelling conventions that its deletion would present all sorts of problems for those accustomed to finding that letter in certain words. Nor is there anything in nature to say that $ and ¢ must be signs for dollars and cents.

Some contend that behind every conventional sign there was at one time a natural sign which for some reason became lost. These arguments are more ingenious that convincing. There is no substantive, objective evidence to support this position.

Look at these signs.

```
          +    -    x    ÷    =
```

Within the context of mathematical signs their referents are "add," "subtract," "multiply," "divide," "equals." Why? Simply because at sometime in the past we agreed these signs would stand for these referents in mathematical notation. The fact that these signs will operate cross-culturally is irrelevant so long as the context remains mathematics. They will remain conventional signs until such time as there is general agreement that they need to be changed.

Signs may be changed. As long as there is general agreement about the meaning of the modification, communication can take place. If we take the + sign and extend the bottom part of the vertical line we now have a sign called a "cross." It may signal two things depending on the context: Christianity or a church.

If, however, the top part of the vertical line is removed and a loop substituted the sign no longer represents christianity. This is an "Ankh," the ancient Egyptian sign for enduring life. You will find a number of these on necklaces, bracelets, and even rings. While they have a degree of popularity as an item of jewelry they do not mean the same thing to the modern wearer as they meant to the ancient Egyptians.

Various other modifications of the basic cross can be made. Each will carry the general meaning of christianity but with a more specialized referent. For example, modifications carry such titles as:

❑ The Cross of Calvary
❑ The Celtic Cross
❑ The Jerusalem Cross
❑ The Maltese Cross

One dictionary illustrates fifteen variations on this sign within the context of Christianity. Like all conventional signs, they are context sensitive. Therefore, one or more those above maybe totally meaningless to you because they have no referents within your particular system of signs.

Here is another variation on the cross to illustrate the conventionality and context sensitivity of signs. This time the arms of the cross are pulled down at an angle and the figure is enclosed in a circle.

This may be recognized by some as a "peace" sign. It was quite popular during the Vietnam War and may still be found occasionally. If, however, we were to return to the 1950s, we would discover that at that time it meant "ban the bomb." The figure was supposed to represent the B-52 bomber and the circle indicated that it should be confined. So we have the same sign but it meant one thing in the 1950s and another in the 1960s.

Colors may also serve as conventional signs. The selection of what the color means is equally as arbitrary within its context. An object with which drivers are familiar is the traffic light. The top color is red (stop), the middle yellow (caution), and the bottom green (go). Why these three colors from the many in the spectrum? Because these were the three agreed upon. Another combination would have worked just as well if we had agreed upon it and we would be none the wiser today.

The placement of the colors is also arbitrary. Granting that whatever is to represent caution should be placed in the middle because in English we process information from left to right and from top to bottom, why should red be on the top and green on the bottom? Wouldn't green on top and red on bottom work just as well? Certainly. But the placement is now a matter of convention and to suggest otherwise would cause confusion.

The color red may also be a sign for other things in other contexts. For example,

1. Danger
2. High Temperatures
3. Anger
4. Blood

Yellow can signify,

1. Caution
2. Dawn
3. Cowardice

And green has these possible referents,

1. Safety
2. Spring
3. Envy
4. Jealousy

The new international road signs have resulted in confusion for those accustomed to the earlier ones. There was one that simply read "Slippery when wet." This is now replaced by a stylized drawing of two curvy parallel lines representing tire tracks with dashes indicating rain drops. Another has a red slashed line drawn through it to indicate trucks may not travel on that street. One convention may be replaced by another but it always takes some getting used to.

This was the case when research discovered that blue was a more visible color than red for lights on emergency vehicles. Some police departments immediately adopted it for their flashing lights but it takes a while to educate people in these matters. As a result, a compromise was reached with one light red and the other blue. Similarly, fire engines and ambulances (as well as some other emergency vehicles) are increasingly being painted a light, lime green. Again, the color was selected because of greater visibility. But there are still those who are convinced that red is the only suitable color for fire engines and ambulances. Those who grew up with these colors for referents will have the same difficulty in adjusting should another color shift be made.

All of this may appear to have little relevance to language as a sign system. The discussion has deliberately avoided that. The purpose is to illustrate how signs operate in controlling and directing our meaning.

# THE NATURE OF SYMBOLS

In the chapter dealing with language from the linguist's point of view an operational definition of language was given:

**Language.** An arbitrary, learned system of vocal symbols, used by human beings to communicate their culture—past, present, and future.

A general definition of "symbol" was given as "something that stands for something else." The caution was also made that later we would have to be more precise. Consider the diagram of sign used a little earlier.

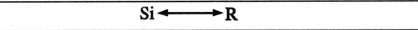

Using the earlier definition of a symbol, there would be no way to distinguish it from a sign. So if permitted to stand, confusion would result. Therefore, a further distinction must be made so we can tell one from the other.

Assume we see a person carrying an American flag. We will use this as a means of distinguishing the difference between the sign and the symbol. The person holds the flag in one hand and with the other strikes a match and touches it to the flag. It bursts into flames and burns fiercely. Then the individual throws it on the ground, steps on it several times, and walks away. What was your reaction? Did you feel anger, disgust, perhaps want to fight? If so, you were reacting to the flag not as a sign, but as a symbol.

If it were possible to witness the burning of the flags of Comoros, Mauritis, Qatar, or Tonga what would your reaction be? Unless you happen to be a native of these nations, probably none. Indeed, it may be that you have never heard of these countries. For you, they are simply signs which have at best a vague referent.

On the sign level, the American flag represents the political and geographical entity called "The United States of America." But if your reaction to the burning of the flag was one of revulsion and anger, then you were reacting to the American flag as a symbol. So we must use another diagram to indicate we are dealing with a symbol and not with a sign.

This diagram for a symbol is also enclosed in a box. Like the sign, **the symbol is context sensitive.** And like the sign, the symbol controls behavior. But we are now talking about a more complex level and type of control than with the sign. The sign and its referent stand in a one-to-one relationship within their context. When you see a red light, you stop! When it turns green, you go. For some, the yellow light indicates caution, for others it is a sign to speed up.

The new diagram has something standing between the Symbol and its Referent. The letter "C" in the diagram stands for "Concepts" or emotional attitudes evoked by the symbol. These emotional attitudes are almost always evoked in terms of opposites: "good - bad," "favorable - unfavorable," "desirable - undesirable," "accept - reject." We are in a very real sense being told how to react emotionally. Further, the solid line indicates there is now a direct tie between the symbol and the concepts but and indirect one between the concepts and the referent.

With the symbol you are reacting **directly** to the concepts but **indirectly** to the referent.

It is now possible to explain your reaction to the burning of the American flag. What happened to the political and geographic entity called the United States when the flag was burned? Nothing! But **symbolically**, we react as though the referent itself was in some way attacked. This is a consequence of our emotional reactions contained in the concepts. In a very complex fashion the concepts compel us to react to the symbol as though it were the referent. So attacking it is equivalent to attacking the referent.

If you are an Israeli, or in some other way emotionally tied to the state of Israel, then you would have the same reaction to the burning of that flag. If, however, you are a Palestinian Arab, a Shite, or a Syrian the concepts standing between the symbol (the Israeli flag) and the referent (the state of Israel) will shift from favorable to unfavorable and rather than anger at the burning of the flag you would feel great joy—just as in some other countries around the world when the American flag is viewed or burned.

We see this confusion of symbol with referent in many areas. High schools and universities will adopt certain animals to represent their institution. Thus we find the Minnesota "Gopher," the Florida "Gator," the Louisville "Cardinals," the Georgia "Bulldogs," the Army "Mule," the Navy "Goat," and on and on. Not infrequently before sporting events it is customary to burn in effigy the opponent's symbol. This is supposed to have the dual effect of inspiring the partisans while enraging the opponent.

Signs do not generate a lasting response. We may feel momentarily irritated by the fact that a natural sign indicating rain compels us to make a decision about whether or not to carry an umbrella or roll up the windows on our car. A stop sign or a yield sign can have the same reaction, especially if we are in a hurry. The rational person, however, does not ruminate about how nature is conspiring against them or how those in charge of traffic control are out to get them. Those who do this are converting signs into symbols and may have problems they are not aware of. Converting signs into symbols when there is no rational reason for doing so is a phenomenon of great interest to psychiatrists and psychologists.

Symbols, therefore, always generate a variety of emotional responses which last far longer than the immediate response to a sign which soon fades. But we continue to think about the subject evoked by the symbol, sometimes long after the symbol itself is removed from our presence. Symbols become part of our emotional baggage which we must carry with us.

Symbols are vital to humans because through them we organize our social relationships, our value systems, and even our personality structures. In other words, through symbols we give meaning to our world on a level far more complex than the simple "stimulus-response" action of the sign. If we were not able to do this, we would not have human language but a primary signaling system identical to that of animals.

Like signs, symbols may be classified as one of two general types. As with the sign, our purpose is to survey the subject not explore it in detail. To do so would require a more complex terminology that we need at this time. These two types are:

> **Universal**: These operate across cultures.
> **Particular**: Symbols which must have a cultural context before they have meaning.

**Universal Symbols.** There is some dispute about the number of universal symbols. Two types are generally agreed upon, however. The first consists of phallic and vaginal symbols. These represent the male and female reproductive organs. The phallic symbolizes fertilization and the vaginal the renewal and continuity of life. The ancients were quite graphic in the representation of these symbols. For illustrations see *Studies in Erotic Art* edited by Theodore Bowie and Cornelia V. Christenson.

The traditional Maypole Dance is a survival of this type of ritualistic symbolism. The Maypole is the phallic symbol and the dance takes place in the spring of the year, the season of fertilization. The dance was performed to insure a good crop during the growing season. The victory wreath, still sometimes presented to the winner of an athletic contest, has its roots in this same type of symbolism but is vaginal. Here you must remember that at one time only males were permitted to perform in athletic events.

**Seasonal Symbols.** In western cultures these have always been clearly symbolic.

> **Spring** — the renewal of life.
> **Summer** — the season of growth, vigor, and strength.
> **Fall** or **Autumn** — harvest and decline.
> **Winter** — death.

Shakespeare works these symbols into a number of his plays. In "Richard III," Richard says, "Now is the winter of our discontent made glorious summer by this son of York" In the musical "Knickerbocker Holiday" there is the "September Song," still occasionally heard.

> *"Oh, it's a long, long time*
> *From May to December.*
> *But the days grow short,*
> *When you reach September."*

The context for these lyrics is a man in his fifties trying to convince a woman in her early twenties to marry him. May represents the time between spring and summer. December is winter and September the fall of the year. Hence the significance of the song's title.

Studies in psychology and anthropology indicate there are other universal symbols. The psychological view is that these are buried in what they call the "collective subconscious" of humans and spring from our primal roots. If you wish to pursue this consult the works of Carl Jung and Bruno Bettelheim.

**Particular Symbols.** These must function within a cultural context to have meaning. Examine the Great Seal of the United States on the back of a bill. On it is our national bird, the American bald eagle. The selection was arbitrary and there some debate in Congress over which animal was most appropriately symbolic the new nation. Some argued for the buffalo, some the bear, others for the beaver. Benjamin Franklin made a case for the wild turkey. In one claw the eagle clutches arrows, in the other an olive branch. The former symbolizes our willingness to defend ourselves if attacked and the latter our desire for peace. So we are saying through the Great Seal, you have your choice.

Within the context of American culture, and others, this symbol carries very favorable concepts (liberty, freedom from oppression, and the right to a fair trial, among many) which stand before the referent which is the political and geographical entity. In areas of the world which disagree with our political and economic policies, then the concepts between the symbol and the referent are highly unfavorable. Finally, there are places where there is no symbolic significance at all to the Great Seal. Here it is simply a sign of the United States.

Explaining how particular symbols evolve is, at least on the theoretical level, a simple matter. In almost all cases they begin as conventional signs associated with a referent. Then something happens which will start people viewing this sign as good or bad, desirable or undesirable, favorable or unfavorable. When this happens the sign will start developing concepts and make the transition to a symbol.

The Navaho Indians, for example, took the basic cross. The arms were bent at right angles in a counter-clockwise fashion, and figures were placed on the arms representing their gods of the forests, rivers, rains, and mountains. This became for them a very potent religious symbol. For those unfamiliar with it, it was just one of those "funny" Indian signs which the Red man was always making.

In 1935, Adolph Hitler took this same basic pattern and bent the arms in a clockwise rather than counter-clockwise fashion. For those who accepted or rejected the principles of the National Socialist Party (acronymed as "Nazi") it quickly made the transition from sign to symbol.

For supporters of the party, the concepts were favorable. For those who rejected the principles as well as the new barbarism which the Nazis ushered in, the symbol developed very powerful negative concepts. And even though the political and geographical entity represented by the symbol ceased to exist in 1945, the symbol still carries strong emotional power.

Time destroys symbols as well as creates them. Hardly anyone today would recognize the symbol for Benito Mussolini's Fascist party in Italy. Like the swastika of the Nazis, it had both positive and negative concepts.

The power of the concepts that stand between a symbol and its referent should never be underestimated. You were asked to visualize the burning of an American flag. Now visualize a copy of the New Testament of the Bible. While you're at it, visualize one of the expensively printed and bound type. For many, this is a symbol of the body of beliefs and principles we call "Christianity." But rather than burning it, as with the flag, imagine that it is being deliberately ripped to pieces.

Was your reaction to the ripping up the New Testament approximately the same as with the flag? If so, then this is also a very potent symbol for you. By destroying the symbol, the referent was in some way also attacked. But as with the flag, what was actually done to the beliefs and principles of Christianity? Just as nothing happened to the political and geographical entity we call the United States, so nothing has happened to Christianity. But for many people the symbol and the thing symbolized become so intermixed that they cannot objectively separate them intellectually or emotionally.

This demonstration with the New Testament was performed before a class studying language and meaning. When ripped apart there were audible gasps of shock and anger from many of the students. Finally, a woman in the class raised her hand and asked what version was used. The title page revealed it was the Revised Standard edition. "Thank Heaven," she said. If it had been the King James Version you would have been in big trouble." So for her the Revised Standard had no symbolic status while the KJV did.

This brief look at the nature of symbols began by observing that through them we organize our social relationships, our value systems, and our personality structures. That is, symbols give meaning to our world in a manner more complex than the simple stimulus-response reaction of the sign. Humans have the unique ability to convert just about any referent they wish into a symbol. For the moment, let's not concern ourselves with whether or not the concepts are favorable or unfavorable. We will simply grant that concepts are there.

A few of the objects we can convert into symbols are:

**Clothes.** Polonius advises his son Laertes in *Hamlet*, "Costly thy habit as they purse can buy; . . . rich, not gaudy. For the apparel oft proclaims the man."

The types of clothes men and women wear will "proclaim" them. For many, being dressed in the latest fashion symbolizes that they are members of the "in" group. This, of course, will vary from social group to social group and what is regarded as "chic" in one will be downright tacky in another.

**Type and Location of Dwelling.** This applies to both houses and apartments. There is hardly a large metropolitan community that doesn't have prestige areas which symbolize affluence and life styles. Would you rather have a town house on Culbreath Bayou or a two-bedroom walk-up in Sulphur Springs? Even though the structure itself may not meet the requirements, the name of the development where it is located can impart some symbolic weight.

**Make and Model of Car.** The situation here is not different from that above. Indeed, there are any number of studies of the American automobile as a symbol. One manufacturer advertises that their product gives you all of the features of a "luxury" car without sacrificing the economy of the "lower priced models." Another says you don't have to "empty your pocketbook to get something that comes from the Black Forest." The same symbol for less money.

This list of "status symbols" could be extended considerably. The important thing is that people believe if they possess the symbol, they also possess the concepts that go with it. A large hotel chain advertises they have "class" and "style." Does this mean that you will also possess these?

This discussion of signs and symbols has been confined exclusively to specific things and objects. One point remains to be made before considering language as a sign and symbol system. The ability to create symbols is a uniquely human process. Because they are such powerful forces in shaping our attitudes and actions, one should be aware of their power.

Sometimes it may not be in our own best interests to react to symbols purely on an emotional basis. They can give meaning on a level that can be either constructive or destructive. No one will die for a sign. But it is not at all difficult to get people to die for a symbol providing the concepts are sufficiently favorable or unfavorable.

# 5

# LANGUAGE:
# A SIGN AND SYMBOL SYSTEM

> "Good mornin'"
> "Hi! How are you?"
> "Fine. And you?"
> "No complaints. Have a nice day."
> "The same to you."

Most of us go through some variation of this verbal ritual several times a day. What does it mean? Not very much when you consider the amount of information communicated. But, then, it isn't supposed to do more than serve a social purpose. You don't expect anything more and neither does the other person.

But suppose you are the one who asked the question, fully anticipating that the response will be "Fine." But instead you hear the following.

"I'm glad you asked. When I got up this morning my throat was sore. My eyes are starting to burn, I've developed a cough, and I seem to be running a fever. My stomach is a little queasy. Do you think I might be trying to come down with a cold or the flu?"

You may never again make the mistake of asking that question of this person. You may even walk on the other side of street to avoid the possibility of a reoccurrence. Why? The person provided you with a great deal more information than you anticipated and the situation, at least as you defined it, required.

These verbal rituals were called "phatic" communication by the linguist Roman Jakobson. Phatic communication is neither designed nor intended to convey a great deal of information. Rather, the purpose is to establish a link between people to show that the lines of communication are open. Not all people, however, observe them. If you are the one who wishes to indicate the lines are open and the other person fails to respond, you may feel you've been insulted.

Another form of phatic communication is found in both face to face and telephone conversations. If you are the speaker you expect to hear noises such as "yeah" or "unh-huh" at regular intervals. These have to occur at twenty to thirty second intervals. If they are not provided by your listener, you become increasingly perturbed and will inject phrases such as "you know" or questions as "do you understand?" in an attempt to assure yourself you're being heard.

These noises are called "feedback" signals. If you doubt this, try reversing the situation the next time you have a phone conversation. By withholding them, you will find the speaker will seek reassurance that someone is out there listening. The first sign that feedback is sought is usually a rise in volume. The extreme range of this is when the speaker finally asks, "Are you still there?"

Phatic communication also seems called for when we find ourselves in situations involving strangers. Psychologists have given this the elegant title of "reducing cognitive dissonance." When in an elevator or a line you might say to someone, "These elevators are sure slow" or "Do you think this line will ever move?" The purpose here is not to enter into a philosophical consideration of the slowness of elevators or lines. You simply wish to open a line of communication between yourself and another human. And it can be frustrating when your gambit is refused and the other person says nothing.

These are examples of language operating much like the primary signaling systems of animals. The phatic utterances may be considered as signs: the referent is "the line is open."

But language operates as a sign system on levels other than the phatic. A man who accidentally strikes himself with a hammer or in some other way hurts himself will exclaim, among other possibilities, "Ouch!" If you see someone in danger of being injured you may shout "Look out!" or "Duck!" just as a golfer is supposed to yell "Fore!" to alert those ahead that a ball is on the way.

Language, therefore, on its least complex level is a system of conventional signs. It is on the level of the word where we can clearly see language functioning as a sign system. An object using ink with which to write is a "pen." If lead is used, it is a "pencil." The machine you wear on your wrist and which you consult to find the time is a "watch." The item containing the words you are now reading is a "book."

In each case there is a direct tie between the sign (pen, pencil, watch, or book) and its referent. But if this were all humans could do with language, our perceptual abilities would be very limited. Communication would be on the level of "Me Tarzan, you Jane." Most, if not all, of the forms we associate with civilization would not exist. It is this ability to move from a sign to a symbol that distinguishes human language from the primary signaling systems of animals. The fact that we have this ability does not, however, mean that we always exercise it. Consider the following exchange.

"What's shakin', man?"
"Things are like, you know, cool. Nothin' heavy."
"That's neat, man. I mean like wow."
"Yeah. Well hang in there."

This, in its way, is not too different from the ritual greeting at the beginning of the chapter. Much of our communication does take place on the sign level. Attempts have been made to quantify this admittedly vague area. Some estimates are that as much as 80 percent to 85 percent of our communication is on the sign or primary signaling system level. Others run as low as 50 percent to 70 percent. But there are many people who always seem to operate on a primary signaling system level when they wish to communicate as in the brief exchange above.

Granting that much of our communication takes place on the sign level, the important fact is that human language also operates on the symbolic, something impossible in primary signaling systems. If there are Pavlovian overtones to the Sign-Referent relationship, they become far more subtle, complex and in some ways sinister when we begin to consider language as a symbolic process.

Symbols have concepts. These concepts are judgmental: good-bad, favorable-unfavorable, desirable-undesirable. The burning of the American flag will invoke very strong emotions for the patriotic citizen. This is in no way different from the reaction a person may have to the destruction of their school symbol. But these are symbols that have referents in the real world.

Through language, however, it is possible to have words which possess symbolic value but which have no referent in the real world. It is on words such as these, symbols with concepts but no referents, that our values, attitudes, and behavior are built and controlled.

To illustrate this, we would have to reconstruct our model of the symbol.

$$\text{Sy} \qquad \text{C} \text{-------} ?$$

The question mark indicates that we don't know precisely what the referent is for the symbol.What is "freedom?" The *American Heritage Dictionary* defines it as,

*1. The condition of being free of restraints.2. Liberty of the person from slavery, oppression, or incarceration. 3. a. political independence; b. possession of civil rights; c. immunity from arbitrary exercise of power.*

The *Random House Dictionary* tells us that "freedom" is,

*1. the state of being at liberty rather than in confinement or under physical restraint. 2. Exemption from external control, interference, regulation, etc. 3. the power of determining one's own actions . . .*

These definitions provide us with a catalogue of characteristics commonly associated with "freedom." We believe that "freedom" is something highly desirable as well as worth fighting and dying for. But there is no specific referent. You can't touch it, see it, smell it, or hear it. There is nothing in the real world we can point to and say with assurance, "That is freedom!" Also note that both definitions contain the word "liberty." What is the referent for this word? The *American Heritage Dictionary* tells us that "liberty" is,

> 1. a. *The condition of being not subject to restriction or control. b. The right to act in a manner of one's own choosing. 2. The state of not being in confinement . . .*

The *American College Dictionary* says "liberty" is,

> 1. *freedom from arbitrary or despotic government, or, often, from other rule or law than that of a self-governing community. 2. freedom from external or foreign rule, or independence . . .*

Like "freedom," "liberty" has no specific referent. In fact, you could substitute one definition for the other with no great loss. Both words are defined in terms of general characteristics. While it is possible to delimit the area, to say these are some aspects of what constitute "freedom" or "liberty," what remains is still blurred.

Another powerful symbol that lacks a referent in the real world is the word "love." Just what does it mean? The *American Heritage Dictionary* says,

> 1. *An intense, affectionate concern for another person. 2. An intense sexual desire for another person. 3. A beloved person. Often used as a term of endearment. 4. A strong fondness or enthusiasm for something . . .*

And *The Random House Dictionary* says:

> 1. *a profoundly tender passionate affection for a person of the opposite sex. 2. a feel of warm personal attachment or deep affection, as for a parent, child, or friend. 3. a sexual passion or desire, or its gratification . . .*

As with "freedom" and "liberty," the definitions of "love" do not give us a specific referent. In fact, the terminology used to define "love" is even fuzzier. What is meant by "affectionate," "concern," and "fondness?" About the only conclusion to reach is that "love" is heterosexual for the editors of *The Random House Dictionary*, "a profoundly passionate affection for a person of the opposite sex," while *The American Heritage Dictionary* prefers a broader interpretation, "another person."

Symbols without referents are said to be abstract. They lack specification. If you look carefully at the definitions of "freedom" and "love" you will note there is a little more to go on with "freedom." Why? Because "freedom" contains references which are in many ways more specific. We find phrases such as not being "in confinement or other physical restraints," "slavery," and "incarceration." But what is meant by "a tender, passionate affection?"

Therefore, there are levels of abstraction ranging from high to low, on which symbols operate. The level of abstraction is the distance between a symbol and its referent, if there is a referent. The greater this distance, the higher the level of abstraction.

Thus it is possible to say that while "freedom" and "love" are abstract, "love" operates on a higher level of abstraction because there is less we can say about it. The problems which levels of abstraction create in the communication of meaning will be examined more closely later. It is sufficient to note that they exist.

Because human language is a symbol system, and because many of these symbols do not have referents, we are able to produce increasingly complex layers of meaning that go beyond the here-and-now of the primary signaling system. Not only can we talk about the present, we can also discuss the past and speculate about the future.

We can also talk about things that never were nor ever will be. For example, the folklore of almost all cultures contains tales of creatures that are purely mythological. There is St. George and the dragon, to mention just one of many. These beasts were reputed to possess all sorts of powers not the least of which was the ability to both fly and breathe fire. The unicorn is another such creation. Medusa was reputed to have snakes for hair and would turn into stone anyone who looked directly in her face. Odysseus met the Cyclops, Aenius the minotaur, and Paul Bunyan had a great blue ox named Babe. These are all "inventions" of humans that have been endowed with varying degrees of symbolic significance.

Because of this ability to create and manipulate symbols, the French-Rumanian philosopher Coran suggested we drop the designations homo sapiens (thinking man) and homo locquins (speaking man) and adopt homo symbolicus (man, the maker of symbols).

Regardless of how you wish to designate our species, there is no doubt that humans are the symbol makers. No other species on earth has this ability. And this ability to create and manipulate symbols can only take place through language.

Just how powerful this symbolic use of language is may be illustrated in a number of ways. Later we will look at the metaphor, taboos, and euphemisms but for now just consider the names of things. There is a large creature that hibernates in winter which we call the "bear." If the meaning is traced back though time, we find it's earliest referent as "the brown animal." Stephen Ulmann, and others interested in problems of language and meaning, argue that this was adopted and replaced a name that is now lost. Why? Because our forebears were afraid if they used the "real" name it would bring the animal into their presence, if not physically, then symbolically.

In primitive tribes we still can find this fear of names. In some, each person has a "public" name that he or she is known by. They also have a secret name. This secret name is carefully guarded because they believe that the person who discovers it will then have power over them. Many people have names that they try and keep secret. Others will have their names changed. How we got these names is, of course, different from the primitive tribes. Some are the result of parental whimsy. But the intent is the same; we believe that the knowledge of this name will, if it gets out, give others control over us.

As we will see when we examine language taboos, there are words that have the same effect as a person's "secret" name. The concepts standing between the symbol and the referent are so unfavorable that we simply do not use them in certain social contexts and are shocked if we hear them used by others. Or at least we pretend to be shocked since there is always a difference between what we publicly profess and privately practice in language and other forms of behavior. Although the referent may not be physically present, the use of the word has the effect of bringing it psychologically and symbolically into our presence.

Therefore, it is always important to remember that in many instances the meaning of a word will not result from any actual association on your part with the referent. Rather, the meaning will be generated from the emotional associations which reside in the concepts. To illustrate this, here is an example from that master symbol manipulator, Adolph Hitler. The following quotation is from his book, *Mein Kampf*:

> *Their final goal [the Jews] is denationalization, is sowing confusion by the bastardization*
> *of other nations, lowering the racial level of the highest, and dominating this racial stew*
> *by exterminating the folkish intelligentsia and replacing by members of his own race.*

One might argue that there is a surface plausibility especially appealing to those hunting for a scapegoat for their own inadequacies. But look at the manipulation of symbols more closely. As our frame of reference, we'll use a device suggested by Stuart Chase in his book, *The Tyranny of Words*. He says that whenever you encounter a communication where the meaning may sound reasonable at first glance, you should check it in a very simple way. All you have to do is substitute the word "BLAH" for those symbols which either have no discernable referent or where you may suspect you being asked to react to the concepts rather than the referent.

Giving Herr Hitler the benefit of every possible doubt, we can render his statement as follows:

> *Their final goal is BLAH, is sowing BLAH by the BLAH of other nations. BLAHING the*
> *BLAH of the BLAH, and dominating this BLAH BLAH by exterminating the BLAH and*
> *replacing them with members of his own BLAH.*

If you believe the words "BLAH"ed have specific referents, consult a good desk dictionary. You will find few if any guideposts to steer you through this verbal morass. What is meant by a "racial stew?" What is a "racial level?" If you really want to have fun, try and figure out what constitutes the "folkish intelligentsia."

This examination of language as a symbol system only begins to open up the subject. Indeed, from the standpoint of the semioticist (someone who studies the interrelationships of signs and symbols within a culture) what has gone before is seriously lacking in both detail and rigor. But since we are using this as means to an ends, not an end in itself, the brevity may be excusable.

To synopsize, the major items to keep in mind about language as a symbol system are:

❑ Human language, on its least complex level, is quite similar to the primary signaling systems of animals but it is far more complex that the one-to-one connection between a sign and its referent.
❑ Through our symbols we are able to communicate about the past and the future, not merely the present.
❑ Human language enables us to develop abstractions.
❑ Since language is also a symbol system, concepts stand between the symbol and its referent.
❑ Some symbols (words) that have no referents. They are composed totally of concepts.
❑ What a symbol means is controlled by its concepts not its referent, if it has a referent.

To the extent we are aware that the meaning of our symbols is determined by the concepts which may have little or nothing to do with the referent, we are in control of our symbolic environment. To the extent that we lose sight of this fact, we are being controlled by that symbolic environment.

# 6

# LANGUAGE AS METAPHOR

> Life is just a bowl of cherries.
> Memories keep turning in the windmills of my mind.
> His plan fizzled out.
> I feel a little strung out today.
> He's always nitpicking my ideas.
> That was a bitter pill to swallow.
> You're just a bull in a china shop.
> That song is a real dog.
> Do you catch my drift?
> Let's tie all of this together.

These statements have one thing in common. **They are all metaphors!** Through the use of metaphors, human language is able to express complex shades of meanings. Although most think of the metaphor as a literary device that somehow doesn't exist except in literature, it is an essential part of our communication.

Simply defined, a metaphor is the comparison of two things, one to the other. What the metaphor does is suggest a similarity between A and B. Ideally, one of these elements should be familiar and the other unfamiliar. Sometimes both are unfamiliar. If we examine a few of the statements above, we can illustrate this.

**"Life is just a bowl of cherries."** This implies that there is some sort of resemblance between life and a bowl of fruit. Just why cherries were selected is a mystery. Some years ago there was a popular song using this metaphor as its title and at the end of the refrain, we are urged to "live, love, and laugh at it all." There may be some deep symbolic significance just as there is with another popular fruit metaphor: "Life can't be all peaches and cream." Which can also be applied to a woman's complexion.

**"That was a bitter pill to swallow."** "That" refers to some unspecified event which undoubtedly had unfavorable consequences for the speaker. Since most persons have at one time or another had to take medicine that was less than palatable, the comparison is on more familiar grounds than the first one.

**"You're just a bull in a china shop."** This is another time-worn expression that ties together the fragile objects usually found in such a shop with the tendency of the animal to knock things about. This presumes, of course, that we are all familiar with the actions of bulls and the breakability of objects in china shops. The validity of this metaphor was tested when an enterprising television show host took a real bull into a real china shop. The animal walked carefully down the aisles. Nothing was broken! Nevertheless, anyone who is the least bit clumsy is labelled with this metaphor.

In literary analysis, it is customary to make a distinction between a **metaphor** and a **simile**. The first is defined as an "implied" comparison, while the second is a comparison using "like" or "as." Thus, in "Life is just a bowl of cherries," we have a metaphor because the comparison is implied. If, however, it was, "Life is just like a bowl of cherries" we would have a simile because of the presence of "like."

Since both metaphor and simile involve comparisons, and since the term "simile" would not add any greater precision to our discussion of language as metaphor, we will arbitrarily consider them as being the same. For the benefit of those who wish to keep the two separate, this does not mean they are the same. Distinguishing between the metaphor and the simile is quite important in literary analysis and joining them as though they were one for the purposes of this discussion is not in any way meant to diminish the distinction in other contexts.

Metaphors, like symbols, may be scaled on the basis of their **level of abstraction**. That is, some metaphors are more abstract than others. The one dealing with the bowl of cherries is abstract because we are uncertain just what the connection is between life and a bowl of cherries. But if we are talking about swallowing bitter pills, the reference is more concrete and hence less abstract. Falling between these two extremes we have bulls and china shops. Most people have been in such a shop although they have never led a bull into one. Usually taking a small child with you is sufficient.

We discover much about our world primarily through metaphors. Why? Because we do not have the luxury of treating each event or situation as though it were unique. We could, of course, try to but this would involve an endless process of definition and redefinition. It is simpler, speedier, and easier to think of the new in terms of the old; to describe the unfamiliar in terms of the familiar. The metaphorical use of language enables us to do this!

In discussing perception, the statement was made that there is an apparent correlation between our control of low frequency words and the ability to make subtle distinctions in meaning. Some suggest there is a similar correlation between our ability to both use and be aware of metaphors and our ability to perceive. For an interesting discussion of this see Julian Jaynes, *The Origins of Consciousness in the Breakdown of the Bicameral Mind,* a book with a controversial thesis but an excellent section on metaphors.

There is, however, no evidence to support an argument for a connection between the ability to create metaphors and the amount of formal education. Indeed, some of the richer metaphors come from areas where there is little formal education. Here are a few collected in rural areas from individuals who had not completed high school. "It's so good I could eat it with one foot in the fire." "I feel like I've been run hard and put away wet." "That's about as much use as wishin' in one hand and spittin' in the other to see which gets full first." "He just keeled over dead as a hammer." "He's got a mind like a mop." "If he ain't bad mouthin' someone, he's puttin' on a poor mouth."

Further, there is no evidence to indicate that the ability to perceive metaphor is learned in any conscious fashion. A brief study was made of students who were trained to isolate metaphors (and similes) in literary analysis courses. The results showed that while they were proficient in spotting these in various forms of literature, this did not always extend to other situations. There was general difficulty in seeing them in sports columns, editorials, as well as news magazines. And even though they used metaphors in their own speech, they were not consciously aware of it. Unfortunately, a follow-up study of their abilities after the class was impossible so these results have only marginal value.

What we may find is a situation not dissimilar to one discovered at the University of Minnesota during the 1950s. Students who took a course in argumentation and persuasion were given a test before and after completing the course. Much to the puzzlement of those involved, students generally scored lower **after** taking the course. However, when they were given another version of the test prior to graduation they scored much higher than their exit scores and significantly higher than students who had not taken the course. The conclusion was that there must have been some delayed benefit. Perhaps something similar would hold true for those studying metaphor through literature.

So we cannot say the ability to perceive metaphor is a skill one can consciously acquire. Nor can we prove that the use of metaphor is in any way of value to our perceptual abilities. Perhaps the ability to perceive metaphorically can even be a handicap. As Hamlet says:

> *And thus is the native hue of resolution*
> *Sicklied o'er with the pale cast of thought.*
> *And affairs of great pitch and moment*
> *With this concern their currents turn awry*
> *And lose the name of action.*

One could argue that Hamlet's perception of the metaphorical possibilities in the situation leads him not to action but to inaction.

Also notice the metaphors Shakespeare uses. "Resolution" possesses a color "hue" that can be obscured by thought "sicklied o'er." "Affairs" become streams or rivers, they flow "currents," and can be diverted "turn awry" by thought which has a "pale cast." So it may well be that Hamlet, like Willie Loman some centuries later in Arthur Miller's "Death of a Salesman" thinks "too much."

There is another thing to note about this quotation. The metaphor is switched. "Affairs" are initially things that take place in the mind but then become "currents". If this is not done carefully the consequence is a **mixed metaphor**. There is no problem in this quotation because the central idea is forcefully underlined.

But improperly mixing a metaphor may cause problems in the communication of meaning. Because a metaphor contains two elements in making its comparison, you must be careful that one element doesn't cancel out the other. That is, one element must be consistent with the other. If they aren't, the image is incongruous. In many instances it's downright funny. Look at these examples:

> ❏ "The defendant, in presenting his alibi, chose the alley he was going to bowl on and the jury just wouldn't swallow it."
> ❏ "This report is a very hard blow to swallow."
> ❏ "This new law gives us a club with some teeth in it. Now we must find someone to coordinate it."
> ❏ "Swimming against the tide can pave the road to success."

Notice how in each, the elements cancel out one another. One has difficulty envisioning a jury swallowing a bowling alley. How does one swallow a hard blow? It's a curious club that possesses teeth. Besides, how does one go about coordinating such a club? And the relation of swimming to paving is at best inconsistent. These are in no way different from the Air Corps general who proclaimed after the first great air raid on Tokyo, "What the Japanese are hearing is the first rumblings of the handwriting on the wall." Or the government official who announced that there existed "a world-wide bottleneck."

There is nothing wrong with mixing a metaphor providing you know what you're about. For example, Ring Lardner in one of his short stories said of a young lady, "She gave him a look you could have poured in a waffle." This works despite the incongruity of the elements in the comparison. But compare this with a statement by a member of the President's cabinet, "If we open that Pandora's box, we're going to find a bunch of Trojan horses inside." Either we're dealing with a very large box or some of the smallest horses ever assembled. Also, there was only one Trojan horse not a "bunch."

There seem to be as many systems for classifying metaphors as there are people interested in the process. So rather than setting up an elaborate classificational system or rehashing some of those set up by others, we will examine just a four of the basic types of metaphor creation in order to see more clearly how they may influence perception and meaning.

## The Anthropomorphic Metaphor.

We create this type whenever we compare a part of the human body to something else. In almost all cases the comparison runs from human to non-human. For example, the object we called a "chair" is composed of anthropomorphic metaphors. Usually there are arms. The objects holding it off the floor are the legs. Chairs also have backs and seats.

A watch has a face and hands, unless it is digital. Hurricanes, needles, and cameras have eyes. The source of a river is the head and where it empties is the mouth. The bottom of a hill is the foot. We find finger cookies, sandwiches, and lakes. Corn has ears and in some cases so may walls.

Laws and regulations may have teeth. Books have spines. Roads have shoulders. If there is something we don't like, we can't stomach it. And there are always people who wish to get at the heart of the matter.

There is hardly a part of the human anatomy that hasn't been pressed into metaphorical service. You should have no difficulty in finding metaphors using the neck, the hair, the elbow, the knee, the knuckle, the bowels, the veins, the liver, and lips. This proliferation of the anthropomorphic metaphor is not difficult to understand. Since we must live in our body, it is only natural to project it on to other things.

## The Synesthetic Metaphor.

This refers to switching the associations of one sense to another. We have five senses: touch, sight, hearing, smell, and taste. We can take a word usually associated with touch and switch it to sound. Thus we can describe a sound as being either sharp or dull. Touch can be transferred to taste: sharp. Many brands of cheese are labeled "sharp," and one is "extra sharp." You may apparently transfer "sharp" to any of the other senses. A smell may be "sharp" as well as eyesight, hearing, the tongue, and one's wit.

There are any number of synesthetic transfers possible in English. We can speak of loud colors where hearing is transferred to sight. Colors may also be soft, where touch is switched to sight, as well as dull, muted, warm, and cool. In a single line from his poem "Isabella," Keats makes three synesthetic transfers:

*And taste the music of that pale vision.*

Taste, sound, and sight are combined. Which is certainly one better than "If music be the food of love, play on."

No one has yet worked out all of the possible synesthetic transfers in our language. Are they some we cannot make? If so, what does this tell us about our perception? Were some transfers possible in the past which we would not think of making today? It is difficult to picture a person with dark hearing or a loud touch.

But since language changes it is not difficult to imagine that sometime in the future synesthetic transfers which we today consider either awkward or silly might be accepted as a matter of course.

## The Allusional Metaphor.

These are drawn from literature, history, philosophy, as well as sources now lost. They are adopted as metaphors without our being aware of their original sources. Nor would it necessarily make any difference if we knew their origins except in cases where we may wish to impress others with the extent of our knowledge; a form of trivial pursuit. Here are two lines from John Donne's "Meditation XVII" which have provided several allusional metaphors.

> *No man is an island, entire of itself; every man is a piece of the continent, a part of the main . . . Any man's death diminishes me because I am involved with all man kind, and therefore never send to know for whom the bell tolls; it tolls for thee*

The mixed up metaphor dealing with Pandora's box filled with Trojan horses contains two examples drawn from mythology. Also a person's most vulnerable spot is the "Achilles' heel"; and the portion of leg, foot, and ankle connection is the Achilles' tendon. A person with the ability to make money from practically any venture is said to have the "Midas touch." When someone is in some way teased or otherwise tempted with things they cannot attain we say they are "tantalized." A party where a great deal of drinking takes place is sometimes characterized as a "dionysian" revel or a "bacchanal." Anything confusing or complicated may be referred to as a "labyrinth."

History provides us with an unlimited allusional metaphors. Thanks to Napoleon it is now possible to meet your Waterloo. At various times, people have been accused of using storm trooper or Gestapo tactics. Few are aware of the fact that when they refer to something as a "blockbuster" they are using a metaphor that has its origins in World War II. Or when they settle a dispute by "burying the hatchet" they are employing one from the colonial period.

The allusional metaphor is much admired by some because it carries an air of learning and scholarship. Unless they are carefully selected, however, the source of the metaphor may be either unknown or vague. As a consequence, meaning is lost or obscured. During the Watergate scandal some years ago an editorial contained the following allusional metaphor:

> *In deciding to ignore the subpoenas for the tapes, President Nixon has crossed the Rubicon.*

This quotation, in context, was given to two classes of college students who were asked if they had ever seen it and then to state as precisely as they could what it meant. Out of over seventy students only two admitted to having seen it elsewhere but none could tell what it meant.

It comes from Caesar's Commentaries. The Rubicon was a river that separated Italy from Gaul (France). Caesar was in pursuit of Pompey. By crossing the river he had committed himself to either victory or defeat. So to "cross the Rubicon" means to take an irrevocable step. You cannot turn back. While the editorial writer's selection of this allusional metaphor was apt, and contained meaning for some, it left two classes of college students confused. But that is an occupational hazard in using the allusional metaphor.

## The Animal Metaphor.

This transfers the assumed characteristics of animals to humans. This label also includes fowls of whatever feather, reptiles of any ilk, and insects of all varieties.

The fox is clever and sly, so are persons who have these characteristics. The dog, in addition to being "man's best friend," is noted for its faithfulness and determination. You can also be dog-tired. Lions are models for courage and pride. Pigs become metaphors for sloppiness and overweight. Chickens serve as models of cowardice and general stupidity as in calling a person a "dumb cluck." You can be busy as a beaver, industrious as an ant, pesky as a fly, slippery as an eel, bird-brained, flighty, stubborn as a mule, and dumb as an ox. If you're not careful, you can make an ass of yourself. If you do, someone may give you the horse laugh.

These four categories are intended give some idea of areas from which metaphors are drawn. There are numerous others. Further, these will change to reflect the changes in attitudes and values of our society. For example, we have adopted in the United States numerous metaphors from sports and games over the past several decades. They become part of our vocabulary and thinking even though we ourselves have never participated in them.

> The ball's in your court.
> Play it as it lies
> He threw me a curve on the test.
> He fumbled the deal.

We also draw metaphors from our occupations—war, politics, sexual activity, government, farming, airplanes, trains, automobiles, and so through an endless list.

There are some interesting questions that one should raise about types of metaphors and their sources. Are some metaphorical patterns likely to be used by one social group than by another? Do certain metaphors dominate during various historical periods? If so, what can we learn by analyzing these patterns?

Metaphors become a habitual part of our speech and our thinking. We use them without being aware we are doing so. This is not meant to imply anything sinister. (Note that the word "sinister" is metaphorical because it means "left-handed.") You simply cannot communicate without metaphors. The problem, therefore, in the communication of meaning is the use of the metaphor in a clichéd fashion where it apparently says something but actually serves as some sort of verbal ritual. In reply to a question of why he wasn't considered for a job, someone was told. "Those are the breaks. You know how the old ball bounces." Any communicative force which "old ball bounces" may have had are now all but lost. If you believe you know what that metaphor means, give it closer examination.

One aspect of this subject that helps enrich our understanding of the role of metaphor in the communication of meaning is to recognize that words which we use as a matter of course were at one time metaphors. The word "sinister" cited above is one such. The metaphor has, in a metaphorical sense, become "frozen" into the vocabulary. Thus the word "window" is composed of two words, "vindr" = wind + "auga" = eye. Literally, the eye for the wind. Hence, a "frozen" metaphor. But we become aware of this only by knowing the etymology of the word. Similarly, the word "curfew" means to cover the fire, literally, "lights out."

This overview of some of the general types of metaphor creation is not the whole story. Its purpose is simply to lay to rest the view that metaphors are something one finds only in literary works. But more importantly, we can begin to see how it is possible for metaphors to interact with one another.

A particular type of metaphor can become so powerful that it literally dominates our perception and puts blinders on us. As a result, meaning is influenced.

# DOMINANT METAPHORS

Metaphors, if they are apt and appropriate, have the potential for sharpening perception, hence meaning. Conversely, they can dull meaning if they are inappropriate. When overworked to the point of being a cliché, they block rather than stimulate thought. (The two sentences above contain one synesthetic metaphor each.) What we will consider now are metaphors in larger patterns to see some of the ways in which they have the potential for influencing meaning and perception; how they influence the ways in which we perceive ourselves as well as the manner in which we view others. These are called "dominant" metaphors because they are accepted as having validity in part or in whole by significantly large numbers of people in a culture.

## The Metaphor of the Journey.

This metaphor is not the exclusive property of Western civilization. It may be found in most cultures having a well developed mythology. In its least complicated form, this metaphor asks you to view life as a journey which begins with birth and ends with death. Another type of journey begins after death. The purpose of this journey varies from one historical period to another. During the "Middle Ages" the purpose was to achieve spiritual salvation. This period is also referred to as the "Dark Ages." Both designations are themselves metaphors.

The legends surrounding King Arthur and the Round Table are filled with all sorts of questing, the most important one being the search for the Holy Grail. The various Crusades may be viewed as extensions of this metaphor into real life. And we find echoes of it in a statement by a senator who said:

> *In searching for a solution to the problems of inflation, I'm afraid we're not going to find any Holy Grail.*

Perhaps the first major use of the journey metaphor in a search for spiritual salvation is found in Dante's epic poem *The Divine Comedy*. The traveller, Dante, journeys successively through limbo, hell, purgatory, and finally paradise—heaven. He emerges at the conclusion of the poem with a deep sense of spiritual salvation. Chaucer, in *The Canterbury Tales*, also uses the journey as the framework on which to hang the stories of the pilgrims who are on their way.

> *. . . from every shires ende*
> *Of Engelond to Canterbury they wende,*
> *The holy blissful martyr for to seeke*
> *That hem hath holpen when they were seke.*

Voltaire, some three centuries later, sends his hero Candide on a journey during which he undergoes almost unspeakable hardships. Voltaire's satirical conclusion is that all is for the best in this best of all possible worlds and we should each learn to cultivate our own gardens.

The journey metaphor is still used today. But it is now redefined. The journey is not a search for spiritual salvation in the religious sense. Rather it seeks social and psychological understanding and through it a salvation of sorts for the human spirit. An interesting transitional example is found in Mark Twain's *The Adventures of Huckleberry Finn*. Huck and Jim float down the Mississippi on a raft. As a consequence of their adventures, Huck comes to the realization that the values he was taught are wrong, that the color of a man's skin is not as important as the type of human being who inhabits it.

Dickey, in his novel, *Deliverance*, also uses a journey down a river as his controlling metaphor. A dam is to be built to harness the power of one of the last wild rivers in Georgia. Four friends elect to take a canoe trip down the river before the dam is completed in order to experience a way of life that will no longer exist. But their experiences and conclusions are quite different from Huck's.

Numerous other examples of the journey metaphor can be cited. Many years ago it was the premise of the TV series, *Wagon Train*. Later, the metaphor was put in space under various titles the most prominent of which is *Star Trek* where the aim was "to boldly go where no man has gone before." Stanley Kubrick used it in his movie *2001: A Space Odyssey*. Elements of the journey are found in *Star Wars*. There is no apparent end to the popularity of this metaphor.

If you view life as a journey, this provides you with a sense of meaning. One presumes that one sets off on a journey with a purpose, even if the purpose is to find out if there is any meaning. Things happen to you on this journey which may be apparently senseless at first. But, we are told, if we look closely, they will have significance. Further, distractions should not divert you.

Numerous reflections of this metaphor are found in our language. Graduating seniors in high school and college are conventionally told they are about to begin "life's journey." One should someday ask the speaker what he or she thinks the students have been on before the ceremony. When we die, our "journey has ended," but while alive we have "paths" to follow and "roads to travel down." In the process you can "lose your way" and even "stray from the straight and narrow." As a final observation on the Journey, some people now take "trips" without physically going anywhere. Moreover, these trips can be both "good" and "bad." When the latter happens, you are said to have "crashed."

## The Metaphor of the Machine.

This metaphor probably started to gain popularity following the invention of the clockwork mechanism. There is no instance found in Shakespeare and while Milton and others spoke of the mind as an "engine," the word at that time meant any agent or means by which something was accomplished, as in the line from John Wilmot, "Huddled in the dirt, the reasoning engine lies."

During the eighteenth century, the clock became a popular metaphor for philosophers and theologians to prove the existence of God. This was the period during which the foundations of modern science were being laid. As new laws of nature were being discovered by Newton and others, and their interrelations understood, order could be seen in what were once viewed as random occurrences. Alexander Pope caught this attitude in his, "Essay on Man," when he wrote,

*All chaos is but some order not yet understood.*
*Therefore that that is, is good.*

Several centuries earlier Copernicus had demonstrated that Ptolemy was wrong. The universe is not geocentric with everything revolving about the earth, rather it is heliocentric with the planets, including earth, revolving about the sun. This created all sorts of theological problems. The earth was no longer at the center of the universe as earlier theologians contended. Copernicus was compelled to recant his findings. During the eighteenth century, his work was rediscovered but the basic theological problem remained. How to resolve it? It becomes quite simple if you view the universe as a complex clockwork mechanism. The existence of a clock means that there must be a clockmaker. Therefore, the clockmaker is God.

Following the Industrial Revolution in England in the mid-eighteenth century and the proliferation of all sorts of machines, the metaphor begins to influence our perception of ourselves, others, and society in general as well as its various institutions. In its basic form we find:

> Society = a machine, therefore, Man = a cog in that machine.

People often refer to the "social mechanism" and question whether or not the "social machine" is functioning properly and whether it is about to "break down."

Once the dominant metaphor of society as a machine is accepted, other metaphorical extensions and perceptual attitudes follow quite naturally. A government appointee was being questioned on a national public affairs telecast about a proposed change in regulations which would make applications for government loans to small farmers more difficult. He replied, "Don't blame me. That's the rule and I can't do anything about it. I'm just one small cog in this very large machine, you know."

A person who occupies a position of major authority is, of course, a "big wheel." Machines are also capable of only two modes, on and off. So we have this as another metaphorical extension. "His ideas really turn me on," or "His ideas really turn me off." Similarly, we can "strip our gears," "idle," "run on empty," "not get started," "run on a broken wheel," "run out of gas." and end up just "spinning our wheels."

If the machine metaphor is accepted, and man becomes a cog, then the next "logical" step is to conceive of a person's function in his job, society, and life in general in parallel terms. For a real machine to function, the cogs and gears must be of a uniform shape. If they aren't, the machine either will not function properly or cease to function altogether. If a machine doesn't function, you search out the part causing trouble and replace it. So if a person is a cog or gear, and isn't performing their assigned function, you replace them with someone who will permit the machine to work. Sports teams, especially when they are winning, are referred to as "well-oiled machines," and the Cincinnati Reds were once called the "Big Red Machine," but when they stopped winning, the main cog, the manager, was summarily fired.

Therefore, when you conceive of a person not as an individual but as part of a machine, the next step is to reason that you can standardize people in the same way as machines are standardized. A good portion of what is called operant learning, as well as behavior modification, has as its base the metaphor of the machine and the person as a cog. And since the function of a machine is to produce, we conceive of ourselves and others in these terms. "He's the product of a broken home." "Education is a marketable product." "Industry is not happy with the products of our schools."

## The Metaphor of the Jungle.

This implies not too subtly that there is a comparison between life, especially in large urban areas, and living in a jungle. The problem here is that for most people the closest they have ever come to a real jungle is the version depicted in movies and on TV. But that hasn't stopped the making of pictures with titles of: *The Asphalt Jungle, The Blackboard Jungle, The Concrete Jungle, The Garment Jungle* to list but four of many such titles found in a film encyclopedia.

If we grant the dominant metaphor of the jungle, as with any dominant metaphor, other extensions become possible. Jungles are inhabited by animals. Therefore, people are "animals." Some are hunters or predators while others are the hunted or the prey. In a jungle, we are told that only the strongest will make it, so we have survival of the fittest. This is sometimes referred to as "Social Darwinism," when the metaphorical extension is applied to society; an interpretation of Darwin's thesis that he never intended any more than he did the survival of the fittest.

When this metaphor is accepted, notice how it influences our perceptions of life and people. Like any metaphor it can become a trap for the mind if we permit it. We may use the jungle as a basis for justifying any type of behavior on our part or the part of others. After all, we are sometimes told, and say ourselves, it's a dog-eat-dog world out there. This is a curious extension because very few people have ever witnessed one canine devouring another. When stretched to its ultimate extension, we may even use the metaphor as a justification for killing.

Few people have ever seen a jungle other than those depicted in the media. Some years ago the United Nations became so disturbed by the popular depiction that the word was dropped and "savannah" substituted. Nevertheless, we still continue to transfer these supposed surface characteristics to modern life while ignoring the deeper, more significant differences. We do not take into account that in a real jungle, stalking, killing, and eating are part of a carefully organized system of survival. There is no verified instance of a homicidal animal that sets out to slaughter a dozen or so of its own kind, or another, for that matter, just for the fun of it. There are few animals in nature, aside from humans, who kill for the sheer pleasure of the act or without apparent motivation.

## The Metaphor of the Wasteland.

This contrasts the barrenness and aridity of the desert with the moral and spiritual barrenness and aridity of modern life. A former chairman of the Federal Communications Commission. Newton Minnow, once characterized television as a "vast wasteland" offering little in the way of intellectual or spiritual stimulation to its viewers.

This metaphor is best realized visually and for this reason is frequently favored by motion pictures. *The Dawn of Man* sequence in Kubrick's *2001: A Space Odyssey* is filmed in a setting that is mostly desert, thus echoing the intellectual state of man at that time. Several years later, *Electroglide in Blue*, opened and closed with a panoramic shot of the Arizona desert. This stood as a visual metaphor for the barrenness of the lives of the central characters. By opening and closing with the same scene, we are told, metaphorically, that nothing has changed or been accomplished.

The wasteland may also serve as a metaphor for a testing ground of a person's values. Normally accepted value patterns are suspended as the individual struggles for survival. The desert becomes a place where a person learns what is or is not important for survival. This extends past physical survival and embraces spiritual and moral survival as well.

But you do not have to have a physical wasteland for this metaphor to function. Large cities, small towns, and even exclusive suburban communities can also become "deserts" in the metaphorical sense. Once the metaphor is established and the comparison accepted the physical surroundings become secondary; spiritual and moral wastelands can exist anywhere.

## The Metaphor of the Prison.

The forepiece of Thomas Wolfe's, *Look Homeward Angel* contains these lines:

> *Naked and alone we came into exile. In her dark womb we did not know our mother's face; from the prison of her flesh have we come into the unspeakable and incommunicable prison of this earth.*

Wolfe suggests two types of prisons, the flesh and the earth. But depending on the situation just about anything may be regarded in terms of this dominant metaphor. Here are a few of the possibilities:

**The prison of the body.** As Hamlet lamented,

> *"Oh that this too, too solid flesh could melt . . ."*

Diet aids suggest that we are prisoners of our body and the only way to free ourselves is to lose weight. A prominent psychiatrist spoke of a patient as being a woman imprisoned in a man's body.

**The prison of the mind.** "I think too much!" lamented Willie Loman in *Death of a Salesman*. The idea of being locked in with your own thoughts can be the same as being in prison.

**The prison of society or the state.** This aspect of the metaphor deals with metaphorical confinement by being part of an institution or a member of a social class. Randall Jarrell used this in his short poem, *The Death of the Ball Turrett Gunner*,

> *From my mother's sleep I fell into the State,*
> *And I hunched in its belly till my wet fur froze.*
> *Six miles from earth, loosed from its dream of life,*
> *I woke to find black flak, the nightmare fighters.*
> *When I died they washed me out of the turret with a hose.*

But there are all sorts of prisons where we can be confined. Quite frequently when one encounters a series of seemingly random reverses, they are said to be prisoners of fate. A person who happens to be in the wrong place at the wrong time becomes a prisoner of circumstance. Someone who cannot control their actions are prisoners of desire. And one should not forget the lament of individual in the popular song of many years ago who found he was just a prisoner of love.

## The Metaphor of the Medical Center.

This metaphor deals with illness but not necessarily the variety you can treat with drugs or surgery. People are "sick," groups are "sick," society is "sick," and perhaps the universe isn't doing all that well. During the Watergate scandals, John Dean, a White House attorney, is supposed to have told President Nixon, "There is a cancer on the presidency." Winston Churchill, Prime Minister of England during World War II, described Nazi Germany as a "festering sore," and a "boil that needs lancing." Various countries have, at various times, been described as the "sick man of Europe." Similarly, our economy is sometimes said to be sick and was characterized during the 1970s as suffering from "terminal inflation."

This metaphor may be extended quite easily to mental as well as unspecified physical ailments. At times we say that people seem to have gone mad or insane. The same is true of groups and society in general. The dominance of this metaphor is not as strong as it once was but is still quite pervasive. We still speak of "curing" society's ills, of performing radical surgery on government spending, and even putting government on a strict diet because it has become too bloated. Preoccupied as we are with health as a personal phenomenon there is little likelihood that the Medical Center metaphor will disappear.

These are six dominant metaphors which influence our perception of life, ourselves, and others. There are others. One that seems to be well on its way to becoming a dominant metaphor is that of the computer. Words from this "language" are slowly but definitely finding their way into our general vocabulary and are used by persons who have never touched a computer. We talk and read about "input," which refers to the opinions of others. One of the interesting extensions of this is "negative input" as opposed to "positive input." If things are put in they must come out, so we have "output," which may also be "negative" or "positive." Establishing communication from one area to another is now "interfacing." When our reactions to a proposal are needed, we are asked to provide "feedback," but you must be careful for positive feedback is more appreciated than negative. What were plans for action are now "programs" in the computer sense not the broadcasting sense. Planning is more often than not "programming," Anything that doesn't make sense is said to "not compute." And earlier when discussing the hemispheres of the brain, the left was said to function as an digital computer and the right as an analog.

Like metaphors in general, dominant ones serve to help us explain the unfamiliar in terms of the familiar. But because they are more encompassing, and because they always carry secondary metaphors with them, their potential for influencing perceptions, and hence the meaning, of large groups of people is far more profound. Like the symbol, an awareness of the potential for influence of perception by dominant metaphors can alert us to the possible hazards of overgeneralizing a complex situation in a readily packaged form. As with the symbol, the problem is whether we will be controlled by our dominant metaphors or be in control of them. As the Cheshire cat said to Alice, "The question is who's to be the master."

# 7

# WHAT DO WE MEAN BY "MEANING?"

If you attempt to find a single synonym for "meaning," the task will prove impossible. Look at these sentences:

> 1. My work has lost its meaning.
> 2. Cloudy skies can mean rainy weather.
> 3. This means war!
> 4. He means well.
> 5. My great grandfather's watch means a lot.
> 6. Democracy means government of, by, and for the people.

In example #1, the most workable synonym is "purpose." "A sign of" would fit #2. In #3, we can substitute "will result in." In #4, try "has good intentions." For #5, "is worth" is perhaps the best. And in #6, we might use "is a symbol for." There are at least fourteen other contexts in which "mean" can function. Consulting either a dictionary or a book dealing with the subject of meaning doesn't help, either.

> "**Meaning**: the sum total of a person's past associations which are called forth when a word is heard or read."
> "**Meaning**: that which is intended to be, or actually is, expressed or indicated; signification; import."

You could justifiably ask what these definitions "mean." What constitutes the "sum total of a person's past associations?" How do we know "what is intended to be?" This borders on mind reading. Is it possible to assess "import?"

Some years ago Ogden and Richards wrote a two-volume work with the title, *The Meaning of Meaning*. The conclusion reached was that "meaning" "means" a number things. There is, therefore, a great deal of confusion as to what "meaning" actually "means." But this is not too surprising because the word has no referent. We are dealing with a highly abstract symbol when the context is human language. The task of determining "meaning" is less complex in the "hard" sciences because it is possible to use empirical data; we can prove that $2 + 2 = 4$, that $19 \times 5 = 95$, and that NaCl is the formula for sodium chloride—table salt.

Rather than rehashing an involved series of philosophical discourses on the nature of meaning, or to attempt an operational definition, as we did with "language," the most expedient thing to do is arrive at some sort of **operational understanding**.

When discussing symbols, we said that they could be classified on a scale ranging from concrete to abstract. These are the two terms to begin with in developing an operational understanding. A word is concrete when there is a specific referent and when the word is not used in a metaphorical sense. All words used as signs are, of course, concrete because they must have a referent. Thus we can define "drunk" as: having sufficient alcohol in the blood to bring about the modification of behavior and the impairment of reflexes, or having .01 percent in the blood by volume.

The first lacks some precision but is never-the-less the one used in some states to define the word for legal purposes. The second is more "scientific" in that it spells out in measurable terms what constitutes drunk. This percentage may vary slightly from one state to another. Tests, however, have shown that it is possible for some persons to be legally drunk because of the alcohol percentage but still not have their behavior and/or reflexes imparted. In both cases, there is a referent for drunkenness and in both definitions the use of the word in non-metaphorical.

If, however, you say "He's drunk with power." or "She's drunk with joy," the word is being used in a metaphorical sense. In this instance, we have a synesthetic metaphor because one sense is being transferred to another. More importantly, "drunk" loses the concreteness it has in the first two definitions.

While concrete words always have specific referents, abstract ones do not. Therefore, we can refer to all words used as metaphors as being abstract simply because their referents are either lost or obscured. And the easiest way to move a word from concrete to abstract is to use it as a metaphor.

Earlier it was shown that words such as "freedom" and "love" are difficult to define because they lack referents. All you can do is narrow the areas of possible reference. Certainly there is a difference in the meaning when you say, "I love you," and "I love ice cream." What, if anything, is the difference in "I'd like to go," and "I'd love to go?" While some might argue to the contrary, there is nothing that you can point to and say with certainty, "That is love!"

Abstract words refer to attitudes—"angry," "happy," "bored," "relieved," "sad"; qualities—"patriotism," "courage," "cowardice," "bravery"; values—"moral," "honesty," "good," "bad"; and ideologies or beliefs—"democracy," "freedom of speech," "communism," "conservative," "liberal."

Abstract words defy precise definition because they lack referents and rely on the emotional reactions of the concepts. All of the words above have very strong favorable or unfavorable emotional associations in their concepts. Also, there is a semantic trap built into the designations—"attitudes," "qualities," "values," "ideologies," and "beliefs." "Courage" was given as an example of a "quality," and "honesty" as one of a "value." One might legitimately ask if courage isn't a value and honesty a quality. Or perhaps these words can be both. Most certainly! You can define them just about any way you wish because they are abstract. This is one of the problems of trying to define "meaning." You must use abstractions to discuss abstractions. Also, this is an excellent example of why human language differs from the primary signaling system of animals.

All of this can be frustrating, interesting, and perhaps even fun. But it doesn't bring us any closer to an **operational understanding** of meaning. The next place to move after "concrete" and "abstract" is to a feature of words discussed earlier. There is difficulty of defining words in isolation because they may, and probably do, have several meanings. That is, they have **polysemy**—various meanings. In isolation, the word "bridge" has several possible specific referents: 1. a structure that spans; 2. a type of dental plate; 3. A card game.

But what about the word in this phrase, "a bridge over troubled waters?" Here, "bridge" is used in a metaphorical sense and cannot be visualized.

But you can be shown a real bridge either physically or in a picture. Similarly, you have concrete referents for "bridge" as dental plate and "bridge" as a game. How and why words develop polysemy is a question to be taken up later. For now, we will simply say that all words have polysemy. Some will have more, others less. With the introduction of polysemy, we can begin to develop an **operational understanding** of meaning a little more precise than the "concrete" - "abstract" division. Two types of meaning are suggested in the three examples above.

## Referential Meaning.

This is the actual thing or object referred to. The simplest way of designating referential meaning is to point directly to the object. Or to show a picture of it.

> What do you mean by a book?
> The object you're reading this from is a book.
> What do you mean by paper?
> Paper is what this is printed on.

In Jonathan's Swift's *Gulliver's Travels* there is a group of philosophers who distrust abstractions. To avoid this pitfall, each carries a large bag filled with objects. When they want to discuss something, they reach into their bags and pull out various objects and arrange them in patterns. This may work in fiction but not in real life. There is really no way to completely free yourself of abstractions. In fact, Swift was satirizing a school of philosophy popular during the eighteenth century by using this absurd example.

Today, the logical positivists mirror Swift's philosophers. They contend the only "true" statements are those capable of scientific proof. Thus, "the rose is red" is a "true" statement because we can demonstrate on the color spectrum that this color exists. But "the rose is beautiful" is incapable of proof because "beauty" is incapable of scientific verification.

Should you wish to follow the example used by Swift, you must first consider the problems of polysemy. This diversity of the possible meanings of words can cause problems for anyone wishing to communicate entirely in referential terms. If you were one of Swift's philosophers, you would have to have several types of "bridges" in your bag. And it would be impossible for you to use "bridge" as a metaphor because no matter how hard you tried there's no way to put "a bridge over troubled waters" into the bag.

The second type of meaning helps resolve most of the problems created by polysemy and trying to deal with words in isolation.

## Distributional Meaning.

This is the meaning a word has when used in a sentence. Or, to put it another way, we provide a context for a word. This context will, in almost all cases, resolve problems of polysemy.

> The bridge collapsed.
> He broke his bridge eating peanut brittle.
> Let's play bridge instead of pinochle.

The combination of referential and distributional meaning is used by dictionary makers, "lexicographers," when they write definitions. Catalogs of contexts are maintained and updated at regular intervals. They collect polysemy. When it's time to revise their definitions for a new edition, they will note something like this:

> Bridge (as a structure)   750 entries
> Bridge (as a denture)     600 entries
> Bridge (as a card game)   500 entries
> Bridge (as a metaphor)    450 entries

The distribution with the most entries will then appear as the first definition and so on through the four examples. They will also note whether it is used as a noun, verb, adjective, or adverb. This combination of referential and distributional meanings which appears in a dictionary is called **lexical meaning**. Another word sometimes used is **denotation** or **denotative meaning**. But **lexical meaning** and **denotation** are not synonymous. A workable distinction is:

> **Lexical Meaning**: the polysemy of a word found in a dictionary.
> **Denotation**: the meaning a word has in a specific context.

A word in isolation may refer to many things. Once it is distributed by providing a context, it will denote one area out of the other possible areas.

Life would be simple if the words in a language meant only in the referential and distributional senses. Unfortunately, they do not. There is a third type of meaning which can override both referential and distributional meaning.

## Notional Meaning.

This type results from the emotional associations, either favorable or unfavorable, which a word will develop through use. These emotional associations are a word's connotations. The term **notional** is used here in preference to "connotative" because a "notion" is a general, vague, not always clearly defined impression one may have about something.

Notional meaning develops in the concepts whether or not the symbol has a referent. These can become so powerful that we react not to the referent but to the concepts. This type of meaning operates on a number of levels.

**Idiosyncratic** or **Individual**. No two people ever have exactly the same experiences. Therefore on the level of the individual, as an individual, our personal experiences with a symbol means we may develop a notional meaning quite different from that of others. For example, most people have a favorable, or perhaps neutral, reaction when they hear the word "tasty" in reference to the flavor of food. A friend does not! Why? Because as an adolescent his family had roast chicken just about every Sunday for dinner. Aside from the predictability of the meal, a relative insisted on proclaiming, "This is the tastiest roast chicken we've ever had." This went on for some years with each chicken being "tastier" than the one the week before. While he did not develop a dislike for chicken, he did for the word. On the idiosyncratic or individual level the word "tasty" carries highly unfavorable connotations for him. Also, he must constantly be on guard when he hears or reads the word or his notional meaning gets in the way. He's not always entirely successful. Further, this enables him to indulge in semantic hypocrisy when served a meal of dubious quality. He can always say it was very "tasty." The host and hostess feel complimented.

If you look into your personal symbol systems, and be honest about it, you will find words which arouse unfavorable, or favorable, connotations in you but not in others. Some areas of psychology use notional meaning as one way of attempting to get at a person's problems. This usually takes the form of word association tests where you are asked to give the first word that comes to mind when you hear another. The list will always contain key or "trigger" words which get at your concepts.

But this is a problem for psychologists and psychiatrists. For our purposes, while we should be aware that notional meaning can influence perception on the idiosyncratic or individual level we cannot be overly concerned with it. If we went around attempting to psych-out other people's notional areas, and try to avoid them, communication would grind to a halt. The only advice is to hope for the best and be prepared for the worst.

**The Group.** We are all members of various groups and our degree of identification with them will influence the notional meanings words may have. A few of the groups we know have an influence on or notional meaning are:

*Political.* If you are a Republican, how do you react to the words "Democrat" and "Liberal?" If you are a Democrat, how do you feel about "Republican" and "Conservative?" Regardless of your political preferences, what is your reaction to "deficit spending," "foreign aid," "welfare programs," "communists," and "fellow travelers?" The intensity of our political identification will have an effect on our notional meanings.

*Religious.* Depending on your affiliation, or the lack of it, what is your reaction to "Lutheran," "Catholic," "Seventh Day Adventist," "Mormon," "Methodist," or "Unitarian?" Do you react to the word "abortion?" To what degree is your reaction controlled by your religious affiliation? In the 1960s a prominent theologian created a great furor when he announced that God was dead. He was using "dead" in a metaphorical sense but persons of some denominations took the term referentially and pages were filled with arguments on both sides, generating more heat than light.

*Racial.* If you are black how do you react to such characterizations as "spade," "nigger," "coon," or "jungle bunny?" If you are Spanish, how about "spic," "greaser," "wetback," and others? This list of racially loaded terms could be extended but we are all aware of the power of notional meaning in racially derogatory terms.

What we don't know enough about is the manner in which the racial group we belong to and identify with may have different distributional and notional meanings for the same word. For most whites, to say someone is "bright" is to indicate they are smart, intelligent, and quick minded. For many blacks the word means to have light skin. Some years ago a white teacher unintentionally caused great amusement among the black students in class when she told them if they studied harder they could be "bright." One of them muttered, "No way!"

*Clubs and Organizations.* Americans are joiners: the American Legion, the National Rifle Association, the American Civil Liberties Union, the Daughters of the American Revolution, the Kiwanis Club, the Rotarians, the Fraternal Order of Eagles, Sertoma. A simple listing of the possibilities would fill pages. Again, as with membership in political and racial groups, the degree of our identification with the interests of the group will influence our notional meaning. If you belong to groups with conflicting interests, you must either reconcile the difference or go though life hopelessly cross-pressured.

**Geographical Region**. You may not consider a geographical region as a "group." But the fact is that the area we come from has an influence on the notional meaning of certain words. The two major divisions here are: 1. Rural - Urban; and 2. North - South - East - West.

There are still certain rural areas where the notional meaning of the word "bull" for the male of the bovine species is such that you should not use it in mixed company. The socially acceptable choice is either "he-cow" in some areas, "cow-critter" in others. Also involved here is a type of language taboo, sex, which is more appropriately discussed later. This is also true of "rooster" in some rural areas. The use of this word in itself is an interesting American peculiarity not found in England. The term most frequently used during the Colonial period was "cock" and it is still used in England to refer to the male of this species. But, again for reasons to be looked at later, the word "cock" developed highly unfavorable notional (it pejorated) meaning in the United States. When it did, two other rural terms, "weathercock" and "haycock" became "weathervane" and "haystack." But "rooster" also developed the same problem and as a consequence you will sometimes find "he-biddy" the accepted term.

Conversely, some words used in rural areas are offensive to most urbanites. A lady of some standing in her rural community in Arkansas called to her small daughter who had a cold, "Melinda! Come over here and let me snot your nose." There is also some urban revulsion to "bitch" when referring to dogs and "in heat" for female animals ready for breeding. There seems to be no such problem when using them as animal metaphors in reference to humans. "Stud" seems to have escaped its notional problems and "to service" in reference to breeding animals is a puzzlement to most urbanites.

The North-South-East-West influence on notional meaning has diminished. This is largely the result of population shifts so that the traditional regional boundaries are not as distinct as they once were. Television and motion pictures, however, help to perpetuate certain language stereotypes, not only for the South but also for rural residents regardless of geographical region. Still found in some areas of the South, especially among older natives, is the distinction between "drive" and "carry." When transporting humans, you are said to "carry" them from one place to another; you "drive" animals. For those who still insist on this distinction, it would be an insult if you offered to "drive" them home.

Notional meaning is so bound up with other factors that you can only generalize about the various types of possible influences. Also, notional meaning is very much subject to change. Words which at one time had favorable notional meanings will develop unfavorable ones. Conversely, unfavorable connotations can become favorable. Or at least not so unfavorable. The word "pregnant" was at one time so charged that it was not used in mixed company, especially if children were present. A lady was "expecting" or "in a family way" or "expecting a blessed event." But they were never "pregnant" and definitely never "knocked up."

Since "meaning" cannot be defined in any precise fashion, the best we can do is arrive at an operational understanding of some factors which control it. In a sense, when we speak of "meaning" we are really talking about a complex set of factors which operate simultaneously when a word is heard or read. There can be no doubt that the word "meaning" represents a very high level abstraction. The fact that we cannot define it even as loosely as we define many other abstract words should in no way prejudice attempts to understand the phenomenon. No one can be completely objective in their language behavior. Recognizing this, it is possible to be aware of some of the factors which control our reactions. This awareness should alert us when we may be adopting courses of action which are not beneficial to either ourselves nor others.

# 8

# HOW AND WHY MEANINGS CHANGE

The following is a close paraphrase of an example from John Algeo's *Problems in The Origins and Development of the English Language.*

> *He was a gentle **harlot** and a happy **bride**. His wife was a teetotaling vegetarian who ate large amounts of **meat** and drank so much **liquor** he was afraid she might starve. But the whole-wheat bread she made from the **corn**, was the best in the county. When not cooking, she liked to feed the **deer** that lived in their **apple** trees, heavy with pears this spring. Although **lewd** for a **boor's** wife, she was quite **silly** and the model of chastity before marriage.*

Something is semantically amiss in this passage. How can "he" be a "harlot and a "bride? If his wife is a teetotaling vegetarian, why does she eat "meat" and drink "liquor?" How can you "starve" from overeating? Is it possible to make whole wheat bread from "corn?" What sort of "deer" live in trees, especially "apple" trees bearing pears? Can a "lewd" person be the model of chastity? Why would anyone want to marry the "silly" daughter of a "boor?"

Despite the apparent semantic chaos this passage generates, all of these words, at one time, made perfectly good sense in the contexts in which they are used. Language changes; the semantic system changes more rapidly than the phonological and syntactic. Our pronunciation has shifted a bit since the sixteenth century. So it was possible for poets to rhyme words that we cannot today. Shakespeare has "grass-grace-grease" as true rhymes. As recently as the eighteenth century, Pope could rhyme "join-line" and "say-tea." We are aware of this because some words are rarely pronounced the way they are spelled. But this is a minor irritation. Syntactically, there have been fewer changes in English since 1625 than there were from 1600 to 1625.

There are several reasons for this stability in the phonological and syntactic systems. A major one was the spread of printing and the increase in literacy. Then public education and, in the twentieth century, radio, motion pictures, and television. These are forces which tend to maintain the status quo in the language, especially education on all levels from the primary through the university.

The comparatively stable nature of the phonological and syntactic systems led linguists to call them "closed" because they are the slowest to change. The semantic system of a language, however, is constantly being modified. For this reason, it is called "open." New words are adopted into the language. When this happens, some words will shift their meanings both connotatively and denotatively. Other words will cease to be used as a part of the active vocabulary in both speech and writing. This is what happened to the words in the opening paragraph. Earlier, we would find:

| | |
|---|---|
| **harlot** | a young boy |
| **bride** | an recently married person regardless of sex |
| **meat** | any food |
| **liquor** | any liquid, alcoholic or not |
| **starve** | to die |
| **deer** | any small animal |
| **apple** | the fruit of any tree |
| **lewd** | ignorant, unlearned |
| **boor** | a farmer |
| **silly** | innocent in the moral sense |

Sometimes the semantic ground can shift very rapidly. Until the time of Korean War you could speak or write the following sentences without fear of being ambiguous:

> "I feel gay."
> "It was a gay party."
> "Let's have a few beers at Ed's, it's a real gay place."

And the line from the old Christmas carol, "Don we now our gay apparel" is certain to provoke at least a smile. Its adoption by the homosexual community brought about a shift in both the concepts and the referent. As evidence of this, the residents on a street in a large midwestern town successfully petitioned the city commission to change the street's name. The name had been "Gay Way." Historically, it had nothing to do with the emotion but was the name of an early settler in the area.

The same type of changes can be noted with other words. "Grass" is no longer something you must mow at regular intervals. "Pot" is not necessarily a cooking utensil. With the help of either, you can go on a "trip" without leaving the room. Lights, stoves, and machinery are no longer the only things "turned on." "Flash" and "ball" when used as verbs have little to do with suddenness or sports—at least in the commonly understood contexts.

Meaning is, therefore, very much subject to change. When meaning changes, the referential, distributional, and notional areas may be affected. There are four types of meaning changes a word can undergo. Sometimes, if you look at the history of a word, it will reflect several of these before the meaning either gains a degree of stability or the word stops being used.

❏ **Generalization of Meaning**
❏ **Specialization of Meaning**
❏ **Amelioration of Meaning**
❏ **Pejoration of Meaning**

## Generalization of Meaning.

This occurs when a word which at one time had a specific referent loses it. Sometimes it is called "radiation" or "broadening" of meaning. The word "cool" has increasingly generalized. We are all familiar with some of the synesthetic transfers such as "cool" colors. But what does the word mean in these sentences?

He's real cool.
Don't blow your cool.
I saw a real cool movie.
I hate cool music.

"Awful" was at one time a very powerful word in its concepts and meant "to fill with awe." This was the sense in which Milton and others used it and it was in this sense that their readers understood it. Since the seventeenth century, "awful" has gradually lost force in the notional area and as a consequence the referent is vague. For most people it has become a mildly intensifying word serving the same function as "very."

I saw an awful good move.
That was an awful bad concert.
I really feel awful.
It was awful awful.

"Nice" meant to make precise distinctions between or among things. There is also some evidence indicating this distinction was overly precise, perhaps even foolish; one that need not have been made. We still have an echo of this in the phrase, "making a nice distinction," but for most such a distinction is felt to be desirable. Like "awful," the meaning of "nice" is now so generalized as to make it impossible to define with precision. There is a vague connotation of pleasantness about it. Or, if not that, at least it isn't entirely unpleasant. "I had a nice time." Perhaps this means "enjoyable" but you cannot be certain. "Be nice to your mother." Here it may be equivalent to "good" or "kind." But what do you do with "Have a nice day.?" The frequency of this phrase has reduced it to a social ritual having little or no meaning.

When words generalize they suffer from "semantic overload." Their polysemy increases to the point where it is impossible to tell what, if anything, they mean. They become "waste basket" words, noises we make to others. They can signify everything and nothing at the same time.

In most cases, however, the generalization is not this disastrous. The word "barn" once meant the building where barley was stored. Today it can mean any large farm building used for storing implements and housing animals. Or we can use it as a metaphor by saying that someone lives in a barn of a house, meaning it is perhaps larger than necessary. Or, parents may admonish a child with a messy room by saying it looks like a barn or "where do you think you live, in a barn?"

Another example of how generalization takes place without causing semantic overload is the word "cardinal." Originally, it meant a "hinge." Since "hinges" are things around which other things turn, we find an extension in the phrase "cardinal principles." Later it came to denote a church rank in the Catholic hierarchy. These men are, metaphorically, the "hinges" around which church doctrine turns. They elect the Pope and also determine policy. Because they wear red as a designation of their rank, the name was transferred to first the color and then to the bird. The word sustains this polysemy with little difficulty and distributional meaning resolves any ambiguity as far as the referents are concerned.

Sometimes a word you are accustomed to using with a precise denotation will generalize without your being aware of it. I had this experience with the word "reactionary." During the 1964 Presidential campaign between Lyndon Johnson and Barry Goldwater, I was discussing the merits of the men with a neighbor. I said that on the basis of his platform, Goldwater was too "reactionary" for my tastes. My neighbor immediately became very indignant; Goldwater wasn't the reactionary, it was Johnson with his welfare programs and the like that would lead the nation down the road to socialism, if not worse.

The communication breakdown arose because I was using "reactionary" in its precise sense: one who wishes to "re-act," to go back to older ways. For my neighbor, "reactionary" had generalized and meant anyone who was out to upset the status quo; he further equated it with the possible destruction of the "American way of life." For him the word was synonymous with "radical." "Radical" has also generalized and no longer refers to someone who wishes to get at the root causes of a problem. There are still echoes of the core meaning in mathematics where "radical sign" means "square root" and in certain forms of surgery where the procedure is called "radical"; an operation to remove your appendix is not "radical," a heart or liver transplant is.

Generalization of meaning, then, is the loss of specific denotations. In its extreme form, semantic overload will result. In most cases, however, the modifications in the concepts or the referents will not be so great that distributional meaning cannot resolve any problem resulting from the polysemy.

## Specialization of Meaning.

This is the opposite of generalization. Words which at one time had general meanings will acquire specific ones. This is sometimes referred as the "narrowing" of meaning. Most of the words used in the opening passage have undergone specialization.

| | |
|---|---|
| **harlot:** | Although somewhat obsolete, the word nevertheless now refers to the female. |
| **bride:** | Specialized to the female. |
| **meat:** | Specialized to the flesh of animals in most nonmetaphorical contexts. |
| **liquor:** | Specialized to liquids containing alcohol. |
| **starve:** | Specialized in non-metaphorical contexts to hunger. |
| **corn:** | Specialized in American English; in England it still refers to any cereal grain. What Americans call corn is either "maize" or "Indian corn" for the British. |

The only words in the passage which haven't specialized are "boor" and "silly." Any person who is rude or clumsy is a "boor." If they are dull and tedious, they are a "bore." "Silly" has also generalized and can now be applied to anything that is faintly ridiculous or inane: "What a silly idea," or "That's a silly looking hat."

Are there any words currently in transition from general to specific? "Expletive" seems headed in that direction. It referred to a word added to a sentence to fill out a construction. "It was nice meeting you." "It" is an "expletive" because the word fills out the construction. When the Watergate tapes were released they were carefully edited to delete words considered offensive. In place of the word or words, the phrase "expletive deleted" was inserted. Although "expletive" meaning a profane or obscene expression was one of the possible definitions, the oft repeated use has assured specialization. Composition teachers may have to search for another term when they want to discuss a student's use or misuse of "expletives."

## Amelioration of Meaning.

This takes place when words which had either neutral or unfavorable connotations lose them and acquire favorable ones. Another term for this is "semantic elevation." Words which ameliorate gain in social acceptability. This may occur when the word either generalizes or specializes. Sometimes it just happens.

Many of the words which today designate particular religious denominations have undergone amelioration. When "Quaker," "Protestant," and "Methodist" were first used they had unfavorable connotations. But this process is not confined to the names of religious denominations. Here are some other words with their earlier meanings:

| minister | a servant |
|---|---|
| fame | a report or rumor |
| luxury | lustful |
| steward | keeper of the pig sty |
| constable | head of the stable |
| marshal | a stable hand |
| engineer | a plotter or schemer |

Thanks to television some words previously carrying heavy unfavorable connotations are starting to lose them. They have completely ameliorated. Their concepts have shifted into a neutral area. Nor does this mean that the words do not still have very strong negative connotations for many people. While words such as "constipation," "diarrhea," and "period" (in reference to a woman's menstrual cycle) no longer have the impact they had at one time, there are still those for whom they possess strong negative connotations.

What about the increasing use of the "four-letter" words especially in movies and on television? Is this an indication they are on their way to being ameliorated? Very probably not. We just hear them so frequently that they have lost the shock value they once had. In most instances they have been reduced, like "awful," to the status of mildly intensifying words.

## Pejoration of Meaning.

This occurs when a word with neutral or favorable connotations loses them and acquires unfavorable ones. It is sometimes called "semantic degradation." This is what happened to "harlot," lewd," "silly," and "boor." A "harlot" is now a whore, a prostitute, or a woman who has indiscriminate sex. "Silly" no longer means innocent but is synonymous with "foolish." A "lewd" person is one involved in proscribed sexual activity. And a "boor" is someone who is rude and unmannered. Some other words that have undergone pejoration are:

| "reek" | smoke |
|---|---|
| "pretty" | cunning |
| "cunning" | learned |
| "sly" | skillful |
| "fond" | foolish |

Depending on one's political attitudes, "liberal," "conservative," "left," and "right" have pejorated. In a like manner, so have "radical" and "reactionary." You could also argue that these words have become so generalized in the process of pejorating that they are all but meaningless. They are all concepts with no referent.

These are the four ways in which words may change their meanings. If we designated Generalization and Specialization as the horizontal axis and Amelioration and Pejoration as the vertical, we can diagram the process as follows:

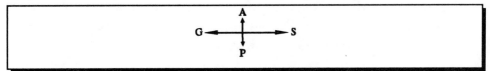

This diagram is useful for plotting the movement of a word not only from one historical period to another but also from one social group to another. In discussing notional meaning, a number of factors controlling it were mentioned. These can influence where you place a word, especially on the vertical axis ranging from Ameliorated to Pejorated. For example, "tasty" most likely would be placed more in the direction of Generalized but above the horizontal in the direction of Ameliorated for many people. Another placement would be more to the Specialized end and definitely below the horizontal and deeply Pejorated. All but two of the words in the opening passage have moved from Generalization to Specialization. Assuming that all of the words had neutral connotations when first used some have moved in the direction of Amelioration while the majority have pejorated. There can be little doubt that "reactionary" had for my neighbor both generalized and pejorated

An instance of how meaning can be influenced by social group is the word "punk" when used in reference to young males. For most whites the word is slightly pejorated and on the generalized end of the horizontal axis. For many blacks the word is highly pejorated and on the specialized end of the axis for it is used to refer to homosexuals. Being aware of these differences should alert one to possible areas of semantic conflict not only between racial groups but political, religious, social, and ethnic ones as well. Regrettably, the work in this area is not detailed and the findings, tentative though they may be, have not received wide attention.

This does not suggest that such knowledge would resolve all inter-group communication problems. But it does give those concerned with reducing tensions something to work with and could thus reduce the possibilities of either misinterpretation or a complete breakdown in communication.

Also, an awareness of the types of meaning changes can be used by those trying to interpret and analyze something from another historical period. Students of literature, history, sociology, psychology, political science, and other academic disciplines run the risk of misinterpreting a passage simply because a word used at the time meant something either slightly or completely different from what it means now.

Thus, when Hamlet says he is going to push aside "all fond recollection" he doesn't mean "pleasant" memories but "foolish" ones. Anyone seeking to interpret the works of Max Weber in *The Protestant Ethic and the Spirit of Capitalism* would do well to remember that the words "bureaucrat" and "bureaucracy" meant something quite different to him, especially in the concepts, from what they have come to mean today. They would also be well advised to check on the meaning of "Protestant ethic" and "capitalism" because these have also undergone a shift in meaning.

## WHY MEANINGS CHANGE

A useful tool for tracing meaning changes is *The Oxford English Dictionary*. Here are found the historical changes in the meanings that English words have undergone since their first appearance in writing. There are thirteen volumes which bring the language into the 1930s. Recently supplementary volumes were published to bring the dictionary up to date not only with meaning changes but also with the new words that have entered the vocabulary.

This is an heroic undertaking. There is nothing equivalent in American English except Mitford Mathew's, *Dictionary of Americanisms*, But this is not as broad in scope and is rapidly going out of date for want of a complete revision or the addition of a supplement. A measure of updating can be found in Harold Wentworth and Stuart Berg Flexner's, *Dictionary of American Slang*, 2nd supplemented edition, 1975, as well as Flexner's, *I Hear America Talking* and *Listening to America*.

Despite the usefulness of these works in helping to trace generalization, specialization, amelioration, and pejoration, they are not too helpful in understanding "why" these changes took place. To find answers to this, the linguist needs the help of the historian, the anthropologist, the psychologist, the political scientist, and sometimes just plain luck. By the same token, these disciplines can draw on linguistics to supply them with information about language and language change which they can use in rounding out their studies.

You cannot study a language without some understanding of the culture, the historical context, and the political atmosphere in which language functions. Nor can any study in other disciplines be more than marginally adequate without an understanding and appreciation of the role of language. Indeed, many of the early contributions to linguistics in the United States were those of anthropologists and it is still one of the most active in its study and analysis. Therefore, using some of the materials and methods developed in these disciplines, which we generally classify as the behavioral sciences, it is possible to approach the question of "why" the meanings of words will change.

Earlier, when discussing the misconception that language should not change, reference was made to *Webster's New International Dictionary,* 3rd edition, and the furor created following its publication. The three major criticisms were: 1. dropping some words found in the 2nd edition; 2. including new words without adding a restrictive label; and 3. listing new meanings before older ones.

These criticisms ignore a fact of linguistic life: your language serves your society. As your society changes, your language must also change. Sometimes these changes are not necessarily those which you, personally, either like or approve. If, for example, you consulted a dictionary published in 1900 or earlier and looked up the word "broadcast" you would find: "broadcast, v. To scatter, as seed or other substances, usually by hand."

With the development of radio the word was borrowed as a metaphor for this new medium of communication. Soon, determined by the frequency of use in this new context, the new meaning pushed the older one into a secondary position. Unless you are using a dictionary constructed on historical principles, this will be the first listed meaning. Here we have an example of one of the reasons why the meanings of words will change.

## Technological Change

Technology will always have an impact on language. The meanings of words already in the language will be modified and, as with "broadcast," the polysemy will be increased. Where there was only one or two possible meanings for this word in 1900, there are now at least fourteen.

It is impossible to find a single technological innovation in a society without finding at least one example of its influence on the language. So numerous are the contributions from the development of various machines that it is not possible to list them. "Spare tire," "a flat," "blowout," "blow a gasket" "get cranked up" and others reflect the impact of the automobile either on the meanings of existing terms or the introduction of new ones. Thanks to the space program we can now "blast off," have a "countdown," and be in "orbit" depending, of course, whether or not everything is "A-OK."

## The Loss of Original Referent

This happens in several ways. One occurs when a word which was the property of a comparatively small group finds its way into general use. The words "hip" and "jazz" have their origins in the houses of prostitution in New Orleans around the beginning of the twentieth century. A "hip" person (sometimes spelled "hep") was some-one who smoked opium. "Jazz" meant to have sexual intercourse, a meaning it still has in some regional and social groups. It was customary to have small groups of black musicians play in the parlors of these houses. While excellent musicians, they had little or no formal training. Consequently, their songs were improvised, memorized, and provided breaks for the individual players to demonstrate their skills on their instruments. During the '20s this style of music gained popularity and "moved up the river" to Chicago. When asked the name of their music, the musicians said "jazz" or "just jazzin' around." Unaware of the origins of the term, it was adopted as the name for this style of music. Some of musicians were in the habit of smoking a pipe of opium prior to performing. This introduced "hip."

Similarly "gig," "riff," and a number of others found their way into general use. Detached from their original referents, they underwent amelioration and acceptance.

Another way change can occur is when a word finds its way into general use primarily because of its novelty. If there was ever a referent it was soon lost and the force lies in the concepts. "Funky" may stem from an older word, "funk" meaning to be emotionally down or depressed. But in many contexts it doesn't carry such connotations. "He really played good; real funky." "That's a real funky outfit." There may still be a referent for some but in general use there is none. The same is true of "nerd," sometimes spelled "nurd." We know it is applied to humans and is pejorative, but there is no referent. The word may be a blend, that is, a combination of "nut" and "turd." "Humongous" and "scuzzy" are also two of many such words which fall into this category. Both of these may be blends.

## New Words Entering the Semantic Field

If someone attempted to draw a diagram to explain the **semantic system** of a language all they could sketch would be a formless blob. There is no shape because the semantic system is in a constant state of modification.

The blob produced today would not be same as one produced next year or ten years from now because the semantic system has changed. The semantic system is the sum total of the ideas capable of being expressed in a language at any given time.

Within the semantic system, however, it is possible to visualize circles which represent **semantic fields**. A semantic field is that portion of the overall semantic system which an idea or a concept occupies. One such circle may represent the idea of expressing ways of having little or no money. Another may represent ways of expressing one's feelings when smoking marijuana. A third could be ways of expressing dislike for another person. A fourth might be ways of expressing the manner of depriving someone or something of life.

The catalog would be endless because we have no way of knowing the number of semantic fields existing within a language at any given time. The "way" of expressing anything within a semantic field is equivalent to a word. Thus if we take the semantic field expressing the idea of having little or no money we could use such words as "poor." "destitute," "bankrupt," "penniless," and "busted" to list five of many. Since each represents a different aspect of the idea, they cannot be used interchangeably with any assurance of precision. We may also place within this circle the diagram given earlier with Generalization and Specialization representing the horizontal axis and Amelioration and Pejoration the vertical. We can now distribute these words in relationship to the diagram. "Poor" would be more Generalized than "bankrupt" and so on. The portion of the semantic field occupied by a word is its **semantic range**.

Now, let's explore the field "to deprive of life" to see what happens when new words come into a semantic field. If we look at English during the early part of the Old English period (around 850 A.D.) we find there is but a single word that has come down to us as "slay." This referred to depriving both humans and animals of life. Towards the end of the Old English period (just prior to 1100) the word "kill" starts to appear with greater frequency. It enters on the Generalized side of the horizontal axis and as a consequence "slay" moves in the direction of Specialization. "Slay" comes more and more to refer to depriving humans of life and also carries the notion of deliberate intent in its concepts. You may accidentally "kill" someone, but you don't accidentally "slay" them. Sometime around 1250, "murder" appears in this semantic field. It enters on the Specialized side of the horizontal axis and is more precise than "kill" or "slay." A person may be "killed" or "slain" in battle but never "murdered." It carried in its concepts both deliberateness and illegality. About 200 years later there is the first recorded use of "execute." This also enters on the specialized side of the horizontal axis but in most contexts it carries with it the notion of an act legally sanctioned. It sounds better to say that the "murderer" was "executed" rather than "killed," "slain," or "murdered" by the state.

In 1618, the *Oxford English Dictionary* records the first use of "assassinate" as a way to deprive of life. This is a more elegant form of murder and is generally reserved for prominent people, heads of state, popes, major political figures and so on. This is a gray area and the question of rank has never been satisfactorily resolved. Was Abraham Lincoln "murdered" or "assassinated?" Was John Wilkes Booth a "murderer" or an "assassin?"

Regardless, when new words enter a semantic field they disturb the ranges of words already in that field and bring about meaning shifts. These may be in any of the four directions listed as "how" meanings change.

The discussion of "why" meanings change could be ended here if the semantic system of a language were made up solely of neat, clearly separated circles. Unfortunately, because of polysemy, this cannot be. A word may occupy a range within two or more semantic fields. The word "bridge," used earlier, illustrates this. Indeed, just about any word functions, or is capable of functioning, in two or more semantic fields. If someone were to say: "That's funny." Does the word "funny" fall within the semantic field of strange and unusual things or does it fall within the semantic field of amusing events? Since no further context is provided, the sentence is ambiguous. But this is a relatively simple problem to resolve. If you are uncertain, just ask, "Do you mean 'funny' in the sense of 'amusing' or 'funny' in the sense of 'peculiar?'"

## Borrowing a Word from One Semantic Field into Another.

Meaning problems usually result when a word is borrowed into a semantic field where the pejorative connotations are strong. When this happens, the semantic range of the word in the field from which it is borrowed will be disturbed.

> Semantic Field A - Words relating to emotions.
> Semantic Field B - Words relating to homosexuality.

The word "gay" is borrowed from A into B. As a consequence, the pejorative nature of B in the minds of many will then result in a feedback to A with the result that its range will be disturbed in the original field.

Similarly, the word "flash" was borrowed from the semantic field of "quick actions." Now, depending on the context, the word can mean: 1. to vomit; 2. to expose oneself; 3. to experience the effects of narcotics; 4. to have an idea. Similarly, "turn on" comes from a machine metaphor and now occupies numerous semantic fields. 1. to arouse interest; 2. to arouse sexually; 3. to use drugs.

To varying degrees, the borrowing of "gay," "flash," and "turn on" have influenced the ranges within their original semantic fields. Whether this disturbance is temporary or permanent remains to be seen. "Grass, "acid," "freak," and "trip" are four words borrowed from various semantic fields by those who use drugs. These words now have general currency even though the users may have no association with what is sometimes referred to as the "drug culture." Nor has there been an effect on these words in their original semantic fields.

Borrowing a word from one semantic field into another where there is a connotative shift in the concepts from favorable to unfavorable results in a feedback into the original semantic field.

## A Connotative Shift in the Concepts Leading to a Change in the Referent.

This is not a variation of the "why" just discussed. Here, the concepts standing between the symbol and its referent (if there is a referent) become so emotionally charged that the referent will change. The classic example of this is "villain." The word was borrowed from French and meant a farmer or a peasant. During the fourteenth century in England there was the "Peasants' Revolt." The farmers "villains" burned a few estates and generally indulged in what those effected would regard as anti-social behavior. As a result, the word "villain" started to develop unfavorable concepts. These gradually build up over the years until the pejorative connotations resulted in a displacement of the original referent. In Shakespeare's day, the word still retained both possible meanings. So when someone is referred to as a "villain" you must examine the context carefully to determine if the reference is to a farmer or the sense in which is now most commonly understood. The words "reactionary" and "radical" are also examples of this happening.

The reverse is possible. A word with neutral or pejorative connotations in the concepts will lose them and in the process of amelioration the referent will change. As the word "minister" became associated with politics and religion, the referent shifted from "servant" to one who serves in some high governmental capacity or who has had formal training in religion.

"Fame," in like manner, is no longer a rumor but now is something to be sought after. "Sophisticated" meant something that was overly complex. Later it came to mean "refined" as in a "sophisticated" person, and perhaps even "intellectually complex" as in a "sophisticated idea."

## A Change in Social Values.

For a number of reasons the attitudes of a sufficient number of people speaking a language will change. When this occurs, words which at one time were regarded as pejorative will ameliorate or move into a neutral position in their concepts. Conversely, changes in social attitudes will cause some words to pejorate. An example of the latter is "mistress." Historically, this is the feminine form of "master." During the nineteenth century there was a change in the attitude about married men who maintained women other than their wives. The word "mistress" was applied to such women and pejoration set in. Today, however, the word does not have the same degree of pejoration it had twenty or so years ago, indicating another change in our social values being reflected in our language

A word which for a number of years was totally pejorated is "abortion." Today we find ads in newspapers for abortion clinics. Not so long ago a newspaper would have rejected such an ad without comment. There are many who regard both the word and the act as totally reprehensible. But since the Supreme Court decision in 1975 upholding the legality of abortions, the word no longer carries the great freight of pejoration it once did. Our social attitudes have shifted to the degree where it now possible to speak and print the word. Whether or not this represents, as some contend, further evidence of the decay of our moral fiber is a subject that cannot be usefully debated.

Sometimes the language has difficulty in keeping up with changes in social values and attitudes. While men and women have lived together without benefit of some sort of ceremony legalizing the relationship this fact was simply not mentioned in "polite" society. Now there are large numbers of couples in all age groups who live together without the benefit of a ceremony. Problem? How does one refer to these situations? "Living together" implies a more permanent arrangement than "sleeping together." Another possibility is "co-house person." The Bureau of the Census has developed the acronym "poselq," which may be loosely translated as "persons of opposite sex living quarters." Of more recent vintage is "significant other"—which is a bit murky since it can also be used to refer to either wife of husband.

## Deliberately Shifting a Word from One Semantic Field to Another.

We do not know if the shift of "gay" from its original semantic field was deliberate but the best educated guess is no. It is quite a different matter when you start calling "janitors," "custodians." Or when children with various types of learning abilities ranging from psychological to physical are termed "exceptional." The purpose here is to obscure the concepts by changing the symbol even though the referent remains the same.

There are four and only four ways in which the meanings of words may change. 1. Generalization; 2. Specialization; 3. Amelioration; and 4. Pejoration. Further, it is usually the case that if a word either generalizes or specializes it will also either ameliorate or pejorate. All four of these are controlled by what happens in one's society as a whole as well as the groups within that society. Although seven possible "whys" for meaning change were given, this doesn't limit explanations of why to one or more of them. As with many things in language, the change may be impossible to trace.

One thing is certain, however. The semantic system changes and will continue to change. To believe you can hold these forces in check is about as productive as believing you can hold an intelligent conversation with a hermit crab or a cheese cracker. But being aware that these forces are in operation can lead to a better control of the meanings we wish to communicate as well as to an awareness of when someone is trying to manipulate us.

We can also use this knowledge as a means of perceiving a little more precisely the meanings of another generation. Sometimes people complain about a "generation gap." What they are really complaining about is a "meaning" gap. Using the same words does not necessarily guarantee that communication will take place. The meanings for different individuals and groups may be different, both denotatively and connotatively.

# 9

# WORDS: HOW THEY GET INTO THE LANGUAGE

*Abactor - benim - concinnate - glother - incrassate - jactation - moonling - pleonetic - reaks - statuminate*

If these words are puzzling, don't rush to a dictionary and look them up. The odds are against your finding any of them. They are no longer a part of the active vocabulary of English. Only the most ardent tracer of obscure words has encountered them.

| | |
|---|---|
| **abactor** | one who steals cattle |
| **benim** | to rob |
| **concinnate** | to put together neatly |
| **glother** | to flatter |
| **incrassate** | to thicken |
| **jactate** | to toss and turn |
| **moonling** | a simpleton |
| **pleonetic** | grasping, greedy |
| **reaks** | practical jokes |
| **statuminate** | to support or establish |

Why did these words drop out of the language? The simplest explanation is that a majority of the speakers of English felt they no longer served any useful purpose so they stopped using them and replaced them. Or it may have been they were used by only a few writers and never found their way into the general vocabulary. The purpose of this chapter is to see how words find their way into the language.

We do not know too much about the rate at which a language will either add words to or drop them from its vocabulary. A branch of linguistics with the impressive title "lexicostatistics" attempts to explain the phenomenon. If we use English as an example, we may say it tends to double its vocabulary every 200 years. But this is based on written records. We have no idea how many words were at one time in the spoken language but never found their way into writing. If they were written, the document is now lost. The results of studies on vocabulary replacement are tentative, sometimes no more than educated guesses.

We do know that anything which affects the culture will be reflected in the language. Frequently these words, which were used in a specialized sense, will find their way into the general vocabulary and we use them without being aware of their origins. Many believe that "high ball," meaning to travel at great speed, comes either from trucking or from the name of a drink. Historically, the term comes from railroading. At one time, the speed at which a train could travel was indicated by a ball suspended from a vertical arm at stations. The higher the ball, the faster the train could travel on that stretch of track. Any small town where a train stopped to take on water was known as a "jerk water." This was then extended to mean any small town regardless of whether or not a railroad ran through it.

When Henry Ford started mass producing cars, we find "jalopy," "step on the gas," "tin lizzie," "road hog," "tailgating," and "hitch hiking" appearing. The process of unionizing added additional polysemy to "scab." Laborers in factories were labeled as "blue collar" workers while those who worked in offices were "white collar" types.

In addition to areas of cultural impact, there are more specific categories of word formation which languages use to pump new, and needed, items into their vocabularies.

**Compounding.** This is a characteristic of the language family to which English belongs. You simply take two words already in the language and combine them to describe a new object. These are sometimes called "self-explaining compounds." The object which tobacco residue is deposited after smoking is "ash" + "tray." The instrument on which letters and other papers are composed is "type" + "writer." (Originally, this referred to the person who operated the machine rather than the instrument itself.) When you go out at night, partial illumination is provided by an object composed of "street" + "light." Your car has a "windshield," "head lights," "tail lights," and a "rear view mirror."

English permits us to adapt "compounding" to the various parts of speech:

| | |
|---|---|
| N + N = N | ashtray, streetlight |
| V + N = N | runway, wishbone |
| N + V = Adj | homemade, heartbreak |

This catalog could be continued at some length. English, moreover, has extended the compounding process and permits the combining of Greek and Latin roots, something not always found in the other languages of our family. We use an instrument called a "telephone" ("tele" meaning distant + "phone" meaning sound) and in the evening we may watch "television" ("tele" + "vision" meaning to see). But German goes within its own vocabulary for the compounds: "fernsprecher" and "fernsehen" where "fern" = distance and "sprecher" = speaker; "sehen" means to see.

While compounding remains our principal source for the creation of new words, there are other means of adding to our vocabulary. In alphabetical order, some of these are:

**Acronyming.** Forming words from the first letter or syllables of a series of words.

| | | | |
|---|---|---|---|
| Self | | Light | |
| Contained | | Amplification by | |
| Underwater | = **SCUBA** | Stimulated | = **LASER** |
| Breathing | | Emission of | |
| Apparatus | | Radiation | |
| | Liquid | | |
| | OXygen | = **LOX** | |

German also does this.

| | | | |
|---|---|---|---|
| FLieger | | GEheim | |
| Abwehr | = **FLAK** or FLACK | STAats | = **GESTAPO** |
| Kanon | | POlizei | |

Many acronyms today are derived from the names of government organizations. These are always spelled with capital letters. While we may not know the specific reference in full, we have some vague notion of what the acronym refers to: NASA = National Aeronautical and Space Administration; NATO = North Atlantic Treaty Organization; SALT = Strategic Arms Limitations Talks; HUD = Housing and Urban Develop. Just how long they will have meaning should these organizations disappear is problematical. Few people remember that the "3 Cs" stood for the Civilian Conservation Corps or that CINCPOA, during World War II was the designation for "Commander in Chief, Pacific Ocean Area." Even at the time WAVES was widely used, few could say it was an acronym for "Women Accepted for Volunteer Emergency Service," the women's reserve for the U.S. Navy.

A recent trend in acronyms is to create one deliberately for an organization. This is done by selecting a word already in the vocabulary whose notional meaning captures in some measure an idea related to the organization's purpose. You then use the letters in the word as a name for the organization.

| | | COngress for | | |
| | | Racial = **CORE** | | |
| | | Equality | | |
| Volunteers | | | Service | |
| In | | | Core | |
| Service | = **VISTA** | | Of | = **SCORE** |
| To | | | Retired | |
| America | | | Executives | |

Most acronyms of this type have a limited life span because the organizations they refer to disappear. Consequently, a dictionary of acronyms is sometimes a useful thing to have when reading about past political events. Despite their relatively short life spans, acronyms will continue to serve a useful, though sometimes confusing, purpose.

**Affixing.** This is the use of prefixes and suffixes to derive new words. No one has yet beat the one created for a song in the movie "Mary Poppins": super + cal + fragil + istic + expe + ali + docious. Fortunately, it hasn't found its way in the language except as a curiosity item.

A prefix such as "de-" can be added to "contaminate" and derive "decontaminate." We can also place it before "mark," "compose," as well as "-liver," "-ceive," "rail," and numerous others. A good desk dictionary will have at least a page or more of words derived with this affix.

Or we can take a suffix such a "-ment" and derive "punishment," "basement," "torment," and "entombment" which is composed of both a prefix and a suffix added to "tomb." A listing of the possibilities for derivation through affixing would result in a fair sized volume. Sample listings of prefixes and affixes in English may be obtained from any number of sources.

Two suffixes have recently regained popularity: "-wise" and "-ize." Why they fell into such disrepute for the better part of a century, at least in writing, is a mystery. We have such accepted words as "otherwise," "lengthwise," "counterclockwise," "criticize," "vandalize," and "tantalize." But people who have no objection to these will become almost apoplectic when they hear or read "temperaturewise," "educationwise," and "costwise" or "concretize," "finalize" and "casualize." While such combinations may be an affront to one's sense of style, "-wise" and "-ize" are suffixes that have all the force of language history behind them.

Similarly, the prefixes "ultra-" and "super-" have gained in popularity. In most contexts they function not unlike the intensifiers "very" or "extremely." In politics it is customary to refer to "ultra-liberals" and "ultra-conservatives." One detergent boasts it will get your clothes "ultra-clean," there's a deodorant to keep you "ultra-safe," and you can brush your teeth with "Ultra-Brite." There is also a detergent to get your clothes "super-clean" if "ultra-" isn't good enough.

A brand of toilet paper assures us its "super soft." And a cleanser boasts it is "super fine." Something may be "super-good," "super-interesting," or "super-nice." All else failing, you may simply use this prefix as a word, "That's super!"

Sometimes an affix will fall into disuse after enjoying a period of popularity. This is the fate of the suffix "-teria." During the 1920s and 1930s it appeared in a number of combinations which strike us today as either peculiar or downright funny.

| | |
|---|---|
| gasateria | filling station |
| washateria | laundromat |
| groceteria | a fast food place |
| bookateria | bookstore |

The extensive use of "-rama" and "-burger" which we have today may strike future generations with the same amusement that "-teria" has for us. Prior to the introduction of "Cinerama" as a movie process in the 1950s, this suffix was difficult to find except is words such as "panorama," "cyclorama," and "diorama." The last two are references to particular types of pictorial display. But a few of the more recent reincarnations provide us with:

| | |
|---|---|
| liquorama | a booze sale |
| beeforama | a meat sale |
| horrorama | several horror movies |
| salearama | store-wide sale |
| cararama | a car sale |

Numerous others can be added to the proliferation of "-burger": cheeseburger - fishburger - steakburger - chickenburger - oliveburger - whopperburger - what-a-burger - ranchburger

**Back Formation.** This is the creation of a new word by deleting an affix (usually a suffix) from an existing word. What we do is extend the rules which enable us to derive nouns from verbs. Thus one who "sails" becomes a "sailor," one who "bakes" is a "baker," something that "cooks" is a "cooker," one who "runs" is a "runner," and one who "hits" is a "hitter." But in the case of the back formation, the noun appeared first and then the verb was formed. This occurred with the following words:

| Noun | Verb |
|---|---|
| peddler | peddle |
| escalator | escalate |
| gypsy | gyp |
| resurrection | resurrect |
| editor | edit |
| sculptor | sculpt |
| panhandler | panhandle |
| mugger | mug |
| electrocution | electrocute |
| reminiscence | reminisce |

**Blending**. This is the combining of two words to form a new one. Unlike the compound where the two words remain intact, the blend removes the last portion of the first one and the first part of the second. Whether this is a conscious or unconscious process is uncertain. What is certain is that it has been going on for some time in English. Here are some blends that are at least a hundred years old.

| | |
|---|---|
| flash + gush | flush |
| twist + whirl | twirl |
| flutter + hurry | flurry |
| spray + twig | sprig |
| chuckle + snort | chortle |

Here are some of more recent vintage.

| | |
|---|---|
| motor + hotel | motel |
| smoke + fog | smog |
| broil + roasted | broasted |
| cafeteria + auditorium | cafetorium |

The recent blends seem to be more conscious creations but that may be because we are historically closer to them. Regardless, the process continues, sometimes with an amazing lack of grace. A zoo recently mated a lion and a tiger. There was much debate as to whether to designate the offspring as a "liger" or a "tiglon." Life will most certainly go on whichever is chosen.

**Clipping**. This is a simple process and one used frequently in English. To clip you shorten a word by dropping something, usually an affix, from it.

| Front Clipping | | Back Clipping | |
|---|---|---|---|
| telephone | phone | ammunition | ammo |
| parachute | chute | brassiere | bra |
| moonshine | shine | hypodermic | hypo |
| periwig | wig | professor | prof |
| defend | fend | examination | exam |
| acute | cute | homosexual | homo |
| omnibus | bus | delicatessen | deli or delly |
| estate | state | obituary | obit |
| estrange | strange | preliminary | prelim |

**Coinage.** Literally, creating a word. You can do this as much as you wish. The only problem is convincing others the word you've coined is useful. If enough people agree, the word will find its way into the language and may even eventually be defined in a dictionary.

Shakespeare is credited with coining over 1700 words most of which are still used. Among those appearing for the first time in his works are "auspicious," "bump," "countless," "dwindle," "hurry," "lapse," "misplaced," and "monumental." When John Milton was searching for a word to describe hell in "Paradise Lost" he came up with "pandemonium" and the word remains. Thomas Jefferson is credited with "belittle," a coinage for which he was roundly criticized by the British who regarded it as a corruption.

Among those added since the end of World War II are "microdot," "automation," "brinkmanship," "biorhythm," "software," "input," "replicate," and "feedback." In addition to being coinages, these also illustrate some of the other forms mentioned earlier. In fact, "acronym" was not coined until 1943. If, however, you feel some of these have no place in the language, stop and consider that during the eighteenth century, Samuel Johnson and Jonathan Swift wished to purge "stingy," "mob," "fun," and "clever" among others as unfortunate coinages serving no real purpose.

Sometimes a word coined as the name for a commercial product will find its way into the language as a "generic" term. Five such are "kleenex," "vasoline," "zipper," "jello," and "bandaid." While manufacturers like to have a product name widely recognized, they live in fear of it becoming a generic term. But with the five examples cited, the courts ruled the names have become so identified with a general type of product (paper tissues, for example, with Kleenex) they can no longer be protected under copyright law. While many people regard "Coke" as a generic for any brand of cola soft drink, it is still protected by law. In fact, the Coca-Cola company maintains a special staff to see that "Coke" is never used as a generic for another brand of cola.

Then there is the multitude of words whose coiners must remain forever anonymous. We will never know who first gave us "plop," "zap," "wow," "skuzzy," "cruddy," "grungy," "grody," and "humongous." Regardless of what some may think of them, they are a part of the active vocabulary of our language. And future users of the language may regard these objections with the same curiosity that we today view the injunctions of Dr. Johnson and Dean Swift.

**Functional Shifting.** This is a fancy way of saying that a word typically classified as one part of speech is capable of being used as another. The noun "father" functions as a verbal in the sentence, "He fathered three children." Or it is a noun adjunct in "He is father confessor for his Scout troop." If we consider "gamble" to be a verb then it is converted into a nominal in "He took a gamble and lost." The adjective "sudden" is an adverbial in "The car stopped suddenly."

There are as many ways of functionally shifting words as there are of compounding but they will almost always fall into one the four major grammatical classifications of words: noun, verb, adjective, and adverb. Thus the word "running," which in isolation we would call a verb in isolation because of the {-ing} suffix, can function nominally, adjectivally, and adverbially:

> Friday is the 25th running of the race.
> Running water is not always safe to drink.
> Some came running.

**Proper Names to Words.** Frequently the name of a person, place, or object comes to signify the meaning of an idea, an action, or another thing. When you "boycott" something by refusing to purchase or participate, you are honoring the memory of Captain Charles C. Boycott, an agent for an Irish landlord who in 1880 was the first person to have this distinction. In the late eighteenth century Captain William Lynch of Virginia meted out summary justice to alleged offenders by hanging them on the spot. Rudolph Diesel is memorialized in the engine he invented. The man who introduced tobacco into France in 1560 was named Nicot and the substance of that plant is nicotine. "Leotard," "dunce," "sandwich," "sadist," "derrick," "braille," "Fahrenheit," "volt," "begonia," and even "America" have their roots in the names of people.

Similarly, the names of fictional and mythological figures add words to the language.

| | |
|---|---|
| quixotic | Don Quixote |
| pander | Pandarus |
| erotic | Eros |
| herculean | Hercules |
| ammonia | Ammon (Egyptian) |

Words are also drawn from place names: ascot - attic - denim - donnybrook - frank - sherry - slave - tangerine.

**Metaphorical Extension.** Here we create new meanings for a word by transferring some of the semantic aspects of another word to it. This is one of the major ways in which polysemy comes about and may be a reason for meanings changing. Thus, since "money" is essential to the purchase of food, and one of the staple foods is "bread," we can then metaphorically extend "bread" and use it to mean "money." Similarly, "clothes" may become "threads," movies are "flicks," "marijuana" is "grass" (among other possibilities). At one time your mouth was your "pie hole," your nose was your "beak," or your "snoot" (both animal metaphors). Someone who is drunk or using drugs is said to be "high" or "bombed."

**Onomatopoeia.** This jawbreaker of a term refers to the creation of words which attempt to imitate natural sounds: baa - tweet - chirp - hoot - quack - pee-wee - dilly-dally - wishy-washy - flim-flam.

## THE PAST IN OUR VOCABULARY

Whatever is important in the culture will be reflected in the vocabulary. This reflection is not only of the present but of the past as well. We have all heard or used statements similar to these:

"If you need any help just send up a smoke signal."
"This has gone on long enough! Why don't we just bury the hatchet?"
"Our economy is on a toboggan ride."
"He got hit with a roundhouse right."
"Don't let them sidetrack you with excuses."

Embedded in these sentences are examples of two influences: "bury the hatchet," and "toboggan" are contributions to both our language and our metaphorical baggage by the American Indians. "Roundhouse," "sidetrack," and "dead head" represent echoes of the influence of the railroads.

Our past is reflected in our language although we may not always be aware of it. This applies not only to events but also to social, political, and religious groups.

When the first settlers came to American they were indeed "strangers in a strange land." They encountered unfamiliar peoples, animals, plants, and geographical features. Since we feel that everything must have a name, our forebears had three options: 1. Transfer names that were familiar. 2. Adopt the names used by the natives. 3. Make up new names.

Consider the names of the thirteen original states:

> Connecticut - Delaware - Georgia - Maryland - Massachusetts - New Hampshire - New Jersey - New York - North Carolina - Pennsylvania - Rhode Island - South Carolina - Virginia

Of these, only Connecticut and Massachusetts are of Indian origin. The others are "New" + the original place names in England or the names of British royalty except for Penn, a British statesman, and Rhodes who was Dutch.

Once political independence was achieved and new states added, twenty-four more names would be drawn from Indian words and tribes, six would be of Spanish origin, three of French, and only one, Washington, for a historical figure. Alaska and Hawaii are respectively Eskimo and Hawaiian. West Virginia seceded from Virginia during the Civil War.

Here are some groups which contributed to our vocabulary during the Colonial period.

**American Indians**. Today, the major contributions of the American Indian are found in place names. We have retained surprisingly few in other areas of our vocabulary. There are ten or so names for animals (chipmunk, raccoon, and skunk), a dozen or more names for plants (hickory, pecan, sequoia, squash, hominy), as well as a few with regional significance: scuppernong, tamarack, and supawn. More generally used and understood are "powwow," "sachem," "caucus," "wampum," "tepee," "mugwump," and "tammany." Albert Marckwardt in *American English* estimates that, aside from place names, no more than fifty words survive to reflect our early contact with the American Indian. Large numbers fell from general use during the nineteenth and early twentieth centuries.

**The Dutch.** Settling in and around New York and areas of Pennsylvania, the Dutch contributed such vocabulary staples as: caboose - cole slaw - boss - yankee - waffle - snoop - spook - stoop - boodle - dope - dumb - cookie - Santa Claus.

**The French**. The primary French contributions come from the Mississippi Valley area from the Canadian border to the Gulf. From these early explorers we have adopted - bayou - gopher - pumpkin - cent - dime - parlay - picayune - sashay - chowder - prairie - rapids - portage - bureau

**The Spanish**. The Spanish contributions come from both the Colonial period and the westward expansion. There are the names of foods: chili - enchilada - frijole - taco - tamale - tortilla. The West is easily identified through such Spanish words as corral - lariat - lasso - ranch - rodeo - stampede - bonanza - wrangle - patio - chaps - sombrero - desperado - calaboose - hoosegow - vigilantes.

**The Germans**. A number of names for foods are of German origin: sauerkraut - pancakes - schnitzel - strudel; as well as any number of exclamations and characterizations: phooey - ouch - nix - loafer - bum - bub - hex - katzenjammer - fresh - spiel.

Following political independence, the waves of emigrants to America helped to enrich our vocabulary. Among the various racial, national, ethnic, and religious groups whose words found their way into general use were the Jews. Although there were large numbers of German Jews who arrived between 1840 and 1865, the so-called "new immigrants," who arrived between 1880 and 1910, were to have the greatest influence. Most of these spoke Yiddish, a Creole composed of German, Hebrew, and various Slavic languages.

The influence is obvious in the names of foods: bagel - blintz - gefilte fish - knish - kreplach - lox - matzo balls - all of which are "kosher."

More significantly for our vocabulary, we have adopted a number of other words which are quite descriptive. Many have heard and frequently used:

| | |
|---|---|
| shamus | a private detective |
| nudnik | a stupid, boring person |
| kibitz | to hover around |
| schmaltz | overly sentimental |
| toches | the buttocks |
| schmuck | a stupid person |
| megillah | a long, rambling account |

And this only suggests the number of words of Yiddish origin. There are dozens more.

The Irish were among the first immigrants with the first group arriving early in the eighteenth century. But the major arrival was after the potato famine in 1846. Despite their large numbers, the contributions to the language are few. "Shanty," "shebang," "shenanigan," "shamrock" and "smithereens" are perhaps the most frequently encountered, Interestingly, all of these begin with the letter "s."

The Italian contributions are somewhat larger but almost exclusively in the area of foods: antipasto - pasta - lasagna - pizza - spaghetti - ravioli - cannoli

Thanks, in part, to Mario Puzo's *The Godfather* and the very successful movies, a few words such as "patrone," "mafia," "cosa nosta," and "subito" can occasionally be heard. And if one wishes to put on an air of affectation, one can say goodbye with either "arrivederci" or "ciao."

Listing all of the groups that have made contributions to the vocabulary is a formidable task. These are just few.

No discussion, however, should exclude the contributions of blacks. Among the earlier contributions are: juke - chigger - banjo - tote - voodoo - okra - goober - gumbo - banana - and gullah. Of more recent vintage are: nitty gritty - rap - to bad mouth - soul food - tell it like it is - peckerwood - right on - shuckin' - jivin' - playing the dozens - oreo - Uncle Tom - honky.

Aside from the vocabulary items, and there are many more than these, we are beginning to see the impact of black speech patterns on general American. This includes, among other features, the lengthening of certain vowel sounds for emphasis such as in "maaan" and "riiight."

In addition to groups of immigrants, events have also stamped themselves on our language. Here are a few.

Indirectly, we adopted a number of military terms from the British and our French allies. "Turncoat" as a synonym for traitor is still sometimes heard. And there are a number of British military terms, "bounty," "draft," "rangers," as well as the ranks "private," "corporal," "captain," and so on.

From the French came "stockade" and "barracks." But words such as "tickens" for overalls, "lobsterback" for a British soldier, and "navy" for a type of pistol have long since disappeared from the vocabulary.

**The Civil War**. In like manner, many of the terms from this period gradually dropped from general use the further we moved from the event. "Johnny Reb," "Yanks," or "Blue belly" for Confederate and Union soldiers are found only in fictional works dealing with the period. So is "contraband," to indicate a former slave who came over to the Union side. "Dixie," as a reference to the South, is still in use. As are: guerrilla - doughboy - firefight - draftee - pup tent - greenbacks - AWOL - war correspondent - unconditional surrender - income tax.

**World War I**. This echoes in a number of words still widely used. Among them: ace - dog tags - shell shocked - basket case - tank - blimp - submarine - whizzbang - red tape - NCO - shock troops - KP - dud - hand grenade - buck private - barrage

Some of these were in use prior to the War but it was the event itself which gave them general common currency. Will they remain in our active vocabulary? Some undoubtedly will but it is impossible to say which ones.

**World War II**. Some of the contributions here are, oddly, not associated with the event by their users. Blockbuster - a type of bomb first used by the British; blitz - from the German "blitzkrieg" meaning lightning war; concentration camp - used earlier but in a limited and different context and was definitely not pejorated; gizmo - the name given to any object you can't think of the name of. The acronym "SNAFU" also has its beginning here.

**The Korean War**. Lasting from 1950 to 1953, this was originally termed a "Conflict." Following as it did some five years after World War II, much of the terminology was simply transferred. Consequently, there are very few terms specifically from this period: honcho - from Japanese meaning the man in charge; moose - also from Japanese meaning girl friend or any woman; chopper - a helicopter; DMZ - a demilitarized zone

**The Vietnam War**. Lasting from 1965 to 1973 (America's longest war), terms in general use reflect both the combat itself as well as the political climate during those years: escalation - increasing in intensity; domino theory - a belief that if one Asian nation went Communistic so would the others; incursion - an invasion; hooch - for house, from the Japanese; fragging - to kill with a hand grenade; grunt - a soldier; defoliate - to spray with weed killer; hawk - someone who favored a hard war; dove - someone who wanted peace.

But events other than wars have influenced our vocabulary. Here are a few.

**The '49ers**. When gold was first discovered at Sutter's mill in 1848 it started a stampede that had a profound effect not only on our nation but on our language, and the echoes of it still resound in our metaphors: hit pay dirt - grubstake - sourdough - stake a claim - didn't pan out - pull bonanza - prospector - mother lode - and, of course, "Levi's" a sturdy pair of pants first manufactured by Levi Strauss.

**Prohibition**. In 1919, the United States Congress passed the Volstead Act ushering in the fouteen-year-long "Great Experiment." We are indebted to it for: crocked - fried - juiced - polluted - sauced - home brew. This, in turn. led to the repopularization of hooch - bust skull - rotgut - redeye - moonshine.

As a consequence, gentlemen such as Mr. Al Capone came along to help supply the demand, and we are lexically indebted to their activities. bump off - take for a ride - gat - speakeasy.

During this period, sometimes called "The Roaring '20s," we find "jazz" adopted for a form of music. Thanks to the actor Rudolph Valentino, "sheik" referred to any handsome man. The then newly "liberated" woman was a "flapper." These are now more than a little dated although they are sometimes used. The same is true of such exclamations as "the bee's knees," "the cat's pajamas," and "the cat's meow." Of interest is the fact that the currently popular "unreal" as a exclamation of awe was used extensively during this period.

**Law Enforcement**. The contributions of the police and other law enforcement agencies should not be overlooked. During the 1960s it became popular for police to be called "pigs" and the "fuzz." "Pig" was first used in this context as early as 1848 so its revival over a century later is hardly original; "fuzz" is found during the 1920s, probably earlier. Prominent among many contributions are: lineup - road block - nab - bust - third degree - hassle - collar frisk - paddy wagon - to shadow - stakeout - undercover - narc.

One of the primary concerns of law enforcement is controlling the traffic in narcotics and other drugs. Those who both supply and use them have their variations reflected in the language. While most of these terms are metaphorical extensions, thus increasing the polysemy of many words in the vocabulary, there is also a great deal of originality in the choices.

| | |
|---|---|
| acid | LSD |
| acid head | an habitual user of LSD |
| angel dust | PCP, an animal tranquilizer |
| bad trip | unpleasant drug experience |
| blow/snort | to inhale a drug, usually cocaine |
| burn out | physical and mental deterioration |

The terminology has a very rapid turnover and varies from one part of the country to another, sometimes from one ethnic group to another. Whether this is a consequence of a desire for secrecy or simply boredom is uncertain.

**The Women's Rights Movement**. The movement to gain equal rights for women is not new. It started in England and the U.S. early in the 19th century. "Women's rights," was first used in the 1840s. A woman who argued for her rights was known in this country as a "suffragist." One of the first was Amelia Bloomer, for whom the garment is named. Belva Lockwood founded the Equal Rights Party in the 1880s and Margaret Sanger was the first to use the term "birth control." She also the popularized the word "diaphragm" as a birth control device. In 1967, "women's liberation movement" was used for the first time. "Sexist" and "sexism" became terms for discrimination against women. A male who practiced either or both was a "male chauvinist pig." "Bra burning" became a popular symbol in the 1970's along with various forms of "consciousness raising." The two major acronyms from the movement are ERA, the Equal Rights Amendment, and NOW, the National Organization of Women.

These are just handful of events that have influenced our language. The next time you describe an easy task as a "cinch," remember your debt to the cowboy and the Old West. From this period we also get "critter," "tenderfoot," "dude," "maverick," "wrangler," and "brand." We are in the Great Depression when we speak of "bread lines," "soup kitchens," "shantytowns," and "food stamps." "Carpetbagger" comes from the period of reconstruction following the Civil War, as does "scalawag," "night riders," and "sharecropper." The Watergate scandals gave us polysemy for "plumbers," "dirty tricks," "stonewalling," and leaving someone to "turn slowly in the breeze." Our attention was called to the fact that money could be "laundered," and shortly after the event another scandal involving the giving of gifts to public officials was termed "koreagate."

Our words, in a very real sense, represent a time capsule which will, if we take the effort, help to open the past for us as vividly than reading a history book. And we are today introducing new words and modifying meanings which will enable future generations to look back and understand us a little better, if they are interested. The past extends into the future in very subtle ways. The metaphors from earlier periods influence our perception of ourselves and the world around us. In like manner we are today determining certain modes of perception for our inheritors.

# 10

# LANGUAGE TABOOS:
## CULTURAL AND GRAMMATICAL

In the 1960s, comedian George Carlin released an album of comedy routines. It was never played on the air. Why? One of the routines contained seven words the Federal Communications Commission ruled could not be broadcast or telecast. Not until 1983, when the pay-TV service "Home Box Office," which is not subject to direct FCC control, presented him in a special concert, was he was able use them.

In 1982, two high school teachers in two different counties in Florida were severely reprimanded by their superintendents. The reprimands were officially entered into their personnel records. What had they done? Parents had protested what they believed to be the inappropriate use of language in the classroom. One had used the word "hell" and the other "damn."

Before the motion picture "Network" was shown on national network television, there was a special "disclaimer" made alerting the viewers that an "offensive" word would occur twice during the film. Although the offensive word was not given, it turned out to be "bullshit." Yet the audience was not cautioned that the words "bastard" and "son-of-a-bitch" would occur with greater frequency in the dialogue.

What makes one word or phrase more offensive than another? The question is easier asked than answered. All languages have rules regarding the avoidance of certain words in certain situations. These rules may be written as laws with penalties for their violation. Or they may be simply "understood" by the majority of the speakers. They will also vary from one culture to another and, of course, change within a given culture as the language attitudes of its members change.

As late as 1962, for example, the Production Code of the Motion Picture Producers of America contained a section on "Profanity." Among the words expressly forbidden were: "broad" (when applied to a woman), "God," "Lord, "Jesus," and "Christ" (unless used reverently), "slut," "damn," and "hell." Living as we do in a more semantically permissive era, such prohibitions strike most as not only quaint but downright silly. Still others may be offended that these were used as examples.

Until the middle of the 1970s these prohibitions were usually observed on the screen despite what people may have said privately. Paradoxically, the motion picture, one of the bastions of language conservatism, is now free of any restraints. The majority of these prohibitions still hold, however, for television although there has been some relaxation. The series "M*A*S*H" first used "son-of-a-bitch," "horse's ass," "fall on your ass," "bust your ass" and "bastard" among others while "hell" and "damn" are standard vocabulary items on almost all programs.

When first published in America, D.H. Lawrence's *Lady Chatterley's Lover* was carefully culled of those passages containing what some regard as the most offensive four-letter word in the language. And when Norman Mailer's *The Naked and the Dead* was published the word was written as "fug," a spelling subtrafuge that fooled no one except the most naive.

But these prohibitions go beyond what are sometimes called "dirty words." Many high school psychology teachers are strictly cautioned against using such words as "phallus," "penis," "vagina," and "sexual intercourse" in their classes although they are used in the textbooks which the students read for their courses.

These are just a few examples of language avoidance. When this occurs, we have a **cultural language taboo**. This is the semantic equivalent of not wearing your hat in church if you are a Catholic or Protestant male, remaining seated when the national anthem is played, or walking through a shopping center, or even in your own front yard, in the nude.

Some taboos are considered so central to the orderly functioning of a society that they are formalized as laws with specific penalties for their violation. This does not refer to violent acts such as rape, murder, or assault. There is hardly a state, county, or city without laws and ordinances regulating how you can dress, the acts you cannot indulge in publicly, and the forms of language you may not use in public places.

Why certain subjects, actions, acts, and words become taboo is a question that can only be answered within the context of the culture where the taboo exists. Sometimes the answers are difficult, if not impossible, to find because the reasons for the taboo are lost or forgotten. Further, what may be a natural form of behavior in one culture is regarded as unnatural in another because it has been defined for whatever reason as taboo. We, for example, think nothing of eating hamburgers, steaks, and beef roasts, unless one is a vegetarian. A visitor from India became physically ill when he saw a tray of freshly ground hamburger. The cow is sacred in his religion and the culture shock brought on by the unexpected encounter was so great that he was not able to control his revulsion.

By the same token, dogs are perfectly edible and in some parts of the world are raised for just that purpose. For most of us, they have not been defined as "food." The thought of sitting down to a meal of roasted, baked, fried, or fricasseed dog would be equally revolting. Similarly, rats, mice, cats, ants, bees, grubs, and grasshoppers are defined as food in various parts of the world. These would have be "cultivated" tastes for Americans. The thought of eating snails is unthinkable to many, but if one acquires the taste and they're called escargot, then they are not longer taboo.

Language taboos operate in much the same way. We are dealing with the same type of situation looked at under the "whys" of meaning change. But now there is a very special difference. The model used was:

$$Sy \longleftrightarrow C \longleftarrow \text{-----} \rightarrow R$$

One thing noted was that it is possible for the concepts to overpower the referent and cause it to change. This is what happened with "villain" when the referent changed from "farmer" to "bad guy." In the case of **taboo**, the referent **cannot** overpowered. It is always the same. Since nothing can be done about the referent, the symbol must change! Here are a few of our more prominent cultural taboos which require varying degrees of language modification when we wish to discuss them.

## Death.

Humans, we assume, are the only creatures who are aware that some day they must die. We are born terminal cases. Some will terminate sooner than others, but terminate we will. While we recognize that death is the inevitable consequence of life, we set up all sorts of language dodges to avoid immediate recognition of the fact. These are almost always in the form of metaphors that enable us to avoid a direct confrontation with the inevitable. Remember, a taboo does not change the referent! To paraphrase Gertrude Stein, "Death is death." Nothing can alter the fact. Since the referent can't be changed, the only alternative is to manipulate the symbol. Therefore, the word is not the thing, as S.I. Hayakawa said, but a way of getting away from it, or at least providing a degree of semantic and emotional distance.

Some years ago, Louise Pound wrote the classic article in this area, "Terms for Dead and Dying in American Speech." She collected several hundred terms and broke them into metaphorical categories. A few she listed are:

**Metaphors for Sleep and Rest.** These are such phrases as "the final sleep," "the sleep of the just," "the last sleep," "gone to (his or her) final rest," and "laid to rest."

**Metaphors of the Journey.** These imply a beginning, a return, or a departure. Someone is said to have "passed on," "passed over," or "crossed over." Or they may "make the last journey," now that "life's final journey" has ended. A recent one stated that the deceased has "started on his heavenly trip," which, considering the present polysemy of "trip" leads one to speculate.

**Literary and Figurative Metaphors.** The bulk of these are usually paraphrases of statements found in literature. "Left this mortal coil" is a not too overly imaginative reworking of Shakespeare's "shuffled off this mortal coil." Some others are said to have "laid down (his/her) burden," "the cord is severed," "the soul has flown," "met the grim reaper," and "joined the silent majority."

**Occupational Metaphors.** The dead person (deceased?) does not necessarily have to be engaged in the occupation alluded to, though some are restricted. "Died in harness" does not require the individual be a horse. Nor does "died with his boots on" mean the person was in the cavalry. These simply indicate the person was active at the time of death. "Answering the last roll call" seems to be reserved for military types. "Answered the final curtain" is for those in the theater. The phrase is now almost a parody of itself when we are told that a sports figure has "gone to that big ball park (gridiron, hockey rink, racetrack) in the sky." When a fighter dies, sports writers can not help but note that he has "answered the final bell."

**Slang Metaphor.** In his short story, "Buck Fanshaw's Funeral," Mark Twain recounts the almost impossible task a miner has explaining to the minister that Fanshaw has "gone up the flume," "throwed up the sponge," "kicked the bucket," and was "scooped." There are far more slang metaphors for dead and dying than any of the other varieties. Nor have they been systematically collected and analyzed to see how they may vary from one historical period to another. Death, therefore, is a major taboo area governing our language behavior. For further examples see Evelyn Waugh's *The Loved One* and Jessica Mitford's *The American Way of Death*,

## Body Functions.

This category, historically, is a recent phenomenon. Until the 17th century, the Anglo-Saxon words were perfectly acceptable for designating what today we must elegantly refer to as "defecation," "urination, and "breaking wind." Shortly after 1600 words in these categories started to accumulate pejorative connotations and until recently retained them. For some they are still strongly taboo in context. For others, the contexts may vary. This, however, has not prevented their return to general use.

When we wish to be polite such reduplications as "pee-pee," "wee-wee," and "poo-poo" may be used. "Tinkle" is definitely onomatopoeic. You may also acronym, "BM." "Poop" and "poot" are still occasionally heard while "poppycock" and "fizzle" have had their referents changed. "Crap" has been reduced to a mild intensifier and is now used on television.

Another bodily function that has undergone a degree of taboo is the condition of your nose. You may describe it as "dripping," or "running," though for some these are borderline terms; "stuffy" and "stuffed up" are better. The substance that drips, runs, or stuffs is less offensively referred to as "mucus," except in some dialect areas. You simply do not in most circumstances refer to it as "snot." To propel this substance from the mouth by expectoration (or spitting) is preferred to saying you "hocked up a goober."

"Vomit" has also developed a degree of pejoration. To "puke," "pitch your cookies," "loose your lunch," "blow chunks" and "flash" are variously employed. "Throwing up" is apparently less pejorated as is "to be sick at your stomach." Just how "barf" will fare is uncertain.

## Body Parts.

The genital areas of men and women have always been under varying degrees of taboo. As a result, quite a few metaphors are available. J.S. Farmer and W.E. Henley in *Slang and Its Analogues* list about a hundred for the penis and several hundred for the vagina. Although the various volumes were compiled and published between 1890 and 1904, it is surprising how many of the terms they record are still found.

Women's breasts are also under a degree of taboo although the possibilities are not nearly so numerous. "Bosoms" and "bazooms" are frequently heard. "Tits," "boobs," "boobies," "cans," and "jugs" have all been used on television without recourse to "bleeping."

The body parts taboo was at one time so strong that it extended to almost every part of the anatomy, animal as well as human. Your torso became the "trunk," while your arms and legs were your "limbs." This, fortunately, was about as far as the tree metaphor could be extended. There is no citation for one's fingers and toes being referred to as "branches." Your knees became your "benders," still found in some British dialects but now obsolete in the U.S. We still find a few reminders of the extension of the taboo to animals when we refer to the breast of turkey or chicken as the "white meat" and the leg or thigh as the "dark."

## Sex.

Attitudes towards the various forms of sexual activity vary from one culture to another, and from one social group to another within a given culture. This is an especially strong taboo in English and is attested to by the ways we must modify our language. The Tampa *Tribune* reported that a man was arrested for using in public what it described as "a four-letter word for fornication."

At its most basic level there is a division of sex acts into two categories: (1) Natural; and (2) Unnatural. The subject is now being debated in the courts. Once they are legally defined, one can only assume that whatever remains must wait for future clarification. Alexis deTocqueville observed as early as 1820 in *Democracy in America* that in a democratic society every moral issue will eventually become a legal one.

Hardly anyone today would have either a positive or negative reaction to the word "swive" because hardly anyone today has heard word. But at one time it meant the same thing as that notorious "four-letter word" which the Tampa paper said is a synonym for "fornication." Why this particular word should have the degree of pejoration it labors under is a unknown. The mystery is further deepened by the fact that in the movies and literature the word is so frequently used as to reduce it to an intensifier. Indeed, if this word is an indication, other four-letter words may undergo the same fate in future generations and lose pejorative force. Like "swive," in a hundred years or so they may simply be regarded as quaint archaisms and people then will wonder why we were ever disturbed by them.

Even the "technical" terms for the various types of sex acts have also undergone degrees of pejoration and, as a result, taboo. Some years ago the musical "Hair" had a song using a number of these words simply chanted. When asked what he thought of the play, composer-conductor Leonard Bernstein said, "I don't see how you can call it music when all you do is string together a bunch of dirty words."

This has been a circumspect discussion of sexual taboos. Despite the deliberate nature of the presentation, many have no doubt been offended. If so, what has been shown is the power of the concept to overpower the referent. We may do it, but we can't talk about it. Or if we do talk about it, we shouldn't.

## Divinity.

The strength of this taboo is difficult to determine. The strictures on avoiding such words as "Jesus," "Christ," "God," and "goddamn" have eased considerably although they are still quite strong in some groups. We still retain words such as "gee," "geeze," "gosh," "golly," "lawsy," "jeepers," "tarnation," "darn," and "dang" to remind us of the strength of the taboo.

Once again we must return to the problem of reconciling what one says publicly and what one says privately. It is not uncommon for persons to denounce openly what they pronounce covertly. The choice is context sensitive with many. Parents may punish a child for using a word which they toss off with no thought of impropriety. Nor is it uncommon for a person to use privately a word they would never think of uttering publicly.

The study of the degree of intensity of this taboo within various social groups would provide very useful information about attitudes and values. Regardless, there can be little doubt that the strength of this taboo has weakened. Whether, as some contend, this is further evidence of the decay of our moral fiber is a point involving more emotion than reason.

## Diseases.

This is a broad category and includes both physical as well as mental afflictions. There was a pioneering public service short film first shown on national television in 1974 which proclaimed "VD is for everyone." This was the first national recognition that people contract venereal diseases. While most feel more comfortable hearing the acronym "VD" the specific names of the diseases in this category, gonorrhea and syphilis, no longer are hidden in our semantic closet.

This is also true of cancer, heart attacks, high blood pressure, alcoholism, and, thanks to advertising, hemorrhoids and jock itch. AIDS (Acquired Immune Deficiency Syndrome) is but the most recent addition and will continue to carry a strong taboo until such time as a cure is found or there is a considerable shift in attitudes regarding the persons who contract it.

While there is still something faintly immoral in the minds of some about mental illness, we are seeing the taboo diminish. The terms "insane," "crazy," "deranged," and "unbalanced" are still used. But we are becoming more aware of and sympathetic to the fact that people do suffer "depression." They can also be "paranoid" as well as "schizophrenic." These latter two terms are frequently used without regard to their possibly having a technical meaning.

These are six of many areas where our taboos influence our language behavior. Some are weakening in intensity while others are still strong and likely to remain so. But whether weak or strong we have the same condition in all cases—we cannot change the referent! Death remains death. Particular body parts, functions, as well as sex acts remain just that. In those areas where the taboo is still strong we must continue to seek new symbols because the concepts will pejorate the older ones.

It is also instructive to see what types of patterns are built through this process of constantly pejorating symbols. What, for example, are the reasons for the lessening of some taboos so we do not have to modify our language behavior? What may we infer from this about ourselves and our society in general?

Are we becoming more or less "profane" and "obscene" in our language behavior? The words we may label as "obscene" or "profane" are drawn from the taboos surrounding body parts, functions, sex acts, and divinity. But these words are themselves difficult to define and are at best unclear as to what they denote. In some contexts, they appear to be synonymous. In others, the "profane" refers to a violation of the divinity taboo while "obscene" stems from the others. There is no simple answer or distinction. Yesterday's acceptable term may become today's taboo. The reverse is also true. There is the possibility our grandchildren may not want us around their children because we're so "foul mouthed."

Or we may not wish to be around them because the words we have been conditioned to regard as taboo have little or no pejorative force for them.

As our culture changes, so will our attitudes regarding taboos. Aldous Huxley, in *Brave New World*, imagines a time when biological conception and gestation take place totally in a test tube. Because there are no identifiable parents, the words "mother" and "father" have no objective meaning. Biological conception takes place only on primitive "reservations" among "savages." Therefore, for those conceived in vitro, the words "mother" and "father" are unspeakable obscenities.

We do not go quite that far, although the word "mother" is a cause for combat under certain conditions. There have been cultural taboos in language since the beginning of recorded history and there is no reason to believe they will disappear. All they will do is change. The question, then, is the degree to which their use influences the communication of meaning. There can be little doubt that in certain contexts, communication is enhanced. In others, it is either blocked or directed into channels other than those intended.

# GRAMMATICAL TABOOS

There is another type of taboo whose violation is considered by some to be far more serious than violating a cultural taboo. Anyone who has written a paper in high school or college has had it returned with one or more of the following comments: "grammar," "diction," "agreement," "usage," "syntax," "prepositions." These were probably keyed to an appropriate place in a "handbook" where you were first cautioned to never again commit this transgression and then provided with ways to avoid a repetition.

In addition, there was a catalog of other terminology to master. There was the "subject" of a sentence as well as its "predicate." Sentences were then written on the blackboard and students asked to come up and "diagram" them. What type of line do you place between the "subject" and the "predicate?" How are "modification" structures indicated? As a consequence, the very mention of the word "grammar" is enough to give many a nervous tic. Others become catatonic.

Recognizing the risks, let's talk about "grammar." What does the word really mean? Rather than rushing to a dictionary, which is not likely to be overly enlightening, we'll begin with a distinction made by W. Nelson Francis in his article, "A Revolution in Grammar." He cautions that we should be careful when we use the word because it can refer to three quite different things.

> **Grammar #1** - The sum total of the meaningful utterances which it is possible to make in a language.
> **Grammar #2** - The scientific study and description of Grammar #1.
> **Grammar #3** - Linguistic etiquette

The following statements, then, are meaningful in terms of Grammar #1:

> He isn't going.
> He ain't going.

In Grammar #2 both of statements are permissible. Why? Because they communicate! They are identical, because the subject "he" is followed by the predicate (a verb phrase). The only difference is that in the first example "isn't" is used and in the second "ain't." Both can exist in Grammar #1 and be described in Grammar #2. Yet, "isn't" is said to be grammatical and "ain't" isn't. Labeling "ain't" as ungrammatical is a Grammar #3 statement; a form of linguistic etiquette.

The first grammar books in English date from the middle of the 18th century. Samuel Johnson published a short grammar at the end of his dictionary in 1755 but it had no impact. Joseph Priestly also published a grammar about the same time with the similar results.

Then, in 1762, Bishop Robert Lowth published, *A Short Introduction to English Grammar*. The echoes of this can still be heard in most of the handbooks published today. He states in his introduction,

> *The principal design of a grammar of any language is to teach us to express ourselves with propriety in that language; and to enable us to judge of every phrase and form of construction, whether it is right or not. The plain way of doing this is to lay down rules. . . .*

This the good bishop did. So, for the first time in English, we have statements about "grammar." But these are not Grammar #2 statements. Rather, they fall under Grammar #3. That is, they do not describe what is there. Rather, they prescribe what should be there as well as what should not.

Bishop Lowth was not being difficult to live with. He was only articulating an attitude held by many scholars of his time. This was, after all, the 18th century, usually labeled the "Age of Reason." Newton, Priestly, and others were discovering the "laws" of nature. These brought order and purpose into what had previously been viewed as a chaotic universe. As Alexander Pope wrote in his "Essay on Man"

> *All chaos is but some order not yet understood.*
> *Therefore that that is, Is Good.*

They were also concerned with the state of the English language. Jonathan Swift proposed establishing an academy on the model of the French. Its purpose would be to "purify," "ascertain," and "fix" the English language. There was a certain amount of change taking place in the language. Most of these changes were felt to be at best undesirable, at worst, a calamity. As the poet Edward Waller lamented:

> *Those who lasting marble seek,*
> *Carve in Latin or in Greek.*
> *We write in sand.*

These were men trained in the "classical" tradition which meant they both read and wrote Latin and Greek. They wanted to see the same precision and certainty in English found in the classical languages; they had no desire to "write in sand." So when he wrote the "rules" for English, Lowth naturally turned to the classical languages, primarily Latin, as the model.

But there were two small problems which Lowth failed to take into account, or chose, for convenience sake, to ignore. First, Latin and Greek are "dead" languages. That is, they represent a form of the language as it existed at the time when the classics were written. Both Latin and Greek continued to change but that change is not reflected in the works studied. Therefore, it is not surprising that the languages represented both certainty and fixity for these scholars.

Second, these languages are "synthetic," not in the sense of "artificial." Rather, grammatical relationships are signaled by inflections placed on the words. Thus the Latin sentence:

*Brutus interfecit Caesarian*

which means "Brutus killed Caesar" could just as well have been written

*Caesarian interfecit Brutus*

the {-am} ending on Caesar tells us it is in the accusative case and he was the direct object of the action "killing," and Brutus performed the action.

English was also "synthetic" in the period from 750 to 1100. But following the Norman Conquest in 1066 it became increasingly "analytical." This means that word order becomes the important way to signal meaning. It makes a great deal of difference in English whether you say "Brutus killed Caesar" or "Caesar killed Brutus."

During this period English also had "grammatical gender" and nouns were classified as "masculine," "feminine," or "neuter" without a necessary regard for the sex, or the lack of it, of the noun. The words for "girl" and "wife" were neuter while the word for "woman" was masculine. This is attested to by the definite article which today has only one form in modern English, "the." There were masculine, feminine, and neuter forms in Anglo-Saxon. "Se" - masculine; "seo" - feminine; "daet" - neuter. This was just for the "nominative" case. There were others for the "genitive," "dative," "accusative" and "instrumental" cases.

During the Middle English period, 1100 to 1500, the language lost most of its inflectional characteristics. Grammatical gender was replaced by natural gender so that masculine referents take "he," feminine "she," and all others "it." For those who breathe a sigh of relief over this "simplification," just remember if it had been retained, we would be none the wiser.

Why these changes took place is more properly the subject for a work dealing with the history of the English language. But why the early grammarians failed to note this change before writing rules is another question. Regardless, when the rules were written, Latin was the primary model. As W. Nelson Francis said, "English was stretched on the Procrustean bed of Latin." There were some correspondences because both are members of the same language family. But each had followed a different path of development. So when correspondences were not found, they were either ignored or invented. In any case, a "rule" was written.

One such rule that all are exposed to at one time or another is: **Never split an infinitive**. In Latin we find:

| | |
|---|---|
| esse | to be |
| fuesse | to have been |

English has no comparable construction. So one was invented. Our "infinitive" is said to be:

| |
|---|
| to + a verb (to run, to hit, to see) |

It is impossible to split an infinitive in Latin because the affix is part of the word. In English, there are two words. We have a part of speech, the adverb, that will fit into just about any slot left in a sentence. Thus we can say:

| |
|---|
| to rapidly run |
| to solidly hit |
| to suddenly see |

The rule is rarely observed except in grammatical drills and the speech and writing of those who would rather have a disfiguring disease than publicly split an infinitive. Historically, infinitives have always been split in English. If the rule were rigidly applied, most government and military documents would require extensive editing—a consumption that one might devoutly wish.

Another rule promulgated at this time was: **AVOID DOUBLE NEGATIVES.** Why? We are told that two negatives cancel one another out and make a positive. Thus to say: "I don't have no money." is to really say that you do have some. The two negatives, "don't" and "not" cancel one another so you have made a positive statement, "I do have some money."

In mathematics, two negatives make a positive. Minus times minus equals plus ($- \times - = +$). Since this was the "Age of Reason" it was argued that the same is true in language. No one can argue with the mathematical accuracy of this statement. Unfortunately, this doesn't square with the way reasonable people use and understand the language for communicating meaning. If saying "I don't have no money" is equivalent to saying "I do," then what about this:

| |
|---|
| "I don't never have no money." |

You are now making a mathematically accurate statement according to the reasoning for minus times minus = plus times minus = minus. In appropriate form this would be: $[- \times - = + \times - = -]$

And if you were to say "I don't never have no money, no how." you have now asserted that you do have money and we're right back to square one for minus times minus = plus times minus = minus times minus = plus. $[- \times - = + \times - = - \times - = +]$

This is a fun game to play if you have nothing better to do. But it really doesn't have much to do with the way language actually operates. The person who uses a double negative does so to reinforce the fact. If you think not, suppose you are asked for $5 by someone who believes in the rule that two negatives make a positive. You reply, "But I don't have no money." The person then says, "Well, in that case, lend me $10." What would be your reaction?

By making such statements as "never split and infinitive" and "avoid double negatives" we are creating grammatical taboos. We know these forms exist in the sense of Grammar #1 because we can describe them in terms of Grammar #2. This, however, becomes irrelevant because they have authority in Grammar #3 - Linguistic etiquette.

Here are some other "rules":

**Pronouns following linking verbs take the subject form.** Thus the 1st person singular in its four forms is:

| | |
|---|---|
| Subject | I |
| Object | me |
| 1st possessive | my |
| 2nd possessive | mine |

Therefore, the proper form should be: "It is I" not "It is me." Similarly with the 3rd person singular: "It is he" not "It is him." "It is she" not "It is her."

This distinction is rapidly disappearing in most spoken discourse and less attended to in writing. The retention of the rule in textbooks and hypercorrect usage is testimony to the staying power of a grammatical taboo once stated and accepted.

**Never end a sentence with a preposition.**

"I don't know what he was looking at."
"That's about all I'll put up with."

There is really nothing awkward with these sentences nor or they "ungrammatical" in a Grammar #2 sense. We certainly know they exist in Grammar #1 because we hear them frequently and have encountered them in writing. One could also argue that in such sentences "at" and "with" as well as other words that might fit these slots, are not functioning as prepositions but as part of a verb phrase. Why not? After all, we know that "to" is an infinitive marker when it comes before a verb and a preposition when it comes before a noun.

| | |
|---|---|
| to run | infinitive marker |
| to the store | a preposition |

**Use "may" to indicate permission, "can" for ability.** Thus, if you are requesting permission, you would ask, "May I go?" But "Can I go" would indicate you have some problem which may prevent your going. This rule only holds when "may" or "can" appears initially in "yes" and "no" questions.

> May I go?
> Can I go?

But if current usage is a valid indicator, few people consistently observe the rule.

**Avoid the comparison of incomparables.** This rule argues that "round" is not a comparable quality. Something either is or isn't. Therefore, one thing cannot "rounder" than another. But the one most are familiar with is "unique." The word means there is nothing else like it. Therefore you should avoid saying that something is "very," "rather," or "somewhat" unique. Again, the observance of this rule is rapidly disappearing, at least for the majority of the speakers of the language.

**Avoid double superlatives.** {-est} is the superlative form of the adjective if it is monosyllabic, "coldest," "hottest," "brightest," "cleanest," and so on. If the adjective is polysyllabic, such as "beautiful," "spectacular," or "enormous," then you use "more" or "most" for the comparative and the superlative. Following this rule, you should then avoid saying,

> "This is the most coldest beer I've ever had."
> "Theirs is the most hottest chili in town."
> "Red is the most brightest color."

Admittedly, there is something slightly awkward about these sentences. But there is nothing "ungrammatical" about them in the sense of either Grammar #1 or Grammar #2. We should remember that in *Julius Caesar*, Shakespeare has Mark Antony say, "This was the most unkindest cut of all." And in *King Lear* the character of France characterizes Cordelia as "most best, most dearest."

**Use {-er} in comparing two things, {-est} for more than two.** If you have two children, one is the "older" and the other is the "younger." If you have more than two, then one is the "oldest" and another the "youngest." An echo of this rule is also found in the caution for the use of "between" and "among." If there are two people it is "between," if more than two, "among." Although still on the books, this rule is also observed with increasing infrequency.

This catalog of rules could be extended. A good traditional handbook will supply others. From what has been said, a logical conclusion would be that we should avoid all rules which regulate the way language is used. Nothing could be more untrue! We should have rules! Regardless of the area, rules must obtain or chaos results. But we are not talking about "rules" in the sense that these are "grammatical errors." They certainly aren't in the sense of Grammar #1. There must be standards appropriate to the area and the subject. But these standards are not something handed down from on high nor are they a part of our language in the sense that they have always been there.

What we are really talking about is a choice between two or more forms which exist in Grammar #1. Choosing one rather than the other is not based on anything within the language. The choice represents a statement of preference. This, then, makes it a Grammar #3 statement, a form of "linguistic etiquette." Since manners and customs change, so will attitudes regarding "correctness" and "incorrectness" in matters of language choice.

As evidence of this, publishers of dictionaries may use "panels of experts" on matters such as those just looked at. The "experts" are never entirely in agreement on many of the items discussed. On the subject of the split infinitive, for example, one dictionary showed that over 40 percent of its "experts" saw nothing wrong with the cleavage.

A final point! Once a statement is made about the way language should be used, you never quite see your language in the same way again. You are always viewing it though the screen created by the statement. And, paradoxically, research shows that people will make judgments about other people who violate one of the rules. But those making the judgments use the same forms themselves. In such cases, the reaction is to the form of the communication and not its content. Meaning results not from what is said so much as the way it is said.

# 11

# EUPHEMISMS or,
# WHEN IS A SPADE NOT A SPADE?

When asked why she had appeared nude in a love scene, a British actress replied:

*I'm fascinated by erotica — as I'm appalled by pornography. Eroticism is rejoicing in love; pornography is debasing love.*

Is there a distinction between erotica and pornography, or is this person playing with words? If you check a dictionary, you will find both words have the same referent. The concepts of "erotica" are less objectionable than those of "pornography." What this person has done is use a euphemism.

A euphemism is the use of an inoffensive term for another considered to be too offensive or explicit. In language taboos, when unfavorable connotations build up in the concepts, and nothing can be done about changing the referent, the only solution is to change the symbol. This is what a euphemism does. All the words used to illustrate different ways of talking about death, body parts, body functions, and sex are euphemisms.

There are two ways to euphemize:

❏ Coin a new word for the occasion.
❏ Borrow a word from another semantic field.

An example of coining a word is what happened to the occupational titles of those who deal with the inevitable by-product of death, the disposal of the body.

Prior to the middle of the 19th century in America, there was no chemical preparation of the body for burial. The deceased was laid out in a coffin, a service held, and interment immediately followed. This practice is captured in the song "Poor Jud is Daid," from the Rogers and Hammerstein musical "Oklahoma" when Curly sings,

*He's lookin' oh so purty and so nice.*
*He looks like he's asleep.*
*It's a shame that he won't keep.*
*But it's summer and we're runnin' out of ice.*

With the advent of embalming during the Civil War, there developed a business whose purpose was the preparation of the body. Those who did this were called "undertakers," a word borrowed from another semantic field. The original referent, one who undertakes a task, was replaced.

At the turn of the century, "undertaker" either developed pejorative connotations or the people in the burying business felt they needed a title with more prestige. The word "mortician" was coined modeled on "physician" but using the Latin root "mortalis," meaning "subject to death." Following World War II, "mortician" either fell under pejoration or a need was felt for still another designation. So "funeral director" came into vogue.

All three terms are still found in the semantic field of titles for those who bury. But somewhere around 1970, there was an attempt to coin yet another term. Using the Greek word "thanos," meaning death, some undertakers - morticians - funeral directors toyed with the possibility of using either "thanatician" or "thanatologist." The first was not well received because of the obvious parallel with "beautician" and other similar job titles. Then, unfortunately, a new discipline devoted to the study of dying and death developed in universities. The people who specialized in this area called themselves "thanatologists." So the term was co-opted. The search, no doubt, will continue. Regardless, the words "mortician" and "funeral director" were coined as euphemisms.

Because a taboo area is central to the functioning of a culture, the language associated with it will be under pressure to pejorate. After a time (no one can predict how long) pejoration will reach the point of no return. When this happens, the concepts overwhelm the symbol and a new word (either borrowed or invented) must be introduced since there is nothing you can do about the referent.

There is always an element of avoidance involved in the use of euphemism. Perhaps we also believe that by changing the word we gain some control over the referent. We play a semantic shell game but now we are both the manipulator and the player.

This game can become more complex than we realize because things connected with the taboo area will also undergo varying degrees of language pejoration. Thus the places where we bury the dead are less frequently called "graveyards" or "cemeteries." We find such euphemisms as "Memorial Park," "Memorial Gardens," "Garden of Memories," and "Memory Gardens." The last three contain some unintended grim humor. After all, a garden is where things are planted.

Another recent modification of language connected with this taboo stems from the process of cremation. Someone thought it was a bit harsh to call the residue "ashes," although this word is still very much in use. There is a move to call these the "cremains." This is bringing about yet another euphemism. The burying of the body is "interment." The burying of the "cremains" is "inurnment." In fairness to Evelyn

Waugh, it should be noted that he first coined the word in his satire, *The Loved One.* Life again gets around to imitating art.

There are a number of areas where the taboo extends from the referent to things associated with it. Consider the place where body functions are normally carried out—in a culture with the conveniences of indoor plumbing. Here you will find a great deal of language modification. Thus "toilet," which once referred to the entire room (wash basin, tub, etc.), now refers specifically to what at one time was called the "commode." And "commode" suffered a similar fate because it meant a table found in the "toilet," when that word designated the entire room. Occasionally, newspaper ads will offer "commode tables" for sale. The designation strikes some people as most peculiar.

In England, the object we call a "toilet" is the "water closet," sometimes simply acronymed as the "W.C." If you wish to be vulgar, you may refer to it as the "loo," a clever pun on "Waterloo." Why this should have become so pejorated in England has not been satisfactorily explained. Nevertheless, a use of the word "loo" by Prince Phillip was sufficient to have him reprimanded in print by the London *Times.* In reply to a question by a reporter he said that the only thing really wrong with living in Buckingham Palace was that the "loos" were always getting stopped up.

When "toilet" specialized to refer to one object, we had to come up with something to call the room. "Bathroom" seems to be the one we've settled on in homes, motels, and hotels. In restaurants and bars, "Men's Room" and "Ladies Room" are denotatively sufficient, or more simply "Men" and "Women." "Restroom" has a bisexual connotation while "Powder Room" or "Lounge" is specialized for women. Sometimes the desire to euphemize in this area is combined with a coy cleverness. When this urge is answered, we get such distinctions

| | |
|---|---|
| Laddies | Lassies |
| Bouys | Gulls |
| Steers | Heifers |
| Outboards | Inboards |
| Bucks | Does |
| Rams | Ewes |

In addition to coining new words, a euphemism is created by borrowing a word from another semantic field into the taboo area. Thus in the taboo area of Body Functions, the words "loose" and "irregular" were borrowed from other semantic fields as euphemisms for "diarrhea" and "constipation." To some degree, the pejorative connotations which these words have developed in their new semantic field are feeding back into the ones from which they were borrowed. This can create a degree of ambiguity should some offer the observation, "I feel real loose today."

The attitude towards these words may be changing thanks to a number of television commercials for products designed to correct the conditions. The carefully avoided "diarrhea" and "constipation" are being recognized as conditions which humans must from time to time endure. In time, "loose" and "irregular" may have this aspect of their polysemy disappear. Although we still find such euphemisms as "la tourista," "Montezuma's revenge," "the South American quick-step."

Words in the Sex taboo referring to "copulation" present equally striking examples of how euphemism can resolve some semantic problems while creating others. Earlier, "swive" and "sard" referred to the same act but have dropped from active use. No desk dictionary currently in the market indicates that "occupy" was at one time also used. In Shakespeare's "Henry IV-Part II" one of the characters exclaims,

> *A captain! God's light, these villains will make the word as odious as the word occupy, which was an excellent good word before it was ill-used.*

And you find these two lines in a 17th century ballad.

> *All that in your beds do lie,*
> *Turn to your wives and occupy.*

Shakespeare's character would be pleased to learn that "occupy" is no longer "ill-used" because it has ceased to be used as a euphemism in the Sex taboo.

But what about such words as "intercourse," "intimate," "relations," and "affairs." They have been borrowed as euphemisms into the Sex taboo and as a consequence the feedback into their original semantic fields severely restricts their possible ranges of use. "Intercourse" has suffered the cruelest fate, especially in American English. In British English it still carries much of its historical meaning, "interchange between persons or groups, communication."

"Intimate" must be used with caution unless followed by the appropriate noun to provide a context. Consider these two sentences.

> They were intimate.
> They were intimate friends.

The first sentence is, at best, ambiguous. The chances are that its all too frequent use in the Sex taboo will tilt the semantics in that direction. There may be some ambiguity in the other sentence but it is not so great. The status of "relations" and "affairs" is not as pejorated as that of "intercourse" and "intimate." But, again, the connotations of the Sex taboo are never far away and will influence the possible meaning. This fact was played on by the late Senator and Vice President Alben Barkley when asked by a reporter why the Senate committee was called "Foreign Relations" while in the House it was "Foreign Affairs." He replied that the Senate, being the senior body was too old to have affairs, they just had relations.

Why do we euphemize? There are several explanations by anthropologists and psychologists as to why taboos exist. Whereever there is a cultural taboo, there is also the need to euphemize. Euphemisms, like cultural taboos, are universal in language behavior. One view argues that the need to euphemise stems from our pre-scientific past when we thought we could through the use of superstition and ritual influence forces over which we had no control nor which could be understood and explained.

If, for example, you said something or used a name and this was followed by misfortune, it was only reasonable to believe the two were in some way related: cause and effect on the most elemental level. We still have this belief today. You will mention something which you hope may or may not take place; then you say, "Knock on wood." As though if you didn't say it, the omission will affect whatever it might be. This is the verbal equivalent of throwing a pinch of spilled salt over your shoulder in an effort to ward off what ever misfortune that act may incur.

This is tied in with the belief among primitive peoples (and not a few modern ones) that the name and the thing are in some way related. Therefore, when you use the name you run the risk of bringing the object or thing named into your presence, if not physically then symbolically. What you must do is come up with a name, either through coining a word or by borrowing one from another semantic field, to eliminate or minimize the possibility. Etymologists, people who study the sources of words and their meanings, believe that some words which we use today came about in this fashion. Frequently cited is "bear," which translates as "the brown one." This word was used when referring to the creature to avoid invoking its presence. What the earlier name was in Indo-European we do not know because the euphemism replaced it and the original is lost.

In the Jewish faith, "YHWH" or "JHVH," depending on the translation, is avoided by the more orthodox and used with caution by others because it represents the name for the supreme being. And the ancient Greeks, who were polytheistic, used the name "Eumenides," which means "the friendly ones" when referring to the "Furies," feared even by the gods.

Therefore, euphemism is born primarily from fear. The fact may be, as some one once suggested, that since euphemizing is found in all languages, it may be part of our genetic baggage. This is a safe argument to make since it cannot be either proved or disproved.

Euphemism is also the result of another type of fear, one different from the fear of bringing the thing named either physically or symbolically into our presence. This is a fear born out of sense of delicacy, perhaps even kindness; the desire not to hurt or offend someone more than is absolutely necessary. We can detect elements of this when we use such euphemisms as "expired" or "passed away." "Passed away unexpectedly" is not as offensive as "dropped dead" or "loss of a loved one" for "death of a relative."

Related to fear in the creation of euphemism is superstition. We speak of a "left-handed" compliment; one that is not sincere and perhaps more than a little malicious. Something threatening is said to be "sinister," and you may also have a "sinister look" about you. The etymology of "sinister" is "left-handed." Just how this connection, and hence superstition, arose relationing it to misfortune is not altogether clear. Perhaps it stems from the fact that the majority of people are right-handed and therefore someone who is not quite like the majority must in some way be suspect.

But fear, for whatever reason, is only one aspect of euphemism. Euphemism is not tied solely to cultural language taboos. Other functions are also served. These will influence not only the choice of words but their meanings as well. For example, the comedy team of Wayne and Shuster have as part of one of their routines a brief exchange.

> "I'm not a dentist, I'm an orthodontist."
> "Same difference."
> "Wait till you get my bill."

Both words have the same semantic field—someone who works on the teeth. In this exchange the "orthodontist" feels his title has more prestige and hence can generate larger fees. The term "dentist" is perhaps too denotative. Here are some other medically related occupations that are perhaps too denotative. Think of another occupational term where the concepts are more heavily loaded on the ameliorative side.

| | |
|---|---|
| eye doctor | chest doctor |
| heart doctor | foot doctor |
| skin doctor | brain doctor |
| bone doctor | butt doctor |
| baby doctor | |

If one is adept at this, the match-up should be something like this:

| | |
|---|---|
| ophthalmologist | thoracic specialist |
| cardiologist | podiatrist |
| dermatologist | neurologist |
| orthopedist | proctologist |
| pediatrician | |

The purpose in playing this name game is to get at an important aspect of euphemism. **They serve to add prestige and dignity** to what might otherwise be rather unexciting, but nevertheless, more denotative referents. At the risk of offending some in the medical profession, you could argue that the adoption of these polysyllabic and difficult to spell titles for their various specializations came not so much from a desire to be more precise or scientific. They were selected to add prestige and dignity.

This aspect of euphemizing is no different from that discussed earlier when examining cultural language taboos. While the process is not different, there is a difference of intent. The purpose now is not avoidance born of fear or a reluctance to offend. The purpose is to bestow prestige and dignity by altering the symbol and at the same time move the concepts from either pejorative or neutral to ameliorative.

When we start examining euphemism from this perspective, we have a new aspect of the subject. This, for want of a better euphemism, is social elegance. To illustrate, some years ago the men who shoveled the coal to fire the boilers to heat the water that warmed the buildings at a large midwestern university were called "stokers." When the time came to renegotiate their union contract, monies were not available to give them the raise they wanted. A possible strike was averted by changing their job classification from "Stoker" to "Thermal Control Specialist." The classification was further subdivided into numerical categories corresponding to the length of time on the job. Thus someone who had shoveled coal for a year or less was "Thermal Control Specialist, 5th class," 1 to 3 years, "Thermal Control Specialist, 4th class," and so on. The referent was still the same. The only thing changed was the job title. "Thermal Control Specialist" certainly sounds more prestigious than "Stoker" and also looks better on a job resume.

The changing of job titles is the semantic equivalent of giving a person a desk closer to the window or a key to the executive washroom rather than a promotion or a raise. Euphemism, in these cases, becomes a means of bestowing status even though the role played is unaltered. There are many examples of euphemisms being used in this way.

| | |
|---|---|
| Press Agent | Public Relations |
| Foreman | Supervisor |
| Clerk | Sales Person |
| Janitor | Custodian |
| Garbage Man | Sanitary Worker |
| Tax Collector | Revenue Agent |
| Typist | Word Processor |
| Window Washing | Glass Maintenance |

Aside from adding prestige and dignity to occupational titles, euphemizing for social elegance has other uses. Buying a "used car" may give a person second thoughts. But what about purchasing one from the "Largest and Finest Selection of Pre-Owned Cars?" Or what about buying a "Fleet Car" where fleet has nothing to do with speed? You may also buy a "Lease" car. Several dealers list their cars as "Collectibles," which is the phase a car passes through before becoming an antique. Also available are "One Owner," "Reconditioned," and "Demonstrators." You could argue that each of these euphemisms has a slightly different meaning. This is true only on the notional level. The meaning is in the concepts and not in the referent. No matter what you call them, denotatively all of these cars are "used."

This also happens with products. Undoubtedly because of its connection with the bodily functions taboo, "toilet paper" is now "toilet tissue," or "bathroom tissue." When the referent is obvious, "toilet" and "bathroom" are dropped; it is simply called "tissue." Similarly, when it became possible to replace a person's real teeth with substitutes, they were sometimes called "artificial teeth" (a reference that is now lost). Later they became "false teeth." This is certainly more denotative but rapidly disappearing. The in-term is "dentures," built on the Latin root "dens," meaning "tooth." Someone made this distinction: dentures fit and cost more; false teeth don't and are less expensive. Further, the stuff we scrub our teeth with is generally known as "tooth paste," but some manufacturers are now marketing their version as a "dentifrice." And a toothbrush maker calls his product a "dental hygiene instrument."

There are many euphemisms for the "hamburger" when it is cooked and sold commercially. One of the earliest of these was "hamburger steak" with the elegance being bestowed by "steak." Some of the other variations found on menus are:

| | |
|---|---|
| steak burger | Whattaburger |
| Whopper | Big Mac |
| Taco burger | beef burger |
| Bacon Burger | cheese burger |
| chili burger | oliver burger |
| rabbit burger | Spamburger |

All else failing, pour some gravy on the hamburger and call it "Salisbury Steak."

There are many other areas where euphemism is used to give social elegance. The examples cited just begin to open up the possibilities. Consider, for instance, one of the consequence of puberty. What do we call it: "acne," "zit," "hinky," "hickey," "pimple," "blossom," or "blemish?" After strenuous exercise, do you "sweat," "perspire," or "glow?" The last term is now almost exclusively regional, primarily in the South. The distinction is that horses "sweat," men "perspire," and ladies "glow."

Whether you sweat, perspire, or glow you will find products to minimize or eliminate "underarm perspiration" as well as protecting you from "perspiration odor." The names of these products become exercises in euphemizing. One would not think of calling such a product "Stink Stopper." But the first of these products was called "Odorono," a name that would not be very likely to attract many buyers today. But there is "Ban," "Right Guard," "Arid," and at least a dozen more.

Similarly, one would hesitate buying a laxative named "Blast-Off" or a diet substance called "Lard Off." The next time you are in a supermarket or a drugstore that handles an array of these products, check the names. Notice how many of them are euphemisms designed to communicate favorable connotations through the manipulation of the symbol.

There are other ways in which euphemisms may be used not just for social elegance but also to obscure the referent.

| | |
|---|---|
| slum clearance | urban renewal |
| prison | reformatory |
| fire (someone) | terminate |
| bastard | illegitimate |
| slums | inner city |
| elderly | senior citizens |
| old age | golden years |
| mentally deficient | exceptional |
| broke | negative cash flow |

No objective argument can be made for one column being "better" than the other. Such contrasts, however, are of great interest to the person studying meaning for they control both behavior and attitudes.

Do we gain, lose, or simply blur perception when euphemism is used in this manner? There is no pat answer. While the question is simple, the response is complex. As with many aspects of meaning, part of the answer lies in the ways which the majority of those using these words perceive the meaning, not in a denotative sense but in a connotative one.

Some authors on the contemporary use of language such as Edwin P. Newman and William Safire believe that we live in a time when euphemism has run amok. Consequently, it has become increasingly difficult, if not impossible, for anyone to say precisely what anything means. The primary targets are the military, politicians, and educators. The question of whether there is more euphemism today than in the past cannot be answered. Certainly, the practice of euphemizing is one with a long history. In the eighteenth century, Jonathan Swift wrote essays condemning his contemporaries for their addiction to what he called "candied" words when there were more familiar and understandable ones in the vocabulary.

Meaning can be manipulated through the use of euphemism. At times it becomes not unlike what George Orwell, in *1984*, called "newspeak." There are numerous examples from the military, politicians, and educators. During World War II, a writer for the Army newspaper "Stars and Stripes" asked why the enemy always "retreated" while we had "strategic withdrawals." He was never given a satisfactory answer.

The Vietnam war, however, focused the attention of many on the use of euphemisms in military dispatches. Their use was intended not for clarifying but for obscuring. Some of the more frequently used ones were,

| | |
|---|---|
| **new life hamlet** | a relocation camp for refugees from the fighting |
| **resources control** | using Agent Orange to kill foliage |
| **counter insurgency** | our guerrillas |
| **pacification** | attacking an area under enemy control |
| **protective reaction** | a bombing raid |
| **escalation** | increase fighting |
| **incursion** | invading the territory of a neutral country |
| **body count** | the number of enemy killed |
| **friendly fire** | being killed or wounded by our side |
| **measured response** | hit them harder |

Such terms are sometimes called "Pentagonese" although it is difficult to say whether they were generated there.

Politicians also contribute their share of euphemisms. Indeed, they proliferate so rapidly that just keeping track of them can be a full time job. William Safire has revised his *Political Dictionary* twice since it was first published in 1968; first in 1972, then again in 1978. He laments that another revision is needed but he hasn't had the time. Some of the more intriguing euphemisms whose meanings have undergone varying degrees of modification (and may have undergone more) are:

| | |
|---|---|
| **activist** | one who works for a cause, usually one whose principles we disagree with |
| **authoritative source** | someone who doesn't want to be identified |
| **bellwether** | a trendsetter whose principles we agree with, as opposed to an "activist" |
| **bipartisan** | mutually beneficial cooperation |
| **brinkmanship** | seeing how far you can push an opponent before war is declared |
| **charisma** | the ability to convince large numbers of people strictly on the basis of personality |
| **destabilize** | to work covertly for the overthrow of a government we don't like |
| **free world** | any governments not aligned with or sympathetic to communism |
| **hardball** | playing dirty |
| **image** | the public impression |
| **moratorium** | to delay a course of action while you try and figure out what to do |
| **reach (someone)** | to coerce them into agreeing with you |

Educators, like the military and politicians, have a ready store of euphemisms. In fairness to teachers, it should be recognized that most if not all of these terms are generated on the administrative level.

| | |
|---|---|
| **underachiever** | a student who has the ability but is too lazy to use it |
| **exceptional child** | one with some sort of brain dysfunction |
| **cognitive deficit** | just plain stupid but not exceptional |
| **decentralize** | to spread something out usually with an increase in the number of administrators. |
| **programmed** | organized |
| **hypothesize** | an educated guess |
| **supersede** | to replace |
| **missions and goals** | the purpose; what we would like to do if you'd just give us more money |
| **academically enrich** | put in more stuff |
| **multimode curriculum** | various subjects |

Those in law enforcement are also prone to euphemizing. The reason for this is not clear. A good part of the answer is undoubtedly the desire to make more elegant the aspects of their profession. There is also a desire to inject an element of objectivity because of the pejorative concepts associated with many of the original words.

| | |
|---|---|
| perpetrator | criminal |
| interrogate | to question the |
| subject | the suspect |
| vehicle | car or truck |
| vacate the premises | leave the place |
| the premises | the scene of the crime |
| restrain | to stop forcefully |
| apprehend | to catch |
| restraints | handcuffs |
| surveillance | watching |

Euphemisms exist in most areas. In some instances, the purpose is to avoid a cultural language taboo. But in most cases there is the need to add prestige and dignity. Or if not that, to make the referent less objectionable by changing the symbol in the hope that the concepts may be altered. Try finding less pejorative words for these.

| | |
|---|---|
| barfbag | manure |
| boobyhatch | nude dancing |
| bug killer | old folks home |
| grease job | rat catcher |
| liar | sleeps around |

The late Bergen Evans, a scholar and lexicographer, said that euphemism is necessary because, "lying is an indispensable part of making life tolerable." Looked at from this standpoint, and without getting into the psychological and philosophical implications of his conclusion, euphemisms are indeed a form of lying. But this is too harsh a judgment to make about euphemisms in general. Speakers of all languages use them so they must serve a very deeply felt need. **It is the purpose of the euphemism which must be considered in the determination of meaning, not the process itself**.

Before determining intent, remember the distinction made earlier. Words are "concrete" if they have a specific referent and are used in a non-metaphorical sense. They are "abstract" if they lack a specific referent. The further a word is from possessing a referent, the more abstract it is. The word "love" has a very high level of abstraction.

How, then, does euphemism fit into this and what are the implications for meaning? Euphemism has the effect of raising the level of abstraction. When this happens there is the possibility you will lose sight of the referent. And when this occurs, meaning becomes at best unclear. Further, the referent may become, at best, secondary to the symbol and its concepts. For example, what is the difference between a "peeping Tom" and a "voyeur?" How does one distinguish between a "dilapidated" house and a "substandard" one?

We all know what a "peeping Tom" is, but what is a "voyeur?" The word certainly sounds impressive. *The American Heritage Dictionary* defines a "voyeur" as,

> *one who derives sexual gratification from observing sex organs and sexual acts of others, usually from a secret vantage point.*

A "peeping Tom" is defined as,

> *one who derives pleasure from pruriently and secretly spying on others: voyeur*

There is absolutely no difference in the referent of these two words. Yet there is a great deal of difference in the concepts.

Because euphemism raises the level of abstraction, several things can happen:

> ❑ The size of the class of things being discussed is increased.
> ❑ When the size of the class is increased, vagueness is introduced.
> ❑ Vagueness obscures the referent
> ❑ When the referent is obscured, meaning becomes uncertain.

The use of euphemism dilutes meaning by raising the level of abstraction. A "peeping Tom" is believed to be a less desirable person than a "voyeur" even though both are engaged in the same activity. Similarly, what is the difference between a "dilapidated" house and one that is "substandard?" The former implies a structure that is about to fall apart and is one step from condemnation. It will not be worth the effort and expense to repair. "Substandard," however, implies the structure may be repaired to bring it up to "standard," whatever that word means.

The problem, then, with euphemism lies in its raising the level of abstraction and thereby obscuring meaning. Whether this is done intentionally or unintentionally is not relevant at this point. Nor is the reason behind the use of a euphemism the point at issue. What is relevant is that meaning can be manipulated through the careful selection of euphemisms because you are playing off of the concepts while the referent remains unchanged.

# 12

# ABSTRACTION, DISTORTION AND MEANING

> *Our school's cross-graded, multiethnic, individualized learning program is designed to enhance the concept of an open-ended learning program with emphasis on a continuum of multiethnic academically enriched learning using the identified intellectually gifted child as the agent or director of his own learning. Major emphasis is on cross-grading multiethnic learning with the main objective being to learn respect for the uniqueness of a person.*

What is this person trying to say? When stripped of the euphemisms, jargon, and dreadful syntax, we find:

> *We are going to take a group of smart students and teach them other cultures. They will set their own pace and be graded on how much they learn about other cultures. The purpose is to make them respect and appreciate cultural differences.*

This well-intentioned person (although the passage reads as though it were composed by a committee) violates the points discussed in the last chapter. The class of things discussed is increased and vagueness introduced; since the referent is lost, the meaning is at best obscure.

A word of caution! This implies a value judgment: euphemism is bad and, therefore, to be avoided. This is not an inaccurate assumption. Some qualification is needed. To the extent euphemisms facilitate communication between or among people, they are desirable. To the degree they obscure meaning (whether intentionally or unintentionally), they are undesirable.

Sometimes stating your meaning too concretely or on a lower level of abstraction will not facilitate communication; it may block it. In such cases, you have not put enough distance between the pejorative connotations in the concepts and their referent. When this happens, the result is not functional but **dysfunctional**. This is a useful word in any discussion of meaning. The "dys-" prefix means "faulty." A word that is supposed to perform a function in the communication of meaning doesn't. Referentially, the words "means" the same, as with "peeping Tom" and "voyeur."

But the connotations in the concepts create trouble. For a teacher to tell parents their child is "dumb" or "stupid" drops the level of abstraction too low for that particular communication situation. The referents are too concrete and their concepts too pejorated. In such instances, wisdom dictates the use of an appropriate euphemism. This will raise the level of abstraction and ameliorate the concepts. You might tell the parents their child is a "slow learner." The kid may not be able to pour water from a boot even with the directions written on the heel. But in this situation that is not relevant. Sometimes the cliche about discretion being the better part of valor is worth heeding (especially when dealing with parents).

Although "dumb" and "stupid" are in the same semantic field as "slow learner" the concepts overpower the referent. As a result, they are dysfunctional. This poses a problem for anyone wishing to communicate with a degree of adequacy. First, how to avoid selecting a word that puts the level of abstraction too low. Second, how to avoid choosing a euphemism that raises the level of abstraction unnecessarily high and obscures meaning. This is just as dysfunctional as pitching the level too low.

There is no easy resolution to this problem. Most people are aware of situations when using a word on a low level of abstraction is inappropriate. But there are times, even with the greatest of care, when the choice will be a poor one. One does not appear at a formal affair dressed in jeans and open-toed sandals. Nor would one ask the host of such an affair, "Where's the john? I've got to take a leak." Euphemizing would not necessarily help: "Where's your toilet. I've got to urinate." While "toilet" and "urinate" may be appropriate euphemisms in some situations, they are not in this one. This is one aspect of using a term which, in the wrong context, becomes dysfunctional. Edward Albee in "Who's Afraid of Virginia Wolfe?" has George say to Martha, "She wants to use the euphemism."

Dysfunction also occurs when a euphemism raises the level of abstraction so high it is difficult, if not impossible, to say what is meant. Here are some examples that move upward into an ever more rarified semantic atmosphere.

> "John has difficulty with motor control."

This simply means that John is clumsy. "Motor control" hoists the level of abstraction too much. Perhaps "lacks coordination" would be a better choice.

> "Alfred should adhere to the rules and standards of fair play in test situations."

If we translate this into a lower level of abstraction, the referent is "Alfred cheats." But by stating it too euphemistically, the meaning is obscured. Perhaps that was the intent. If so, it was successful.

> "Your child is unable to ingest learning because of low normative data supply."

This brings us referentially full circle to the initial example. All this means is that the kid is stupid. The parents may feel less hostile when told this simply because they are not too certain what it means. But sometimes parents can make distinctions within a semantic field that inject an unexpected level of abstraction. One mother told a teacher, "My son may be dumb but he's not stupid." Obviously, in her semantic system, "stupid" is more specialized and pejorative than "dumb."

The process of raising the level of abstraction higher than the situation demands is not confined to the field of education. Richard Altick, in his excellent little book, *Preface to Critical Thinking* cites the example of a plumber who wrote a federal agency to tell them that hydrochloric acid did an excellent job of unplugging clogged drains. He received the following reply.

> *The efficacy of hydrochloric acid is indisputable, but the corrosive residue is incompatible with metallic permanence.*

He wrote thanking them and received this reply.

> *We cannot assume responsibility for the production of toxic and noxious residue with hydrochloric acid and suggest you use an alternative procedure.*

He again thanked them for agreeing with him. Very shortly he received a third letter which said,

> *Don't use hydrochloric acid. It eats hell out of the pipes.*

There is another aspect of levels of abstraction that, in part, involves euphemism. This is stating an idea in an overly complex manner. Technically, this is called "circumlocution." "Circum-" meaning "around," and "-locution" meaning "to talk." Or, on a lower level of abstraction, to talk around a subject. Less technically, it may be called "circumblundering." Regardless of the term, and "circumlocution" is the one generally encountered, you express yourself in an unnecessarily complex style whether speaking or writing.

In "Hamlet," Polonius advises his son Laertes that, "Brevity is the soul of wit." ("Wit," at that time, meant knowledge or wisdom.) He then ignores his advice with a long winded excursion that only clouds his purpose. The poet Robert Southey said, "Words are like sunbeams—the more they are condensed, the deeper they burn." And George Orwell, in his essay, "Politics and the English Language," quotes a passage from *Ecclesiastes*.

> *I returned and saw under the sun, that the race is not to the swift, nor is the battle to the strong, neither yet bread to the wise, nor yet riches to men of understanding, nor yet favor to men of skill: but time and chance happeneth to them all.*

He then translates the passage into a form he believes might be used by a government official. Or, as he says, "English of the worst sort."

> *Objective consideration of contemporary phenomena compels the conclusion that the success or failure of competitive activities exhibits no tendency to be commensurate with innate capacity. But that a considerable element of the unpredictable must inevitably be taken into account.*

Orwell concludes, "But if thought corrupts language, language can also corrupt thought."

Here are some examples of wordiness. Each raises the level of abstraction more than necessary.

| | |
|---|---|
| "at that point in time" | "then" |
| "in the capacity of" | "as" |
| "in a great many instances" | "frequently" |
| "on numerous occasions" | "often" |
| "exhibits an inclination" | "tends" |
| "in regard to this matter" | "about" |
| "affirmed his intention" | "agreed" |
| "make a concerted effort" | "try" |
| "due to the fact that" | "because" |

The last chapter listed examples of euphemisms used in various professions. Any profession will develop a technical vocabulary. This is necessary to express ideas with precision. But frequently the technical language is used to either obscure meaning or to state simple ideas in an overly complex way. It may also become a "semi-secret" language, the purpose being to block the outsider from understanding what is meant. When language is used in this fashion it is called "jargon." And jargon always raises the level of abstraction, especially for someone not familiar with the terminology.

The example used at the beginning of this chapter is pure jargon. What is meant by "cross-graded," "multiethnic," "individualized," and "learning program?" Equally puzzling are "enhance the concept" and "continuum of multiethnic academically enriched learning."

But education is not alone is this. Sociologists and psychologists are frequently cited as jargon generators. Malcolm Cowley, in his article, "Sociological Language Patterns in Linguistic Transmogrification," (a title designed to parody sociological language) wondered why things are never "divided" but are "dichotomized"; why opposite views become "polar foci," and "total dissolution of a marriage" can't be called divorce. He notes that "slums" are now "inner cities" and that a neighborhood in transition to a slum is called "interstitial."

Leo Rosten deplores the increased use of what he calls "psychobabble." This is largely generated by "pop-psychology" and intended for mass consumption. Among the examples he cites are,

> "get into your head"
> "get in touch with yourself"
> "I know where you're coming from"
> "fully aware in the now"
> "having a heavy experience"
> "a high energy experience"
> "getting your (my) head together"
> "psyched (freaked, grossed) out"

Although some psychiatrists admit puzzlement about the precise meaning of many of their terms, they still continue to use them. More importantly, they have found their way into the general vocabulary of many. While psychiatrists are quick to point out that "insane" is a legal term and not a professional one, what is a "neurotic?" At what point does a person's behavior exhibit "neurotic tendencies?" When does this behavior become either "schizophrenic" or "paranoid" or both? Do you suffer from an "Oedipus complex?" And how goes things in your "collective subconscious?"

Sociologists and psychologists are not the only professions generating jargon. Linguists are no longer certain what some their terms mean. Technical words which at one time had specific meanings are now generalized to the point of confusion. "Bilingual education" at one time meant teaching a person another language. Now it can meaning teaching a subject to a non-native speaker in that person's native language.

"Diglossia" referred to a country possessing two or more languages but where one had more prestige than the other(s). Now it may also refer to dialects of a single language where one of the dialects has more prestige than another. But since it is also used in its earlier sense, confusion abounds. As a result, it is conflicting with "bidialectalism," which means using two or more regional or social dialects.

Whether you call it "jargon," "psychobabble," "Pentagonese," "bureaucratese," or "gobbledegook" the effect is the same as far as the communication of meaning is concerned. The level of abstraction is raised and meaning declines. At best it is obscured, at worst obliterated. Why? When you cannot tie high level abstractions into lower level ones, meaning in the referential and distributional senses becomes a chancy thing and we run the risk of not knowing what is being talked about—although we may think we do. Further, we may take action based on what we think we know. This could lead to undesired consequences either for someone else or for ourselves.

In the musical comedy, "The Best Little Whorehouse in Texas," the Governor is supposed to be answering questions from reporters as to why he hasn't taken action to shut down the house. In reply, he sings a song called "The Side Step." Instead of replying directly, he says he stands "four-square" for God, motherhood, and "the American Way of Life." The refrain boasts, "now you see me, now you don't." When one reporter asks another what was said, he replies, "Marsey doats and dosey doats." Setting aside the fact that the Governor is circumblundering, he pitches the level of abstraction so high that no one can figure out what he meant even if he had spoken directly to the questions.

A Secretary of State was asked by a reporter how his talks went with the minister of another nation. He replied, "We found the talks to be constructive, fruitful, and mutually rewarding." Beyond this he would not elaborate. What does "constructive" mean? Was something accomplished? Is this what is meant by "fruitful?" Was some sort of agreement reached on whatever points were discussed? Or does this mean that nothing was accomplished and more talks will be held in the hope of reaching an agreement? Does "mutually rewarding" mean that both parties learned or gained something from the discussions?

These are unanswerable questions. There are no lower level abstractions they can be plugged into with any degree of certainty. We simply do not know what, if anything, was achieved during the talks. There is a surface note of optimism in the statement. But once you attempt to find the reason for it by delving for lower levels of abstraction, the only conclusion one can reach is that very little, if anything, was communicated. The Secretary of State, like the Governor, has danced his version of the side step.

Here is an example taken from a national news magazine. The quote is deliberately broken after the first twelve words because they set the level of abstraction. "On the basis of a responsible report from a high government official . . ." The following seem to be fair questions to ask if one wishes to get at lower levels of abstraction.

**What is a "responsible report?"** Can we assume that "responsible" is synonymous with "reliable?" This would seem to be the case but we cannot say with certainty.

**What does "report" mean?** Is this a written document that you can read for yourself? Is it a verbal statement? If so, is it not then equivalent to a "rumor?" If, indeed, this is a "rumor," what is a responsible rumor, granting that some may be more reliable than others?

**What is a "high government official?"** Does this designate his position in the governmental hierarchy? To reduce this to an absurdity, he might be "high" in the sense that his office is the fifteenth floor of whatever building it may be in. Or he might be "high" in the sense that he was stoned out of his skull when the reporter talked to him. But setting aside the absurd possibilities, consider again the statement, "On the basis of a report from a high government official . . ." There is nothing by way of lower level of abstractions this can be referred to. If you think you "know" what this statement "means" give it a closer look.

Finally, look at the level of abstraction in this course description from the catalogue of an Ohio university cited by Terence Morgan in his article, "Public Doublespeak: On Beholding and Becoming,"

> *Personal Development for Men - 1½ credits: Training in the art and science of achieving success in the business world without sacrificing human values or life-styles. Course includes grooming essentials, dress options, effective communication skills, and the prerequisites of poise.*

What is the "art and science of achieving success?" What is meant by "human values?" Does "life-style options" mean different ways of living? "Grooming essentials" could include regular bathing, brushing the teeth, and seeing that one's fingernails are clean. However, the "prerequisites of poise" is a boggler. This could mean anything from standing or sitting in a reasonably upright posture to knowing when to shake hands, not picking your nose in public, and putting your handkerchief over your mouth when you sneeze.

When language is used this way, it is sometimes called "fuzz phrasing." Fuzz phrasing is the connecting of abstract words in a manner which seems to communicate more than is actually said. You can set these up like a Chinese menu and take one from each of the various columns. There is apparently no limit to the number of columns but three seems to be the most productive number.

| Column A | Column B | Column C |
|---|---|---|
| universal | ambivalent | adaptation |
| aggregate | societal | motivation |
| prior | elitist | synthesis |
| uniform | differentiated | polarity |

There are only twelve words in this chart but look at the possibilities for abstracting someone out of their senses and still have them believe you are saying something. Think of how impressive it is to mention "universal elitist adaptation," or argue for a "uniform societal synthesis." If you wish to add more words to each of these columns the possible combinations for fuzz phrasing a person into catatonia are countless.

Another way of raising the level of abstraction is through the use of "buzz words." These are terms which rely primarily on their concepts for effect rather than referential value. Or if they have referential value, it is not important. The aim is to trigger an emotional response, almost a "knee jerk" reaction. Unlike fuzz phrases, buzz words most frequently occur singly though they may also be found in pairs.

Branding an idea as "ultra-liberal" or "ultra-conservative," depending on your particular position, is buzz wording because no one really knows what these hyphenated compounds mean. One may also talk about "brainstorming" an idea, developing a "data-based" hypothesis, looking for ways to "enhance the image" of something all of which should take place within the proper "conceptual framework." This can result in "ongoing" benefits although you may wish to "replicate" your work at a later date.

There is nothing wrong with communicating on a high level of abstraction so long as it is possible to tap lower, more denotative levels. Indeed, there are some areas that can only be discussed through high level abstractions such as religion or philosophy. But there must always be some foundation on which the discussion rests. More importantly, the deliberate use of high level abstractions for the purpose of obscuring or obliterating meanings should be guarded against.

One consequence of using buzz words is "labeling." What is called to mind if you say someone is a "politician?" For many the concepts separating this symbol from its referent are not too favorable. This is in no way different from calling a person an "ultra-liberal," an "ultra-conservative," a "radical," or even a "terrorist" without some understanding of what the label means and the evidence to support its application. What can be done for people, can also be done for ideas. "The whole plan for a national health insurance program is socialistic." Or an action. "Don't do that! It's silly!" Or an object. "You may call it art, but I call it junk."

A "label," therefore, is any word that classifies (or appears to classify) a person, idea, action, or object. The examples of labeling cited are all pejorative but they can be ameliorative as well. What is meant by "classify?" To classify is to put someone or something into a category. Or, to use a popular metaphor, "pigeon-hole" it. Whenever we do this, meaning results not from the referent but from the category of classification.

Earlier, "stupid" and "slow learner" provided two different classifications in the same semantic field. The semantic range of "stupid" is different from that of "slow learner." "Stupid" is more pejorative in its concepts. "Slow learner," however, is both more generalized and ameliorative. Both are labels and both determine the manner in which we perceive the person to whom they are applied. Labels, therefore, influence perception and meaning.

Another way to put it is that this classification helps us define what we are labeling. Or at least we believe it defines. It is this definition that provides the meaning. In his book, *The Phantom Public,* Walter Lippmann says we do not see something and then define it. Rather, we first define and then we see. He called this process "stereotyping." That is, we select a few familiar features from a complex of features (defining) and on the basis of these, we stereotype (seeing).

Imagine you are presented with a photograph of a man in his early fifties. He's well dressed; tie, vest, and jacket. The hair is neatly trimmed. He wears glasses and is holding a pipe. What can you say about him?

You may select some features as being more significant than others. Just as someone else, presented with the same photograph, would make his or her selection. Is he a business man? Perhaps he's a lawyer, a college professor, a judge, a politician, or someone who is out of work and going for a job interview.

Regardless of the label we apply, we can never be certain of its accuracy until more information is obtained. Yet, we continue to perceive and act on the basis of this classification. We think we "know" something about the individual. In Lippmann's terms, we have "defined" the person and then we "see" him. Gordon Allport and Leo Postman, in their article, "The Basic Pattern of Distortion," take the "defining" and "seeing" of Lippmann and discuss it as a three step process: "leveling," "sharpening," and "assimilation."

**First Step - "leveling."** Here you reduce a complex situation to just a few easily recognized, familiar features.

**Second Step - "sharpening."** The features selected are now out of context. Because they are, they assume an importance they might not have otherwise.

**Third Step - "assimilation."** The sharpened features are then placed in a context that is familiar and apparently makes sense.

In discussing signs, it was said that context provides meaning. Without a context, any sign is capable of a number of possible meanings. Because we frequently encounter signs without contexts, we supply one based on our past experiences. Frequently, we supply the wrong context and come up with the wrong meaning. This is one reason we make mistakes. Our past experience with similar situations leads us to a conclusion that is inaccurate. This is essentially what can happen in the three step process of leveling, sharpening, and assimilation.

Allport and Postman cite the example of an oriental who was taking a vacation in 1942. He stopped to put gas in his car and also buy some film for his camera. Shortly, thereafter, he was stopped by the state police. The station owner had reported there was a Japanese spy in the area taking pictures of military installations. The situation had been leveled to three features: oriental = Japanese; wartime = spy; film = taking pictures of military installations. Because they were taken out of context, these were sharpened and assimilated into a context that apparently made sense to the person who called the police. Ignored was the fact that the man was Chinese and there were no military installations within a hundred miles.

Meaning, then, is more often than not expressed through labels applied to persons, actions, ideas, and objects. But labels are always simplifications. In his book, *The Nature of Prejudice*, Gordon Allport points out that any label condenses many features. These features, he says, are grains of sand. Using a label is like pouring these grains of sand into a particular shaped container. We frequently forget that the same grains of sand could just as well fit into a container of an entirely different shape. We have the same amount of sand, it is simply in a different container. The shape of the container defines for us.

Let's say the first container is labeled "slow learner" and the second "stupid." The grains of sand will fit either of the two. The only thing changed is the shape of the container. Suppose that among the features which the label lumps together are "honest," "trustworthy," "loyal," "reverent," and so on. Because of the labeling, features are omitted which would offer a sounder basis, or at least another basis, for perception and meaning.

If Allport's metaphor of grains of sand and containers is puzzling, think of the mirrors frequently found in amusement parks and carnivals. When you look into one of these mirrors, all of the parts are there but their relationship to the whole is distorted. This is essentially what a label does. If we place this hypothetical person in front of a mirror labeled "stupid," that feature becomes distorted and emphasized at the expense of other features. We could just as well place this person in front of a mirror labeled "loyal." If so, that feature would be emphasized and the one indicating stupidity would be minimized. Yet the person so labeled might still lack the ability to know when to open an umbrella. Should we place the person in front of a mirror labeled "slow learner," the image is both distorted and blurred. The blurring results from raising the level of abstraction, a natural consequence of euphemizing.

This same process operates whether you are using labels from the same semantic field or whether you have the option of selecting a label from among a number of semantic fields. In either case, when the label is chosen, it prevents either cross-classifications or alternative ones. This creates what Allport calls a **"label of primary potency."** A label of primary potency is a word that classifies and blocks possible cross-classifications.

A label of primary potency magnifies one or several features out of proportion to their true significance. Whatever we select is no longer in a context so the process of leveling leaves those remaining features sharpened. Assimilation will follow. Here is a hypothetical individual and some of his features.

1. He participates in various sports whenever possible. Label of primary potency = athlete. (Notice what would happen if "jock" were used rather than athlete.)
2. He has graduate degrees from several universities, writes for professional journals, and gives talks on subjects in his area of expertise. Label of primary potency = scholar.
3. He works in a decision making position for the federal government and has twenty years experience as a civil service employee. Label of primary potency = bureaucrat.

There are three potential labels of primary potency to select from. Each emphasizes a different set of features. From among these, "bureaucrat" is selected. This label, for most people, carries strong pejorative connotations. We are compelled by its use to ignore his athletic ability, his scholarly accomplishments, as well as his being a good provider for his family, a caring husband and father, regular church attendance, and a number of other features that could just as well serve as labels of primary potency.

When a label of primary potency is applied, three things are lumped together in a reckless manner. First, we have the defining attribute. In the case of the label "bureaucrat" it simply means someone who is employed in some capacity in some branch of a highly structured organization. This organization may be governmental, military, industrial, or educational. The second thing is "possible attributes." These result from either our first hand experience or what we have heard or read. Since "bureaucrat" is largely pejorative, the concepts may contain items such as a person more concerned with rules and regulations than with human beings. The third element now enters and that is the conjuring up of either non-existent or imagined attributes. We know that "bureaucrats" enjoy putting people through time consuming procedures. They do little if any real work if they can avoid it, and will do anything to protect and preserve the system which permits them to exercise this power.

In mathematics, the whole may be equal to the sum of its parts. But in using a label of primary potency, the part becomes the whole and the other parts are ignored and disappear. Notice what happens within a single semantic field.

**Labels Involved in Some Way with Teaching**: educator, professor, instructor, teacher, schoolmarm.

"Educator" is about as high as the level of abstraction can be raised in this semantic field. The word, for most people, is ameliorative although it is generalized. What are defining attributes of an "educator?"

Quite simply, a person involved in some manner with the educational process. What are the probable attributes? In addition to teaching, we assume the person thinks a good deal about the aims and goals of education and will write as well as give talks of the subject. What are the non-existent or imagined attributes? These can be filled with a number of items.

Now, drop down to the last term in this field, "schoolmarm." What is the defining attribute? No different from the one for "educator"—someone involved with the educational process. But the ameliorative aspects of "educator" are now missing. The connotations are largely pejorative and the probable as well as the non-existent attributes have undergone a similar shift.

In all semantic fields used to classify people, ideas, actions, or objects, there is the potential for a number of words, each with its own semantic range. Further, each is capable of becoming a label of primary potency on a range from ameliorative to pejorative depending on which is selected. In the field below each word carries this potential.

| Racial Terms for a Particular Group | |
|---|---|
| Black | Nigra |
| Afro-American | Nigger |
| Negro | Spade |
| Colored | Coon |

Here we find the same thing as found with the semantic field dealing with education. This arrangement, however, was not one that was made up but was worked out by a group of Blacks between the ages of twenty and thirty-five in Liberty City (Miami), Florida in 1975. A different age group would probably provide a different ranking. Since the list was made sometime in the past, this would also have an influence on both the terms and their ranking. For example, both "African-American" and "person of color" have come into use. Where would these be placed?

Allport regards all labels of primary potency as pejorative. This is understandable since his topic is the nature of prejudice. But this would be too narrow a restriction on a most useful term.

The two examples cited demonstrate that labels of primary potency may be either pejorative or ameliorative; favorable as well as unfavorable. This depends on the meaning you wish to communicate when you select the label. There is a range of choice whether the label comes from a single semantic field or from different semantic fields.

Sometimes people are insensitive to the fact that labels of primary potency lurk about just waiting to be misapplied. When this happens, the inept choice of a label will lead to communicating a meaning other than the one intended. This was the case some years ago during the first Israeli-Arab war when a mediator from Washington suggested that the two sides get together and discuss their differences like "good Christians." A teacher who always addressed male students as "boy" was puzzled by the amount of resentment this aroused in his black students. To him, the word was not a label of primary potency. It was to his black students, and a highly pejorative one.

There is nothing inherently evil in the process of labeling. The human mind craves order (though this is at times debatable). Regardless, one has to have at least the appearance of order. So labels are used. We should, however, realize that they distort because they call our attention to just a few features out of many. Meaning, therefore, results from the few feature on which a label focuses. Whenever this occurs the potential for miscommunication and misinterpretation exists.

The same caution Walter Lippmann gives in his discussion of stereotyping could just as well apply to the process of labeling because labeling is one important aspect of creating and using stereotypes. Lippmann says you cannot avoid stereotyping. Similarly, you cannot avoid labeling. The problem becomes one of holding your stereotypes lightly. Also, you should be willing to modify them, or discard them completely, should evidence indicate that modification or change is needed.

Nothing has been said about the deliberate use of stereotypes and labels to distort for whatever purpose. But both stereotypes and labels do distort. Yet we must use them for they help us to sort things out. At the same time, we should always be aware that the label, like the stereotype, only carries partial meaning. There will always be features omitted which are equally important in influencing perspective, perception, and meaning.

# 13

# STANDARDS, STYLES, AND KEYS

"Grammatical Taboos" looked at the role of the "purist" in influencing language attitudes, especially those grounded in "Grammar #3 - Linguistic Etiquette." During the 1950s and 1960s, a cigarette manufacturer managed to offend them by proclaiming, "Winston Tastes Good, Like a Cigarette Should." While those handling the advertising for a fast food chain stirred up the keepers of the flame with, "There Ain't No Reason to Go Anywhere Else."

The first example offended because, it was argued, "like" is a preposition being used as a conjunction. Therefore, the ad should have said, "Winston Tastes Good, As a Cigarette Should." Since the intent is not to inflict grammar, the discussion will be left to that found on p. 757 of the *American Heritage Dictionary of the English Language*. It is quite complete.

There were two objections to the second example. The first was the use of "ain't." Again, consult the *American Heritage Dictionary*, p.27. Second, "ain't no" constitutes the use of a double negative. That, according to Linguistic Etiquette is a forbidden construction because two negatives make a positive. So what the advertiser is really saying is that you should go someplace else. Anyone who believes this is indeed the advertiser's intent should also beware of people selling bridges.

Such constructions are usually labeled "non-standard." This means you might be able to get away using them in some situations but they should be avoided if possible. When you say something is "non-standard," this assumes there is an entity called "standard." So the problem is to define what is meant by "Standard English." The *Random House Dictionary of the English Language* defines it as,

> The English language as written and spoken in both formal and informal usage and that
> is universally current while incorporating Regional differences.

The *American Heritage Dictionary* has no entry for "Standard English." But under "standard" there is a separate entry with the label "Linguistics," which states, "Conforming to established educated usage in speech and writing."

Several questions should be raised about these definitions. First, what is meant by "literate" people? Does it mean anyone who can read, write, and cipher to fifteen without removing a shoe? Second, what does "universally current" actually imply?

Is it "universal" only in the sense that it applies to those who read and write English? It could certainly not be "universally current" among those who have no knowledge of the language. Third, what constitutes "educated usage?" Does this mean educated in the formal sense of having worked one's way through a curriculum designed to award a diploma or a higher degree? There is no need for a definitional expedition to find answers to these questions. But one should consider the implications of the assumption that there is a "Standard" "universally recognized" by "educated people."

If there is a "Standard," it is certainly not "universally recognized." Since language changes, it follows that "Standards" will also change. At various times during the 19th and early 20th century all of the following words were considered "non-standard" by various editors in the United States.

> jeopardize
> balance [the money you have in the bank]
> bully
> stingy
> belittle
> sham
> fun
> doodle
> clever
> mob

The list could be extended many times over. Imagine trying to get along without these words in our vocabulary. There are, today, very much a part of "Standard" English.

But the idea of a "Standard" is not simply a matter of words. It applies to pronunciation and syntax as well. How do you pronounce the words "tomato," and "either" or "neither?" Most Americans pronounce the central vowel in "tomato" the same as the vowel in "mate." "Either" or "neither" have the same vowel as in "neat." But in some dialects of American English, these vowels match those in "hah" and "high" respectively. Which of the two is "Standard?"

Some years ago, I visited a man I had graduated from high school with. He had gone straight from school to work. I went to college and into teaching. I dropped my car off for an oil change while we visited and asked the mechanic to give me a call at my friend's house when it was ready. We chatted for an hour or so when the phone rang. Knowing it was the garage calling, my friend picked up the phone and said, "Let me talk to him. The way you talk, it'll cost you money."

Obviously what I thought was "Standard," he did not. Perhaps the way I talk would have cost me money in that situation. Therefore, "Standard" is controlled by time, geography, social group, and education. Time, here, is the particular historical period; geography is the part of the country you happen to be in; social group is the one you most identify with on a regular basis; and education is the number of years you have put in. Looked at in this way, trying to define "Standard" becomes difficult perhaps even impossible.

"Standard" English is, in reality, a convenient fiction and does not exist in any agreed upon, definable form though we pretend it does. William Labov says that "Standard" English is best explained through the attitudes of people towards certain vocabulary items, pronunciations, and syntactic forms. People will regard some of these as "correct" even though they do not always use them in their own speech and writing. When looked at in this way, "Standard" English becomes both a subjective and relative way of using the language. Or, to return to Grammar #3, a form of "linguistic etiquette."

People regard their dialect as "Standard" unless taught otherwise. All other varieties are evaluated accordingly. This evaluation is usually downward. How does one function in this confusing situation? The best advice is that of Dr. Henry Lee Smith. The variety of the language which guarantees the maximum amount of cooperation and the minimum amount of interference is the best one to use in that given communication situation.

How does "Standard" English relate to meaning? It does so in this way. The variety we use may either favorably or unfavorably affect the reaction of our listeners or readers. In these instances, meaning results not from the content so much as from the envelope carrying the message—your vocabulary, your pronunciation, and your grammar (Grammar #3, that is).

Language and meaning, therefore, function on a variety of levels which may have little or nothing to do with the actual content of your message. This is an easy fact to forget or to recognize but one that must be taken into account. When this occurs, it is a very natural step to assume that one form of the language in more desirable, therefore "better" than another. This, then, becomes your "norm," or "Standard." Many of these norms are composed of the do's and don'ts derived from the taboos first set down by Bishop Lowth in 1761.

One of the earliest, and certainly most influential, attempts to square normative language behavior with social reality was made in John S. Kenyon's article in the October, 1948 issue of *College English* "Cultural Levels and Functional Varieties of English." He tried to bring some system and order into an area that was rapidly approaching chaos; at least from the standpoint of those charged with teaching composition. But like the definitions of "Standard" English, the categories he proposed, as well as his discussion of them, create, unintentionally, a form of linguistic etiquette and prejudice. He speaks of "semi-literate" speech and writing; of people having "an ignorance of good English," as well as the inability to use the language on a "cultivated level."

The Kenyon article is significant because the general approach he outlines has carried over into a number of handbooks on all levels from elementary school through college. These handbooks adopted his views and are still found with appropriate changes in terminology to avoid plagiarism. The article went far, though that was certainly not Kenyon's intention, towards establishing the "convenient fiction" of "Standard" English as a cardinal principle of language instruction. What emerges from Kenyon's discussion is a model of the language that looks something like this.

```
  I -  Standard English
        A.  Formal Standard
        B.  Informal Standard
 II -  Nonstandard English
        A.  Illiterate & Semiliterate
        B.  Slang
        C.  Shoptalk
        D.  Jargon
```

The two major categories as well as the subcategories are discussed giving the sentence types and vocabulary characteristics of each. "Formal Standard" is primarily spoken rather than written. The sentences are compound or compound-complex and tend to be "periodic." That is, the meaning is suspended until the end of the sentence. The vocabulary items are polysyllabic and low frequency. "Informal Standard" is both spoken and written. The sentences are shorter and have a "direct" movement. The vocabulary items consist of both low and high frequency words. "Nonstandard English" is primarily spoken rather than written. Each of the subcategories is then discussed with their "defining" characteristics.

A model of this sort is useful so long as you do not take it too seriously. Remember that a model attempts to provide a way to examine the components of a complex process. But the model is not the process. Further, it captures the process it purports to represent at a particular point in its operation. Models become dysfunctional when they are taken as literal representations. This, unfortunately, is what has happened with the various variations on the Kenyon model. They do not represent language as it actually functions but only language from one perspective. Models have value for providing insights only. When they become a straitjacket for the mind mischief and misrepresentations about language occur.

"Standards" are frequently yoked with "styles." Since style is the manner in which something is written or spoken, it is not the case that the two go together as easily as it would appear on first examination. Frequently style is referred to as "formal," "informal," or "colloquial." A person's manner of writing or speaking is termed either a "fluid" or a "cramped" style depending on whether the critic likes or dislikes it. This brings up one of the major problems of trying to discuss style systematically.

You may point to some features which constitute style, but you cannot do much more because any such listing must be so general that it cannot possibly apply to all writers or speakers.

One of the better general discussions of this is found in Strunk and White's *The Elements of Style*. But even this useful little book points to the problem of defining style. At a Conference on College Composition and Communication a session was held on the use of Strunk and White as an adjunct to the teaching of composition skills through reading literature. One of the speakers distributed three quotations and asked the audience of well over 200 to grade them as though they were freshmen compositions. They were also asked to mark any sentences or constructions which violated the cautions of Strunk and White. The grades on each ranged from A to F. There was no general agreement on the offending material. The passages were from non-fiction work by George Orwell, Ernest Hemingway, and William Faulkner.

Further, what is a favored style during one period will not be in another. The arguments about this go back well into the eighteenth century. Jonathan Swift criticized one of his contemporaries for writing in "that peculiar manner of expressing himself which the poverty of our language compels me to call his style." Mark Twain took James Fennimore Cooper to task in "The Literary Offenses of Fennimore Cooper." Walt Whitman was criticized by Ralph Waldo Emerson for his "formlessness." The same types of charges have been levelled at just about every writer at one time or another.

Little, therefore, is gained through a synopsis of the various attitudes toward style. One way to approach the subject of standards and styles, if we wish to consider them as roughly equivalent, was first set down by Martin Joos in *The Five Clocks*. Here he discuss what he calls the five "styles of discourse." These were later reworked by H.A. Gleason, Jr. in *Linguistics and English Grammar*.

Instead of using "styles," Gleason calls them "keys." He prefers this term because a "key" is something that opens and will work only in certain social situations, just as a key will not necessarily open all locks. Despite the change in terminology, the approach is still the one set down by Joos. Gleason's model is:

---

**Keys of Discourse**
❑ Intimate
❑ Casual
❑ Consultative
❑ Deliberative
❑ Oratorical

---

Each key has its own social and linguistic characteristics.

## Intimate Key.

This is a private, semi-secret form of the language developed within families or among intimates. Vocabulary items take on special meanings within this context. There is a great deal of "over-talk" where two or more will speak at the same time with sentences over-lapping and frequently left unfinished. Intimate keys are rarely used in public. It is possible for a single family to develop several intimate keys, one between husband and wife, father or mother and children, and one or more among the children if the family is a large one.

## Casual Key.

This assumes a high degree of mutual interest, attitudes, and values among the users. There is a great deal of slang which, as Gleason notes, is a prime indicator of being "in" with the group. The slang has a high rate of turnover as new words are constantly being sought to replace those either adopted by other groups or become over worked. There is again a certain amount of "over-talk" but the frequency is not as high as in the Intimate Key. Sentences tend be less open ended; that is, they are completed. If there are interruptions, enough information will be supplied so that one feels free to interject. This shared information results from mutual interest in the subjects discussed.

## Consultative Key.

This key is central, the one everyone must possess according to Gleason. Here we find "turn taking." One person will talk and then the others. A basic feature is the use of overt "feedback" signals among the users. At regular intervals you will say "right," "mmm," "uh-huh," and the like. Speakers expect these indicators to signal agreement or disagreement. They help then adjust the rate of delivery and go more slowly if there is disagreement or misunderstanding. This type of modification is not needed in the Intimate Key and is rarely found in the Casual. While sentences may be left unfinished, the frequency is not as great as in the Casual Key. Also, the sentences are more elaborate. This is the key we most frequently communicate in when we are outside the home and away from our casual groups. Therefore, it must be possessed with varying degrees of fluency by every speaker.

## Deliberative Key.

This is used when speaking to medium or large groups. The feedback signals characteristic of the Consultative Key are either missing or take a different form. Rather than verbal noises, you will find frowns, smiles, body posture, and nodding of the head in either agreement or disagreement. Sentences in the Deliberative Key are more complex. There is little dropping of words. The vocabulary tends to shift in the direction of low frequency words. Finally, you make a conscious effort to avoid repeating yourself except to emphasize or underline a point. Sentence transitions as you move from one part to another of your presentation are more apparent.

In the Casual and Consultative Keys there is a high frequency of "and" to signal transitions. In the Deliberative Key you will find "however," "therefore," "nevertheless," "after," and so on. These are sometimes called "logical indicators" which signal either that a conclusion is to follow or that reasons are to be given for believing a conclusion already stated. They also serve to indicate you are about to present another point of view.

## Oratorical Key.

This is the most elaborate of the keys of discourse. Everything is carefully planned in advance and you may even speak from a prepared manuscript. It is not unusual for the material to be practiced several times before being delivered. The sentences are complete and the various devices characteristic of public address will occur. That is, gestures will be sweeping and intended to emphasize the points being made. The voice is carefully modulated ranging from a whisper to a shout depending on the needs of the situation. This key is characteristic of ministers delivering a sermon, lawyers addressing a judge and jury, most political speeches especially those given at the two major nominating conventions. Speeches given before and following a swearing into office always seem to evoke this key as does the President delivering the State of the Union address to Congress.

Here is a contextual situation. Someone has made a statement and you doubt its truth. Since the intimate key defies reproduction, we'll have to skip it. But the other four keys might look like this:

| | |
|---|---|
| **Casual**: | Bull! |
| **Consultative**: | Are you sure? |
| **Deliberative**: | Do you have any evidence to support that? |
| **Oratorical**: | On the basis of what you have said thus far, I can only conclude there is no basis in fact for accepting the validity of your assertion. |

This is one of several possible models for understanding how language signals meaning on different levels and in different communication situations. The same caution applies to this modification of Joos by Gleason as that given when looking at the one by Kenyon. This is simply a model and nothing more. We are trying to see how the parts relate to the whole. So don't permit it to become a set of blinders and focus attention too narrowly. James Sledd once stated that "all grammars leak." By this, he meant that no grammar is sufficiently complete to explain everything about a language. Similarly, we can paraphrase Sledd and say that "all models leak." Ignoring or trying to plug the leaks in a model leads to the invention of "exceptions" to the rule. What you are doing when this happens is ignoring the facts in an effort to preserve the model. The model must be changed to fit the facts, not the other way around.

There are, for example, some problems in the Joos-Gleason model. Most prominent is the assumption that we all speak the same dialect and therefore have the same keys. But what about the possibility you will find the keys operating differently in different social dialects? If this is so, then all sorts of complex possibilities open up and makes their basic model a useful one for understanding why meaning problems arise when people from different social dialects communicate.

Assume we have Speaker A from one social dialect and Speaker B from another. Further, assume that within each of the dialects can be found the Casual, Consultative, Deliberative, and Oratorical Keys. BUT, the match up is:

| Speaker A | Speaker B |
|---|---|
| Casual | ............ |
| Consultative | Casual |
| Deliberative | Consultative |
| Oratorical | Deliberative |
| ............ | Oratorical |

There is the possibility that if Speaker A uses his Consultative Key, Speaker B will read it as the Casual Key within his dialect. Or, if Speaker B uses his Deliberative Key, Speaker A will hear it as his Oratorical Key. In the first instance Speaker B, not realizing that his Casual Key is Speaker B's Consultative Key, may feel that A's tone is too familiar for the situation. In the second instance, Speaker A, whose Oratorical Key is a match for B's Deliberative Key may feel that B is being too formal.

The problems become further compounded when one wishes to communicate with people representing a number of various social groups where even trying to figure out the various possible matches would tax the capacity of a computer. In situations of this sort, meaning is at hazard.

One should recognize that there will always be a Key mismatch. The chore is to minimize it as much as possible. This is best accomplished by emphasizing the emotional over the rational. As Bart Maverick observed in the old TV series, "You can fool all of the people some of the time, and some of the people all of the time . . . and those are damn good odds."

There must be a "Standard" to operate by when framing a communication. But it is not some concrete thing that all people subscribe to. Indeed, one could convincingly argue there are a number of "Standards" and the problem is determining which one best fits the situation. What may be acceptable in one instance may be totally inappropriate in another.

Two models have been presented in an effort to try and get at some of the problems one should consider in both sending and receiving meaning. But all these models do is provide insights into the types of problems one encounters. They may also be useful in helping to avoid them. But neither model, nor any of the others that could have been given, is totally satisfactory as an explanatory device. The fact to remember is that meaning, in many instances, may not result from the content of the message but from its form.

# 14

# INTONATION, KINESICS, AND PROXEMICS

There are other factors operating within language which influence meaning. Frequently, these become more important in controlling and determining meaning than the words and the sentences in which they are placed.

| He is my brother. |
|---|

This sentence begins with a pronoun [he] followed by a linking verb [is] followed by the first possessive [my] and ends with a predicate nominal [brother]. But this sentence has four different meanings depending upon which word is stressed.

| |
|---|
| HE is my brother. |
| He IS my brother. |
| He is MY brother. |
| He is my BROTHER. |

Why does each mean something different? This aspect of language is called "paralanguage." "Para-" is the Greek prefix meaning "beside" or "beyond." "Paralanguage" refers to those features that operate "beside" or "beyond" language to influence meaning.

Strictly speaking, only the items discussed as "intonation" are considered "paralanguage" by linguists. Kinesics and proxemics are regarded as "non-verbal" communication. But in other areas intonation, kinesics, and proxemics are considered "non-verbal."

"Non-verbal" can refer to a number of things apart from language itself which influence meaning. Color, for example, communicates meaning. Colors are said to be "loud," "warm," and "cool." When you are angry you see red. Jealousy and envy are green. Cowards are yellow. Black is for mourning (in most western countries). White represents purity and cleanliness. Such items as type-faces, clothes, manner of dress, and length of hair could all fall within the area of non-verbal. While these subjects are important in any discussion of meaning, they would lead to areas more general than the one we wish to examine.

Further, there is the complication that while there are forms of non-verbal communication which communicate one meaning in your culture, they may communicate quite different meanings in others or they may communicate no meaning at all. Similarly, the aspects of paralanguage which we have in our culture and language may not function quite the same way in another or they may not function at all. You have to find out how the other system operates. Therefore paralanguage may be considered as an area of non-verbal by some and as a separate category by others. Just make certain you know who is talking about what in which circumstances.

The feature of paralanguage that makes the same sentence have four possible meanings is intonation. This is the "tune" the voice plays when we speak. One problem many people have when they read is that the words on the printed page lack this "tune." We must play the melody ourselves. But we can never be certain the one we select is the one the author intended. Without the tune to guide us, and without an appropriate context to help supply the meaning, some written sentences remain hopelessly ambiguous.

> I can't praise him too highly.

Does this mean that the writer has a very high regard for the person or no regard at all? Without a context you cannot say.

Intonation is a combination of three interwoven features. **Stress** - the degree of loudness of softness with which syllables are pronounced. **Pitch** - the rising and falling of the voice from one level to another. And **juncture** - the short pauses that occur in the stream of speech which may influence maning.

Since juncture is not that important for our considerations here, a brief bow in its direction is sufficient. These short pauses in the stream of speech are sometimes so brief as to not be consciously detectable to the native speaker although they do influence the semantic system. For example, "ice cream" and "I scream" have the same stream of sounds. If we let the "+" represent a pause, these may be phonemically transcribed as:

> /ays+krim/ = ice cream
> /ay+skrim/ = I scream

But the interest is in how stress and pitch influence meaning. Without going into a highly technical discussion of this aspect of intonation, please accept the following on faith.

English has four degrees of stress: primary, secondary, tertiary, and weak. Of these, the one of most immediate interest is primary, the strongest. For our purposes we will use /'/ and place it over the vowel receiving primary stress. To see how primary stress can control meaning, look at this sentence with NO primary stress added.

> He dislikes scratching dogs.

This can mean two things depending on where the primary stress is placed. If it is placed over the letter "a" in "scratching," the sentence indicates the person does not like to scratch dogs. But if placed over the "o" in "dogs" the sentence now means the person doesn't like dogs that scratch.

In English, we can change nouns to verbs by shifting primary stress. Not all nouns in English are capable of being converted, however. Among those that can are

| Noun | Verb |
|------|------|
| rebel | rebel |
| produce | produce |
| content | content |
| permit | permit |
| present | present |

We may also change adjectives to noun adjuncts by the shifting of primary stress.

| Adjective | Noun Adjunct |
|-----------|--------------|
| 1. black bird | black bird |
| 2. right hand | right hand |
| 3. green house | green house |
| 4. small arms | small arms |
| 5. long island | long island |

In the first pair, there is the difference between a bird that is black and the name of a type of bird. In the second, "right" is roughly synonymous with "correct" when it is adjectival or to your hand, as opposed to your left. In the third, the adjectival indicates the color of the house is green but as a noun adjunct the house belongs to someone named "Green." With the fourth, the adjectival refers to someone with short arms while the noun adjunct is a dealer in pistols and revolvers. Finally, the adjectival indicates the island is long; the noun adjunct refers to the name of an island—Long Island.

The shifting of primary stress to signal a shift of meaning in the semantic system in one way we make puns in English. For example, following the 1984 presidential election, there was a picture of the unsuccessful Democrat candidate Walter Mondale standing in front of a white Iowa farm house. Someone remarked, "I guess Mondale found out that every white house isn't a White House." The primary stress over the first "white" signaled it was used adjectivally, the color of the house. But shifting it to "House" indicated the presidential mansion at 1600 Pennsylvania Avenue. Despite what one may think of puns as a form of humor, the ability to create them through stress shifting indicates an awareness of this feature of intonation and its ability to control meaning.

These statements about primary stress apply only to English. All languages do not have the same stress patterns. If we were to translate the "white house" pun into French - "maison blanc" the humor would be lost because French is under even stress and the distinction we make between the adjectival and the noun adjunct forms doesn't hold. A native French speaker would not hear the pun and also consider this rendition of the language not only peculiar but also harsh.

Interacting with stress is pitch. This is the rising and falling of the voice as we speak. There are also four levels of pitch. These are labeled with numbers from highest to lowest, almost like musical notation.

> 4 - extra high
> 3 - high
> 2 - normal
> 1 - low

We never hit these precisely when we speak because the human voice is like a trombone and slides up and down the scale. Regardless, we all use and recognize these levels. The differences between one person's 2 and another's is only a matter of differences in voice quality. You will recognize the other person's and they will recognize yours. 2+3+2 indicates the utterance will continue; 2+3+1 is for finality; "the sentence is over." If you try to practice these consciously, you will find yourself trying to hit them as though they were absolutes rather than relative. The consequence will be a most contrived form of speech, almost like that produced by a voice synthesizer.

Both stress and pitch interact to control meaning in English. We can now explain why the four variations of "He is my brother." can mean four different things depending on where we place the stress.

> HE is my brother.

Since the primary stress is on "HE" this pulls the voice up to the 3 - high, level. After that it falls to a 2 - normal level on "is" and holds there until "brother." It will briefly rise again to a 3 on "brother" but rapidly fall to a 1.If you do not drop to the 1 but move from 3 to 2, this signals you have not completed the sentence, that something more will follow.

By using this 3+2+3+1 pitch pattern with the first primary stress on "HE" you've communicated there are several males present and only one of them is your brother. You are designating him for the benefit of someone else.

```
He IS my brother.
```

"He" is on a 2 level. The primary stress on the "MY" pulls the voice up to a 3. But the voice quickly returns to 2 and the 2+3+1 pattern is repeated. This indicates that a question has been raised as to whether or not this person is related to you. You are, by placing the primary stress on "IS" affirming the fact that he is, indeed, your brother.

```
He is MY brother.
```

Again the voice begins on the 2 or normal level and is sustained through "is." Now the primary stress "MY" pulls the voice up to a 3 and this is followed by a rapid 2+3+1. The meaning now is that the person you're talking to had best be on guard. The person is your brother and you will defend him if necessary.

```
He is my BROTHER.
```

Here the voice moves along the 2 level until it reaches "BROTHER." Then it hooks suddenly to a 3. There is a rapid drop to somewhere between 2 and 1 followed by another slight hook in the direction of 3. This indicates that the person has done something that makes you question whether he is in fact related to you. Or if he is, you'd be just as happy not to acknowledge the relationship.

We can, and do, play all sorts of games with primary stress and pitch. Frequently, they communicate more meaning than the words themselves. This is difficult to illustrate without the voice present. Imagine that some one asks you, "Want to go see a movie?" You reply in the affirmative. "Yeah." How would you say this to indicate you are not particularly thrilled at the prospect? This time, you want to indicate you are very eager to see the movie. Notice how both the stress and pitch will vary. The response is still in the affirmative, but each has a different meaning.

There is a cliche that says: "It wasn't so much what he said as it was the way he said it." We have all experienced roughly similar situations. In Owen Wister's novel *The Virginian*, the hero cautions the villain Trampas, "Smile when you call me that." So the way you say something can be just as important as what you say.

Stress and pitch also serve as indicators of our physical and emotional states. Have you ever asked, or been asked, if something is the matter or if you're not feeling well? Conversely, you may be told, "You certainly sound cheerful (or happy) today." Someone might ask, "What are you angry about?" and if you express puzzlement they may reply, "Well, you certainly sounded mad." In this regard, a best selling "how to" book to instruct the reader on how to succeed in business without really trying, has a chapter on how to conduct yourself during a job interview conclude with this advice. "Above all else, sound sincere!"

There may be a more meaning carried by intonation than the simple advice to "sound sincere." An electronic device called the "Voice Stress Analyzer" can detect minor variations in speech patterns which are said to indicate whether or not one is lying or telling the truth. Just how accurate this device may be is hotly debated. Some believe it is more reliable than the traditional lie detector. Others argue that it is subject to the same problems and records nervousness as lying; both are equally unreliable primarily because we are not able to define "stress" with any precision.

What is a stressful situation for one person may not be for another. The point is not the accuracy of such a device. Rather, it is that there are features in our stress and pitch patterns which are quite subtle and difficult to detect. Whether or not this indicates lying is another question.

But most of us must deal with what we can hear, unaided by any electronic device. This conveys a large part of the meaning, whether accurate or inaccurate. We know that in English the normal sentence intonation pattern is 2+3+1\ ["I'm going."] indicating finality. If, however, the pattern is 2+3+2- ["I'm going"] this tells us the sentence is not finished and something else will follow.

No discussion of intonation and meaning can be completed without recognition of the social functions which the tunes of language play. A greeting, for example, is all tune.

> "Mornin'. How are you?"
> "Fine, thanks. And you?"
> "Can't complain. Take care."
> "You do the same. And have a nice day."

There is little or no content, all one listens for is the tune. President Franklin D. Roosevelt was convinced that at many governmental social functions it made no difference what you said as long as your voice played the appropriate tune. The story is that he tested this at one function by shaking hands with each of the guests and saying in the most pleasant of tones, "Glad you could come. I just killed my mother." Everyone but the British ambassador simply smiled and said how happy they were to be there. He replied, "Jolly good! The old girl's had it coming for years."

There is also an apparent connection between intonation and certain psychological states such as paranoia and schizophrenia. People with diagnosed cases of paranoia have a tendency to employ a 2+2+2 or a 2+3+2 intonation pattern with only infrequent use of the normal 2+3+1. There are also some changes in the syntax which take place so that the logic is difficult to follow. In some forms of schizophrenia syntax and semantics disappears and the words tumble out in random fashion, called "word salad." The research is still inconclusive but it appears to hold promise as a possible diagnostic tool. That is, the symptoms for certain psychological disorders may first appear in verbal behavior before manifesting themselves in other forms of behavior. If this in accurate, it may be possible to anticipate problems before they become acute and require more dramatic, not to mention expensive, forms of therapy. But this is still speculative. Whether you are speaking, listening, reading or writing the vocabulary and syntax only supply one level of meaning. Operating in conjunction them are stress and pitch.

# KINESICS

You are talking to someone across a table. As you speak, they are quietly drumming the fingers of the right hand on the table. The eyes are not fixed on yours but stare off into the distance. They then make an attempt to stifle a yawn. At this point you ask, "Am I boring you?" They answer, "No. What makes you think that?"

The answer lies in the three signals they gave: the drumming of the fingers, staring off in the distance, and the yawn. These signal boredom; they would to most people.

These actions are part of what makes up kinesics; the correlation of facial expressions and body movements with meaning. The systematic study of these was first made by Ray Birdwhistle in his book, *Kinesics & Context*. Popular attention was called to the subject by Julian Fast in *Body Language*. Neither book is to be approached lightly. Birdwhistle's is quite detailed and, at times, mind-numbing. The Fast book is superficial to the point of irrelevancy in many places.

One problem in examining the connection between kinesics and meaning is distinguishing between (or among) movements which are socially and culturally significant and those which are idiosyncratic—peculiar to a single individual rather than a social group or a culture. For example, there is a person who will start to twist a piece of his hair when discussing serious matters. He does not do it in simple conversation. His friends know this and when he starts, the signal is, "Fred's getting serious." Since this is not a generally used gesture, there is no pattern on the social or cultural levels; it is idiosyncratic to him. If everyone did the same thing, then we have socially significant kinesics.

A speaker wearing glasses will from time to time remove them with the right hand. They then take the little finger of his left and runs it across the bridge of the nose. Using the thumb and index finger of the left hand, they lightly massage the bridge of the nose. They then replace the glasses. Birdwhistle says the first part of this gesture (the removal of the glasses) is idiosyncratic while the rest is socially conditioned and can have several meanings. Since people who wear glasses will frequently remove them when they are about to make a point, then perhaps the gesture has kinesic significance.

In addition to the idiosyncratic gesture, which is of interest to psychiatrists and psychologists, there is the problem of gestures which cause cross cultural interference. The same gesture in two different cultures means something different in each. For example, in most western cultures it is customary to bunch the fingers of the right or left hand together when you wish to emphasize a point. The palm of the hand is turned upward. The thumb rests somewhere between the tips of the middle two fingers. The hand is then shaken several times for additional emphasis. An American who spent many years in Saudi Arabia stopped using this gesture when talking He discovered it is equivalent, in that culture, to "shooting a bird" or "giving the finger."

The same gesture, two cultures, two very different meanings.

Anthropologists have collected data on cross-cultural kinesics and how they correlate with meaning. Such information can be of great value given the international nature of our political and business dealings. Knowing the simple hand gesture mentioned signals something different in Saudi Arabia should enable us to avoid it and the offensive meaning carried. We should remember that our way of doing things is not the only way.

When American males are introduced, they customarily shake hands. This gesture is also repeated among friends who have not met for awhile and business associates. In India, the greeting is quite different. The palms of both hands are placed together with the fingers pointing toward the chin. The head is then quickly bobbed and the greeting is complete. Some years ago a new American ambassador to India slipped his kinesic grip. He was greeted on his arrival by the Indian prime minister who gave the traditional gesture of greeting. The American extended his right hand. Fortunately, the Prime minister, who had been educated in England, helped to cover the gaff by rapidly extending his hand. Several months later, two Russian officials visited India but when they stepped off the plane, they gave the traditional Indian greeting. They had studied up on their cross-cultural kinesics.

In America, when we wish someone to go away, we will raise a hand, usually the right, and wave it toward the individual with the palm facing out. The movements are rapid. When the same gesture is used by someone from Latin America, it means "come here." If we wish to indicate we want the person to "come here," we turn the palm toward us and then wave. But this same gesture in England is used to acknowledge the greeting of a crowd.

Sticking out the tongue is regarded as a gesture of contempt and is supposed to be used only by children although adults are known to use it on occasions when nothing else seems to do the job. In China, given the appropriate context, sticking out the tongue indicates either surprise or mock horror. In Tibet, it indicates politeness. But in some central Pacific cultures it is used to show negation. In this case, an American might think the individual is being rude when he is merely indicating he disagrees.

Cross-culture kinesics is fascinating. Citing examples would consume many pages. That would not be to the point. The point is we are sometimes so close to our modes of communication we cannot observe them objectively. But comparing ours with others helps to provide perspective and a degree of objectivity. Potentially embarrassing and awkward situations can also be avoided.

Birdwhistle has recorded over thirty movements of the face and head area which influence meaning. For example, there is the nodding of the head. A single vertical nod can mean either recognition or possible agreement depending on the context. "I'd like you to meet Mr. Walters." The single vertical head nod indicates recognition, usually followed by the traditional hand shake. "Do you think this will work?" The single vertical head nod will now signal agreement.

A single horizontal head nod, accompanied by a slight elevation of the shoulders, will signal partial interest at best, or, at worst, indifference. The lifting of both eyebrows indicates surprise but raising only one shows skepticism or doubt. The "furrowing" of the brow with an accompanying dropping of the eyebrows can mean puzzlement, doubt, thought, or perhaps even pain. "Wrinkling" the nose indicates either displeasure or disagreement. When a person is angry, we say they are "flaring" their nostrils. When surprised or awed, the mouth will drop open and the eyebrows raised. When angry, we compress the lips, lower the eyebrows, and perhaps raise one corner of the mouth, usually termed "snarling," to signal the same meaning.

This list of gestures relates only to the brow, nose, lips, and eyes and is by no means complete. Sometimes the gesture alone will be sufficient to carry the meaning. In other cases, these will influence the meaning of the words which the gesture accompanies. Or sometimes they can run counter to one another as in the line from the old song, "There's 'no, no' on your lips but there's 'yes, yes' in your eyes."

Gender differences are reflected in kinesics. There is a difference between the American male and female walk. The male has a rigidity. As a consequence, the buttocks show very little "roll" or "bounce" when he is striding along. Females' do. There are also masculine and feminine sitting postures. If he does not have his legs crossed, the male will have the knees flexed on the vertical. The female will have the knees together. Whether these developed because of different modes of dress is not important. The pattern is established. Just what effect the wearing of shorts and slacks will have on this aspect of female kinesics must wait for further analysis.

Regardless, for a male or a female to use a gesture characteristic of the opposite sex is immediately noted and probably commented on. Birdwhistle and Gregory Bateson, to name but two, discovered in working with different cultures that each has kinesic patterns which are readily identified by the natives as being either typically masculine or feminine. A culture will stereotype these gestures so that a male who uses female gestures is classified as feminine, and vice versa. In American culture, men do not (typically) walk either holding hands or with their arms around each other's waists. Yet this practice is quite common among men in the Middle East. Just as in American culture, it is not regarded as seemly for a man to cry in public.

Yet this is also quite common in the Middle East. When Senator Edmund Muskie, who was running for the Democratic nomination for president, broke out in tears while denying some possibly slanderous remarks that had been made about his wife. Many political analysts attribute his loss of the nomination to this public display of emotion.

One area of kinesics where little material has been either collected or analyzed is how gesture may vary from one social group to another within a culture. The types of movements discussed operate across large segments of American culture. But there is always the question of whether there are variations which influence meaning within ethnic and racial groups. Tentative evidence indicates yes. But we know next to nothing about their intensity or their influence on meaning. Black males, for instance, have a different mode of walking than white males. The black carries the body more loosely and there is a fluidity of movement not usually found in white males. Some white males are starting to imitate this. Again, only time will reveal if this imitation will have any lasting effect on white male kinesic patterns.

Some kinesic differences between blacks and whites started to be recognized when busing to attain racial balance in the public schools was mandated. White teachers who had had few, if any, black students in their classes read, or more accurately misread, the kinesic behavior of some of their black students. White students usually signal boredom and lack of interest by:

> ❑ Slumping posture.
> ❑ A head nod and turn, usually to the right, accompanied by a raising of the shoulders.
> ❑ The eyebrows are raised accompanied by a widening of the eyes and a movement of the pupils up and to the right.

Many black children have this same set of kinesic features. But it does not signal boredom or indifference, it signals embarrassment. So, when a black child is asked a question by a white teacher, or is placed in a similar stress situation, this is the form of kinesic behavior that may result. In most cases the white teacher is not aware this signals embarrassment. They read it as boredom or indifference, which is the meaning they are accustomed to assigning through their experience with white students. The child signals one type of meaning but the teacher assigns another. The consequences of such a kinesic mismatch are easy to imagine. This is an isolated example. More work needs to be done if teachers and students from different racial and ethnic backgrounds are going to communicate effectively. This information, however, should be for the teacher's benefit not the student's.

The problem for anyone studying the interplay of motion and meaning is not too different from that facing anyone studying the broader field of language and meaning. How does one separate the significant (that which carries meaning) from the non-significant? Edward Sapir says in his essay, "The Unconscious Patterning of Behavior in Society,"

> *Gestures are hard to classify and it is difficult to make a conscious separation between that in gesture which is of merely individual origin and that which is preferable to the habits of the group as a whole . . .*

Birdwhistle appears to be of two minds on the subject. In *Kinesics & Context* he says,

> *Like other events in nature, no body movement or expression is without meaning in the context in which it appears.*

Yet in a panel discussion dealing with paralinguistics, kinesics, and cultural anthropology, he states,

> *I am in very much agreement with the position, that under no circumstances would all body motion, all movements of bodies in space be subsumed under something called kinesics, anymore than I think that all sound made in all circumstances is to be subsumed by linguists and paralinguistics.*

We are apparently back to the metaphor about how to separate the chaff from the wheat. The problem of how to do this is vexing. It is also one that must remain unresolved until we know more. All we can do at the present is state there is a relationship. Again, we are in a position of having to say we don't understand all we know and we know very little.

We do know there is a correlation between the degree of authoritarianism in a government and the manner in which its military conducts itself in formal marching and other ceremonies. Everyone has seen film clips of the Nazi "goose step." This is a completely artificial and highly disciplined form of movement. The legs are kept stiff at the knees and the arms move in a mechanical fashion across the chest. When a weapon is carried, the free arm is moved in this fashion. This same movement is characteristic of the Russian military and not a few South American dictatorships.

Contrast this with a column of American soldiers marching. The knees are flexed. The swinging of the arms is far less rigid. While there is a uniformity of movement, it is more natural and less machine-like. Only in highly formal situations such as the changing of the guard at the Tomb of the Unknown Soldier or in a funeral procession will the gait of the American military be modified. But even in those situations it doesn't approach the highly artificial. What the psychological implications are for these differences is left for others to explain.

Before departing from the military, note how much can be communicated through the simple act of saluting. The hand salute is a ritualized movement showing respect and recognition of authority. This is elaborately described in the handbooks and diligently practiced by all recruits under the careful supervision of a drill sergeant. The fingers of the right hand are tightly pressed together. The arm from the shoulder to the elbow is held rigid at a 45 degree angle from the trunk of the body. The arm from the elbow to the fingertips is brought up crisply to a position where the fingertips are slightly above the eyebrow.

By varying the nature of the salute, an enlisted man is capable of insulting, enraging, ridiculing, or flattering an officer all without the risk of being court martialed for insubordination.

---

- ❏ To flatter follow the formal salute as described in the manual.
- ❏ Partial lack of rigidity. This could indicate the two are on suffi-ciently familiar terms to dispense with the formality. Or it could mean the enlisted man really doesn't think much of the officer.
- ❏ Movement of the hand and arm in the general direction of the eye but the motion is not completed. This is customary when officers are returning the salute of an enlisted man. If used by an enlisted man, it may signal complete contempt.

---

While we know that a great deal of meaning is communicated through both facial expression and body movement, we do not as yet have instruments precise enough to separate the significant from the non-significant. Most medical schools have at least one course for students to familiarize them with kinesic signals as an aid to diagnosis. Persons who screen job applicants also use some aspects of kinesics in evaluating prospective employees. So meaning and kinesics are linked with intonation and other aspects of language in subtle ways. There was a popular song, "Every Little Movement has a Meaning All Its Own." The second line is: "Every little feeling by some gesture can be shown." This should be kept in mind.

## PROXEMICS

The term **proxemics** was first used by Edward T. Hall in *The Hidden Dimension* to refer to the ways space and distance influence the communication of meaning. We are aware that the size of offices in a large corporation is related to the status of the position. The larger the space, the higher the status.

Sometimes it extends even beyond that. The central office of a large manufacturer is housed in a four story building. The first floor contains the general reception area with a receptionist who takes visitor's names and contacts the office of the person they wish to see; a large mailroom screened off from the reception area; a complex communication room is visible to the visitor through large glass windows. The second floor houses the offices of those who conduct the general business of the company. An office consists of an open bay arrangement set off by partitions about three feet high. On the third floor are the middle management people whose offices are essentially the same type of bay arrangement but with glass dividers that stretch to the ceiling and permit more privacy. The floors are not carpeted on either the second or third floors. The fourth floor houses the executive offices. There are office suites each with a secretary who acts as a receptionist. The floors are carpeted and there are drapes on the windows. Finally, those on the fourth floor park in a garage under the building, those on the third floor have their parking spaces outside but covered so when it rains they will not get wet. Those on the second and first floors must park in whatever other space is available and chance the elements. So the status structure of this company is reflected in the proxemics of its organization.

One subject Hall discusses is architectural space and how it is utilized both within buildings as well as between them at different historical periods. He argues that the use of space is an index to the ways in which a culture views both the world and the place of the individual within it. The cathedral at Chartres in France was built during an intensely religious period. There are high, vaulted arches that both draw the congregation's attention upward and impress on them their own insignificance. By way of contrast, many modern churches are designed to integrate the individual into the ritual of the service. While impressive, the intent is not to overwhelm or inspire awe but to draw together.

Most court houses are designed on the Chartres principle. The doors to the courtrooms are almost always huge and out of all proportion to their function. The judge sits in a large chair on a raised dias which also is larger than actually needed. The intention is to impress you with the power and majesty of the law.

Space may be used to create psychological moods. Adolph Hitler was aware of this when he helped design the room in the Reich Chancellory where foreign dignitaries were received. The doors were huge, perhaps ten or twelve feet high. The floor was highly polished squares of black and white marble. Upon entering, there was nothing in front of the dignitary but open space. Hitler stood beside a davenport at the far end of the room. Persons who walked this distance were at an emotional disadvantage by the time they reached the Fuhrer. But this is just one aspect of proxemics.

Regardless of the culture, all people are surrounded by an imaginary bubble. This is their "space." A popular phrase in psychobabble is for someone to complain they only want their own space and not have others getting into it. The fact is well documented that how a person regards space is an index of personality type. People who are extroverted, very outgoing, have comparatively small bubbles. They also tend to regard others in the same way. They will touch you, grab an arm when making a point, and put their arm around you.

Introverts, as well as people given to violence, have large bubbles. With extreme introversion, the bubble will fill any space they occupy. Just by entering the room, you threaten their space requirements. They will retreat as you move toward them even though you may be ten or more feet away initially. In some cases they will move to the furtherest corner and cower. The violent personality will attempt to move the offending person from their space as rapidly as possible. Such extreme cases are best left to the psychiatrist and psychologist.

As a general rule people from Germanic languages (and that includes the English) have larger bubbles that those from the Romance languages. If you come from Italy, Spain, France, or South America, your bubble extends from 1½ to 2½ feet. For people from England, Holland, America, Sweden, and the other Germanic language areas, the bubble extends from 2½ to 4 feet.

This presents a problem when someone from a Romance language has a conversation with someone from a Germanic. There develops a conflict of distance. What seems "normal" speaking distance for someone from Spain will represent "invasion of privacy" for most Americans, English, and Germans. They feel the person is trying to get inside their bubble. The likelihood is they will start to back away—sometimes all the way across the room. Those from the Germanic languages feel those from the Romance are "pushy" while those from the Romance feel the Germanic are aloof by backing away and trying to keep them at a distance, perhaps even avoid them.

This can be seen in other areas. When we drive, we tend to transfer our bubbles to the front and rear bumpers of our cars. We are told we should keep one car length for every 10 miles per hour of speed between ourselves and the car in front. This is not always observed but we usually try and keep a reasonable distance. Driving in France, Spain, or Italy can become a chore for many Americans because they always have the feeling that the car behind them in trying to climb into their trunk.

What does this have to do with language and meaning? It relates in this way. Hall says that we segment space into four general zones. The size of these zones vary from one culture to another, as noted with the bubbles of Germanic and Romance language speakers. The American defines them as follows:

**Zone #1 - Intimate Distance.** This ranges from direct contact to about eighteen inches. This is touching distance. Here the senses are operative and acutely focused. You can hear respiration, perhaps even feel the breath as well as smell it—not to mention other odors. There are numerous products on the market to avoid the pitfalls of intimate distance: mouthwashes, soaps, breath mints, deodorants, powders, and perfumes. After all, no one really wishes to "offend," especially in the courting season.

We may also transfer intimate distance. Thus a husband and wife may be across the room from each other at a party. But he will become uneasy if another male gets too close to her. Or she will become disturbed when another female approaches him in what she defines as her intimate zone. This doesn't just apply to husbands and wives. It also operates whenever two people regard each other as intimates.

Some situations necessitate "enforced" intimate distance. These occur when you are compelled to be within eighteen inches of others: on elevators, in various means of public transportation, on crowded streets, malls, and at public events. Sometimes even short periods of "enforced" intimate distance makes Americans uneasy. Consider what happens on a crowded elevator. People will either stare at the wall, the lights indicating the floor, or at the back of the person standing in front of them. Some times they become so acutely aware of the situation they will make a remark either about the speed of the elevator or the weather in an effort to reduce their uneasiness. The other alternative is to regard those around them as "non-persons." There is evidence to indicate that extended periods of "enforced" intimate distance such as one must undergo in large cities and crowded tenements increases the incidence of violence.

**Zone #2 - Personal Distance.** This begins at eighteen inches and extends to four feet. The usual distance is 2½ to 4 feet. This is the space where most conversations take place. You may permit someone inside the 2½ feet boundary but only for short periods of time. If someone wishes to whisper a confidential piece of information, this is permissible. But they are expected to withdraw as soon as the communication is complete.

**Zone #3 - Social Distance.** Extends from four to twelve feet. This is the distance at which business and other formal transactions take place. For people who work together on a regular basis, the appropriate distance is four to seven feet. There is usually some sort of a barrier such as a table or desk to insure that distance is maintained. As you move beyond seven feet the formality of the situation increases.

There are various ways to break up social distance in business offices. One configuration is to have a desk with one or more chairs in front of it. This pushes you out four to five feet. If the office is sufficiently large, there may also be a table with several chairs around it. In addition, there may be a couch and several comfortable overstuffed chairs. Such an arrangement permits persons who controls this space at least three options. If they remain behind the desk, one set of expectations control the communication. Or they may suggest you sit at the table. This is another possibility. The third is to sit on the couch. There are other variations to play on this theme. The more important the individual, the more the office will permit variations.

**Zone #4 - Public Distance.** This is reserved for formal situations. Either a single individual is addressing a group or a formally constituted body, such as a commission or board meeting on public business. The minimum distance in these situations is thirteen feet. There is almost always some sort of raised platform, perhaps even a railing, to separate the individual or the body from the general public.

In a courtroom, the place where the judge sits (still called a "bench" even though it is a comfortable chair) is at least three feet above the level of the room. This is also the case with county commissions, boards of education, and the hearing rooms in state and federal legislatures. The effect is to increase the formality of the situation. For very important public figures such as a mayor or governor, and always the president, a minimum of twenty-five feet is necessary.

Proxemics, like intonation and kinesics, influences both language and meaning. But how? In the discussion of "Standards, Styles, and Keys" one of the models was the "Keys of Discourse" developed by Joos and modified by Gleason. The five keys were:

These keys may be tied into the four zones as follows:

| | |
|---|---|
| #1 - Intimate Zone | Intimate Key |
| #2 - Personal Zone | Familiar Key |
| #3 - Social Zone - 4 to 7 ft. | Consultative Key |
| #4 - Social Zone - 7 to 12 ft | Deliberative Key |
| #5 - Public Distance | Oratorical Key |

This is a movement from informality to formality not only in the way that language is used but also in the types of gestures and expressions. The problem becomes one of selecting the Key of Discourse appropriate to the situation. If one or the other is inappropriate, the meaning you wish to communicate may either be misunderstood or lost altogether. Although they were discussed as separate entities, intonation, kinesics, and proxemics are always tied together.

An exact science explaining these ties is neither practical nor possible. Important questions, however, need to be explored.

Are certain types of intonation patterns called for in each of the proxemic zones? In the oratorical key and the public distance situation, there is an overemphasis on the various three aspects of intonation, especially stress. Note this the next time a politician or a minister speaks. Are certain kinesic patterns more appropriate for the expression of feelings in certain situations and inappropriate in others?

As Hamlet advised the players:

> . . . *suit the action to the word, the word to the action, with this special observance, that you o'er step not the modesty of nature.*

An awareness of the interaction of intonation, kinesics, and proxemics with language will not automatically guarantee the appropriate meaning will be either communicated or received. There will always be the possibility of giving inappropriate signals. Or that someone may be doing so deliberately. It may also be the case that when communicating cross culturally the same intonations, kinesics, and proxemics will have meanings different from those you possess. Actions indeed speak louder than words. They will frequently communicate a great deal more meaning than referential, distributional, and notional meanings of the words themselves as well as the sentences in which they occur.

# 15

# SOME PROBLEMS:
# THE MANIPULATION OF LANGUAGE AND MEANING
## Is English Racist?

The responsible use of language should be of increasing concern. We are constantly bombarded with messages urging us to adopt a particular course of action whether it is the purchase of a product or to adopt a position on an issue. The individual must be the one to develop standards for analysis and make the decision on whether or not to act. But action should be based not so much on emotion as reason. The balance between the two is not always easy to achieve. Emotion without reason can lead to the simplification of complex issues.

In a speech before the National Council of Teachers of English annual convention actor, writer, and director Ossie Davis said,

> . . . .*Words have a power over us: a power we cannot resist. . .you and I have had our deepest physical reactions controlled, not by our wills, but by the words in the English language.*

His subject was "The English Language is My Enemy." The question he raised: Is the English language racist? Some of the evidence he presented is compelling. *Roget's Thesaurus of the English Language*, lists 134 synonyms for "white."

Among them are "chaste," "cleanliness," "clear," "fair," "purity," "unblemished." When the list is examined for ameliorative and pejorative connotations, the majority range from mildly to strongly favorable with the preponderance being favorable. Only synonyms such as "pale," "ashen," and "gloss over" could be considered pejorative. To tell a "white lie" implies that the untruth was told with the best of intentions and not to be taken too seriously. The *American Heritage Dictionary* , lists various compounds with the word "white."

| | | |
|---|---|---|
| white collar | white flag | white paper |
| white elephant | white magic | white slave |
| white feather | white noise | white tie |

Only three of these, "white elephant" (something you don't really want), "white feather" (cowardice), and "white flag" (to surrender or ask for a truce) are pejorative. "White slave" meaning to transport women for purposes of prostitution, is now obsolete.

Roget has fewer synonyms for "black" but none has favorable connotations. Among these are "dismal," "malignant," "obscure," "sinister," "smut," "sullied," "unclean," "wicked." Some of the compounds in the *American Heritage Dictionary* are,

| | | |
|---|---|---|
| blackball | blackguard | black magic |
| black belt | black humor | blackmail |
| black book | black market | blackjack (weapon) |

When comparing the synonyms and compounds of "white" and "black" there is little doubt that the concepts in the semantic field of "blackness" are uniformly pejorative while those associated with "whiteness" are ameliorative. To the extent we find this, we can say that the English language is racist. This, however, is the result of historical accident not deliberate manipulation.

Words relating to "black" or "blackness" developed pejorative connotations very early in the history of our language. Our linguistic forebears were highly superstitious. They believed evil spirits walked the night and foul deeds took place in the dark. Even the night air was regarded as unhealthy and people closed their windows to keep it out. And this was considerably before even a minority of them had ever seen a black person. There is little evidence Shakespeare had seen a black when he wrote "Othello: the Moor of Venice."

But historical fact should not be used as an excuse for denying the fact that the potential for prejudice is built into the semantic system of our language. Nor should we dismiss the fact that this bias is frequently exercised either unwittingly or with deliberate intent. We should not forget that English is capable of expressing prejudice in a number of ways toward both racial and ethnic groups. Nor should we forget that English is not unique in this.

Time has removed much of the pejoration in the concepts of "redskin," "red devil, and "red man" when applied to the American Indian. But we still carry a not too subtle reminder this was once the case when we call someone an "Indian giver." Similarly, if we manage to get someone to reduce the price, it is not uncommon to say, "I jewed him down." Few people today remember that a shovel was once an "Irish spoon," a brick was "Irish confetti," and a wheelbarrow was both an "Irish buggy" as well as an "implement that taught the Irish to walk upright." Taking a few drinks before acting is getting "Dutch courage." Any confused situation can be referred to as a "Chinese fire drill."

English, like any language, is prejudiced in the ways it may refer to certain racial and ethnic groups. Sometimes this results from historical accident as in the case of "black." At other times the resources of the language are deliberately manipulated to show prejudice as when Latin Americans are called "greasers," "spics," or "wetbacks." Orientals are sometimes disparaged as "slopes," and any native of an underdeveloped country a "gook."

Mr. Davis suggests that the English language must be changed or, as he puts it, "reconstructed" to remove the prejudice. But this, according to cliche, is something easier said than done. The solution lies in the attitudes of people for they, after all, are the keepers of the language. If we concentrate on changing these, then the language will of necessity follow.

## Is English Sexist?

We are now in the process of trying to alter the language in just the manner Mr. Davis supports. That is, the language is being examined with the intent of removing as many sexist overtones as possible. Collectively, we have for centuries referred to ourselves, regardless of gender, as "mankind." The available labor force is "manpower." Those of the feminine gender are called fe(males) or wo(men). When an unspecified generic noun such as "student" is used, the textbooks say the masculine pronoun "he" should be used if there is nothing else in the sentence to indicate the sex of the student. To avoid this, a group of teachers in Dade County, Florida suggested introducing a new pronoun, "hem," to cover both the third person singular and the plural when the reference to sex is not specific. Two other attempts to get around the problem are "he/she" and "(s)he."

Since the mid 1960s, groups concerned with women's rights have campaigned with some success to purge the language of words they believe are prejudicial and substitute ones which do not convey discriminatory sexual attitudes and stereotypes. Casey Miller and Kate Swift say in their article, "One Small Step for Genkind," "Sexist language is any language . . . that assumes the inherent superiority of one sex over another."

There can be no doubt that in many respects the English language is sexist. Again, there is a historical reason. Women, for centuries, were regarded as the "weaker sex" and not entitled to the same rights accorded men. This attitude is reflected in cliches. The husband is the "breadwinner" who "brings home the bacon." Not until 1920 could women vote in this country in presidential elections. And it has only been since the 1970s that married women could purchase items on credit in their own name without having their husbands cosign. So, in a sense, women have inherited a situation not unlike the semantic prejudice which blacks are trying to counter. The argument that English is sexist is as compelling as the one for the language being racist.

This is frequently expressed in very subtle ways. What, for example, is the difference between a "lady" and a "woman?" The difference is caught in these two sentences.

> At fifteen, she was already a lady.
> At fifteen, she was already a woman.

The first communicates that she was already versed in the social graces attributed to "ladies." The second suggests both physical development and sexual awareness.

Note the differences in connotations between "master" and "mistress."

> The picture was painted by an old master.
> The picture was painted by an old mistress.

An unmarried, mature male is a "bachelor," but an unmarried, mature female may be a "maiden lady," a "spinster," or an "old maid." These now seem to be yielding to "single" and "career woman." But the first three are not entirely out of the language and may still be encountered though not with the frequency in years past.

Allein Pace Nilsen, in her article, "Sexism in English: a Feminist View," reviewed the words in a disk dictionary and isolated those relating to males and females. She concluded that the dictionary entries reflect a bias against women in several unexpected ways.

1. Men's names are used to indicate more words than women's. "boycott," "chauvinism," "derrick," "lynch," to list a few. By her count, there are more than a hundred such words. She found but two drawn from women, "bloomers," and "mae west."
2. In certain pairs of words, the feminine form has sexual connotations while the masculine does not.

   | | |
   |---|---|
   | master | mistress |
   | sir | madam |
   | call boy | call girl |

3. Words where the male form serves as the base with the appropriate suffixes added to indicate the female. Linguists refer to such forms as "marked" because of the suffixes.

| | |
|---|---|
| usher | usher(ette) |
| waiter | wait(ress) |
| hero | hero(ine) |
| poet | poet(ess) |
| steward | steward(ess) |
| actor | act(ress) |

In general use, some of these distinctions are rapidly disappearing. "Poet" is now used regardless sex. "Waiter" and "waitress" and "steward" and "stewardess" are now simply "serving persons," and "flight attendants."

4. Women are far more likely to be identified as food; something to be consumed. "Tomato," "dish," "peach," "honey," "sugar," although the last two are apparently bisexual.

She concludes with the observation that in youth a woman is a "chick," after marriage she may feel "cooped up." Then she may "henpeck" her husband. She raises her "brood," suffers an "empty nest" syndrome when the children leave, and finally ends up an "old biddy."

Other instances of sexism in English have been pointed out a number of times. When a female enters what has been traditionally a male profession or occupation that fact is frequently considered worthy of note.

| | |
|---|---|
| a lady doctor | a lady barber |
| a lady lawyer | a lady bus driver |
| a lady professor | a lady trucker |

Dr. Robin Lakoff points out in "Language and Woman's Place" that the areas where women have more complex vocabularies than men have little concern to the male and carry with them the connotation of triviality. Thus, most men do not have, or feel the need for, extensive vocabularies for colors, cooking, and sewing. A survey of 100 males showed that well over 90 percent had no idea what words such as "hem," "pleat," and "dart" meant within the context of sewing. The general reaction was indifference. "After all," one said, "that's stuff that women do."

Lakoff also notes that certain adjectives are regarded as female: "adorable," "charming," "divine," "goodness," "lovely." Her study revealed that women also use far more "tag" questions than men.

> We are going, (aren't we)?
> You will be on time, (won't you)?

The "tag" really isn't needed. Lakoff points out that this form is used when the speaker is making an assertion but is uncertain or lacks confidence in the truth of the statements. Further, she notes that it is "unlady-like" for women to make strong statements.

Marjorie Swacker made a study reported in "The Sex of the Speaker as a Sociolinguistic Variable." It has been duplicated several times with the same results. The findings demonstrate just how mythic some beliefs about how women use language really are. These myths were held by women as well as men. In a controlled study involving equal numbers of men and women in the same age group and equivalent sociocultural backgrounds, she asked them to describe three pictures as thoroughly as possible. The responses were tape recorded and transcribed for checking and rechecking. Perhaps her most interesting finding was that men are far more verbose than women. In their descriptions, the women averaged 3.17 minutes while the men babbled on for 13. This is a 4 to 1 ratio. A cross check of the descriptions showed that women were more accurate in their details while men seem to hedge their descriptions with "looked like," or "seemed to be."

By now, most are familiar with the efforts to remove sexist overtones from the language. Anthropologist Peter Farb titled one of his last books *Humankind* rather than "Mankind." But Casey Miller and Kate Swift (mentioned earlier) argue against both terms. They believe that "genkind" should be substituted. It is from the root "genus," meaning species. Some businesses and academic institutions have mandated that the individual heading a committee no longer be designated either as "chairman" or "chairlady." The title is to be either "chairperson" or simply "chair."

Persons delivering a talk at a professional meeting frequently receive a "style sheet" for the preparation of their material. One such issued by the Conference on College Composition and Communication was four pages long, single spaced, and did not address itself to the format of the paper. Rather, it indicated the types of words and syntactic structures which may be construed as sexist and, therefore, avoided. Among the many items were the generic "he" mentioned earlier. Also to be avoided were:

| | |
|---|---|
| mailman | use "mailperson" |
| salesman | use "salesperson" |
| fireman | use "fireperson" |
| feminine | use "female" |
| masculine | use "male" |

Since the talks were to cover problems in student compositions, there seemed to be little opportunity for any of these being used. Therefore most of the speakers were spared the necessity of modifying their syntax and vocabulary.

Publishers are equally sensitive to possible problems and issue similar "style sheets" to prospective authors. Or it is sometimes the case that the manuscript will be returned with editorial suggestions for deleting references deemed offensive. A religion professor insisted on using the generic "he" over the objections of his editor and while it was a matter of heated argument, "he" prevailed. Despite the fears of his editor, there were no repercussions.

If this appears to make light of efforts to modify the language, such was not intended. The subject, however, is one that lends itself to satire when the positions are stated too arbitrarily and dogmatically. One such crusader advocated the immediate purging of any and all words having racist or sexist overtones. Such a suggestion may have merit in theory but little in reality.

First, there is the question: "Who is to make the decisions?" Does one operate the way a government agency did and appoint a panel of "experts?" Their task was to go through the index of job classifications used by the Bureau of the Census, and change any titles which indicated racial or sexist bias. They had very little difficulty with the former but it took a number of years to complete the latter. Even then the finished version was not to everyone's satisfaction, including some on the panel. Further, these changes in job titles make it difficult for researchers who wish to compare census data over several decades.

Another question is: "To what degree will we be cut off from our cultural heritage if restrictions on references which might possibly be construed as either racist or sexist are rigidly enforced?" Would books such as Mark Twain's *Huckleberry Finn* and plays such as O'Neill's *The Emperor Jones* be dropped from the curriculum and removed from the libraries? Or would they be revised to remove the offensive language? What about the books and plays where women are depicted in ways considered submissive or subservient? Since they cannot be revised, would they be banned?

One way to get perspective on such arguments is to consider those developed by persons wishing to reform English spelling. There is the classic case of George Bernard Shaw who vigorously fought for reform and left a large sum in his will to establish an academy for this purpose. He felt our spelling was at best illogical and at worst chaotic. One of his examples was that if there was any logic in our spelling, "fish" should be spelled "ghoti" with the "-gh-" representing the sound in "enou(gh)," the "-o-" representing that in "w(o)men," and the "-ti-" the sound in "na(ti)on." Another reformer urges that the letter "c" be dropped from the alphabet since it can be easily replaced by either "k" or "s." "Cage" would be come "kage" and "cider" would be "sider."

There is a historical reason for English spelling being the way it is. At the time our spelling started to standardize, there were some sound changes taking place in the language. These spellings were set before the sound changes were complete. This is why it is possible for Shakespeare to make puns on "reason" and "raisen" as well as "grease" and "grace" because both pairs were pronounced alike at that time. This is also why it is possible for Alexander Pope to rhyme "tea" and "say," "join" and "line" where we cannot. Looked at objectively, English spelling is not as illogical or chaotic as some would have us believe. There are problems but they are no greater than one can find in any language. Reform, therefore, would accomplish little and create problems of unthinkable proportions considering the quantity of material in print that would have to be revised.

There can be little argument that English is both racist and sexist. This is historical accident not planned. But language is not something that can be changed by edict, especially the semantic system. You cannot arbitrarily delete words without doing serious damage to the fabric of your semantic system. So we are confronted with a circular problem.

Before you can change the attitudes of people, you must first change the language. But before you can change the language, you must change the attitudes of people.

At the present, we are too close to these problems to be completely objective about them. This applies to both the analysis as well as possible solutions. Witness the difficulty of having Americans accept the metric system as our basic unit of measurement. It may well be that in some future generation, meters, kilometers, and the other freight of metric terminology will become part of the active vocabulary of our great grandchildren and they will look on yards, miles, feet, ounces as quaint words that no longer have any meaning. What we are confronted with in racism and sexism in language is a problem that must be resolved through evolution not revolution no matter how well intentioned the motives.

## The Manipulation of Language and Meaning

*. . . Nothing so aids the advance of corruption and ideas but also all the words and phrases making up a language. . . . A generation that has formed itself linguistically around the primitivisms of "like," "cool," "man," "feel," and above all, "you know" will not be a difficult generation to enslave politically, socially, and culturally. Weaken, corrupt, dissolve the authority of language in a society, and the rest follows rather easily.*

This quote from sociologist Robert Nesbitt was cited earlier. A concern about what is happening to language and meaning is not recent. The problem, however, is not that language and meaning are being manipulated to control attitudes and behavior. Tracts, leaflets, and essays designed to enlist support for a position or a course of action have been published since the invention of moveable type made possible the beginnings of mass communication.

Consider the opening lines of the Declaration of Independence:

> *When in the course of human events it becomes necessary for one people to dissolve the political bands which have connected them with another, and to assume among the powers of earth the separate and equal station to which the laws of Nature and of Nature's god entitle them, a decent respect for the opinions of manking requires that they declare the causes which impel them to this separation.*
>
> *We hold these truths to be self evident: that all men are created equal; that they are endowed by their creator with certain inalienable rights; that among these are life, liberty, and the pursuit of happiness.*

A moving and compelling statement; one that has controlled the attitude and behavior of Americans for over two hundred years. Its purpose was to enlist support for the Colonies separating from England. There are few who would argue that the situation did not warrant such action. The problem, then, is not the manipulation of language and meaning but the purposes behind the manipulation. The moral and ethical implications of the manipulation can only be touched on and their development left to a more appropriate forum.

But we should be aware of some of the complexities involved. Citing the opening lines of the Declaration of Independence suggests one such complexity best phrased as a question. Does democracy, as a form of political governance, pose special problems in the use of language and the interpretation of meaning? In the early 19th century, a Frenchman, Alexander de Tocqueville, came to the United States to study our prison system. When he returned, he published in 1830 *Democracy in America*. He set down his perceptions of the emerging nation and the implications, as he saw them, for the people and their attitudes. One section deals with language in a democracy. He wrote,

> *[Democratic peoples] are passionately fond of generic terms and abstract expressions. These abstract terms which in democratic languages, and which are used on every occasion without attaching them to any particular fact . . . render the mode of speech more succinct and the idea contained in it less clear. But with regard to language, democratic nations prefer obscurity to labor. . . .*

Is there something built into the democratic process that inclines us to use language, as de Tocqueville characterizes it, in a "generic" way? Generic terms are, by nature, reasonably high in their level of abstraction and difficult to pin down denotatively. Consider, for example the words "love" and "freedom" discussed earlier. Nisbit cites the words "like," "cool," and "you know." They seem to say something but exactly what? What is meant by the statement, "Man, that's heavy." when the reference is not to a weighable object but something someone has said? Where are the referential and distributional meanings in that sentence?

We hear complaints about politicians "talking around" a subject and never stating precisely what they mean. Presidents have at various times characterized their aims as a "New Deal," "Fair Deal," "Square Deal," while we hunt for the "New Frontier" which will lead us to the "Great Society." When this happens, we will return to "those values which have made America great." There is a high degree of abstraction in all of these. They communicate on the gut level but are difficult to equate with something on a lower level of abstraction much less something denotative and concrete.

A question frequently asked is: "What did the framers of the Constitution 'mean' when they said as they did in the 1st Amendment,

> *Congress shall make no law respecting the establishment of religion, or prohibiting the free exercise thereof, or abridging the freedom of speech; or the right of the people to peaceable assembly, and to petition the government for a redress of grievances.*

A good part of the Supreme Court's time is spent trying to interpret what the framers of the Constitution meant. Does the word "no" mean exactly that? Does pornography fall under the protection that single word? To further complicate matters, different Court with different Justices have at different times come up with widely different interpretations.

But is the passion for generic terms and abstract expressions the result of our form of government? A differing view is suggested by Edward H. Carr in his book, *The New Society*. He believes the problem is not the form of government but the movement following the Civil War from what he calls "individual democracy" to "mass democracy." In this regard, it should be noted, collective nouns were more often than not treated as plurals. So we have "the enemy are" but more significantly, "the United States are." Following the war, we find "the United States is." In a "mass democracy" Carr argues that one markets ideas and individuals in much the same way as a product. The appeal is to "non-rational" or emotional; it is not to reason but to "gullibility."

Walter Lippmann in, *The Phantom Public*, explores the subject from another perspective but arrives at the same conclusion.

> *Since the general opinions of large numbers of persons are almost certain to be a vague and confusing medley, action cannot be taken until these opinions have been factored down, canalized, compressed, and made uniform. The making of one general will out of a multitude of general wishes . . . consists essentially in the use of symbols which assemble emotions after they have been detached from their ideas. . . . The process,*

*therefore, by which general opinions are brought to cooperation consists of an intensification of feeling and a degradation of significance.*

In other words, to return language as a symbol system, one concentrates on the concepts (where the emotions reside) in such a way that the referent becomes irrelevant. The manipulation of meaning, then, is the manipulation of concepts so that emotions are intensified and significance diminished. Or, in Lippmann's view, degraded.

There is another factor to consider. The movement (to use Carr's terms) from individual democracy to mass democracy following the Civil War coincides with two other major changes in American society. The first is the development and rapid expansion of industry and technology—especially the latter. A listing of the inventions beginning, alphabetically, with the adding machine and ending with the zipper shows that the majority of them followed the Civil War.

David Potter, in *People of Plenty*, says that technology makes it possible to produce new products faster than people have a need for them. The task, therefore, becomes one of "educating" people to become consumers. If you have a product, you must create a need to use or consume that product. But you must also have the technology which enables you to create that need in a speedy, economical, and efficient manner. Enter the rotary press, radio, television, and, of course, those who specialize in ways to create the need.

Gyles Brandreth, in *The Joy of Lex*, looks at how to create this need through the manipulation of the "blurb" to convince people to purchase a particular paperback book from the thousands that are on the shelves. He calls it his "Bantam Blurb Generator." It looks, in part, like this.

| COLUMN #1 | COLUMN #2 | COLUMN #3 |
|---|---|---|
| a tempestuous | magnificent | best seller |
| an emotional | terrifying | best seller |
| a captivating | outrageous | best seller |
| a sensational | celebrated | best seller |
| a brilliant | spine-tingling | best seller |

His list is longer but this sampling is sufficient to begin the game. Column #3 is held steady but you may interchange the words in Columns #1 and #2. One possibility might be "a tempestuous, spine-tingling best seller." Another "a sensational, terrifying best seller." You may add to this list in any way you wish. He then quotes a number of blurbs taken from the backs of Bantam books. Here are three. "A high octane inferno raging to a terrifying climax on the Canadian coast." "A sweeping novel of three recklessly passionate women and three generations spawned in wealth, lust, and betrayals of Bloomtown, Texas." "A scorching epic that will entice, terrify, and grip you as it soars towards its shocking climax."

These are examples of what Carr meant by "the appeal is no longer to the reason of the citizen but to his gullibility" as well as illustrating what Lippmann called "an intensification of feeling and a degradation of significance." Each contains the "generic terms and abstract expressions" that de Tocqueville noted in 1830. What is a "high octane inferno?" What does it mean to be "spawned in wealth, lust, and betrayal?" And what constitutes a "scorching epic," especially one that both "soars" and "shocks?"

A good part of our communication today, especially as regards people, institutions, and ideas is through the creation and manipulation of "images." The *American Heritage Dictionary* lists as its fourth definition of "image":

> *a.  the concept of something that is held by the the public. b. the character projected by someone or something to the public.*

It is not uncommon to hear such statements as,

> "We're projecting the wrong image."
> "We're going to have to change our image."
> "His image has to be modified."
> "We've got to create a new image. The public isn't buying the one we have."
> "We can't do that. It doesn't fit our image."

Some years ago a soap manufacturer decided to market a new brand of bath soap and call it "Cleopatra." It was perhaps a coincidence, perhaps not, but the high powered media campaign was timed to the release of a "super colossal extravaganza of epic proportions" bearing the same name. The television ads showed an attractive young women dressed to resemble Cleopatra getting on busses, walking though malls, or just strolling down the street. All eyes followed her, supposedly to admire the quality of her skin. But the odds are that anyone dressed like that would attract attention. The movie was both an artistic and financial disaster. And so was the soap. One of the executives responded when asked why the product was being pulled from the market attributed its demise to the fact that it "projected the wrong image."

One can draw some small comfort from this failure. While we may be manipulated through our language, it is not yet an exact science nor is it likely to be. But to once again quote Bart Maverick, "You can fool all of the people some of the time and some of the people all of the time. And those are damn good odds."

When analyzing images, remember the items discussed under "labeling." A label will communicate a certain set of features. But anything, or anyone, is capable of bearing a number of labels each with its own set of features. Therefore, any label will distort whatever it purports to describe. The problem is not the distortion but the degree of it, as well as its purposes. We might all profit from the admonition Oliver Cromwell gave to the artist commissioned to paint his portrait.

*I desire you will use all your skill to paint my picture truly like me, and not to flatter me at all;, but remark all those roughnesses, pimples, warts, and everything as you see me; otherwise I will never pay one farthing for it.*

There is little likelihood, however, that anyone would like to have their image revealed "warts and all." The problem is not covering them up but the intent behind it. And this gives rise to yet another problem - one of responsibility.

Responsibility cuts in two directions: First, there is the responsibility of the person using the language to communicate meaning as accurately and precisely as their abilities permit. Second, there is the responsibility of the person on the receiving end to sort out the misleading from the substance; to establish some sort of middle ground between complete gullibility at the one end and total skepticism (even cynicism) at the other.

Will Rogers said he believed nothing he read and only half of what he saw. This is too skeptical. Nevertheless, it is well to cultivate a "systematic doubt" about what it is we read and hear when the purpose is to persuade us to adopt an attitude or path of behavior. The complete skeptic takes the position of some who contend that all of the juices have been squeezed from the language. That the constant and continued manipulation for whatever purposes has made it useless. Or, if not useless, then constantly suspect. Little is gained and much lost from adopting this attitude.

Neil Postman in his article, "Language is America," views language through the metaphor of a river. He sees the constant manipulation of meaning without any regard for responsibility as a polluting factor. His question is to what extent can we continue to pollute this river of language before it loses the ability to sustain meaning? This can happen only if people permit it. That is why one should shy away from the position of the pessimists. Also, what else do we have to communicate with? We cannot adopt the position of Swift's philosophers and lug about sacks filled with objects. Nor can we, like the characters in a play humorist Max Schulman created, go about sniffing "meaningfully" on benzedrine inhalers. We must develop the "systematic doubt."

What these materials have tried to do is provide the implements for building this systematic doubt by examining various aspects of language and meaning. In the final analysis, you must be the one who develops the criteria on which this doubt is based. Also, while we know a great deal about language and meaning as a uniquely human phenomenon, we do not as yet understand the implications of what we know in a moral and ethical sense. Not unlike an atomic physicist, we can create all sorts of destructive devices. But where does the responsibility for their use lie?

There is much more to learn and analyze about language and meaning. Some of the generalizations made may have to be modified or changed completely as more is known and deeper analysis becomes possible. The restructuring of present conclusions should not be distressing. All responsibly acquired human knowledge is based on the principle that as new information becomes known we must be prepared to modify or change our views if that information indicates the necessity. If you were a physicist who learned the subject in the first quarter of the twentieth century you would have had to have changed your views as many as three times. Einstein brought about the modification of Newtonian physics. Since then both have been modified. This does not mean that everything learned must be forgotten. It does mean that in the light of new information, ideas once held as true must now be modified or discarded.

Granted, language is not as empirically based as physics and the other hard sciences especially when meaning is added into the equation. While some have attempted, no one has successfully reduced meaning to the same rules found in mathematics. This can be done with the phonological system and to a degree with the syntactic. But the semantic system continues to defy precise classification for a number of reasons.

Meaning serves society and to a large degree helps shape its modes of perception. But people change, societies change, and language, in particular its semantic system, must change to reflect this. To the degree that we are aware of the factors which may control language and meaning we are, to that degree, in control. To the degree that we are unaware, we are controlled.

Novelist and essayist Aldous Huxley wrote,

> *Words are indispensable but also can be fatal. . . . Never before have so many listeners been so completely at the mercy of so few speakers. Never have misused words . . . been so widely and disastrously influential as they are today.*

> *[These are] good reasons for disliking the idea of universal education in the rational use of language . . . . Such training seems (and rightly so) profoundly subversive.*

This material, therefore, is subversive. Language was examined and questions raised about what language can do both in fact and theory in the formation of attitudes, perceptions, and values. Some regard the questioning of these as subversive.

Having discussed the potential of the metaphor to shape perception and through it meaning, it seems appropriate to close with one. These materials may be looked upon as the product of a rope factory. What you may wish to use this rope for is, in the final analysis, your responsibility. The same material can be used to make a noose or a ladder.

# BIBLIOGRAPHY

Note:    *This listing makes no pretense at being comprehensive.*

Berry, Lester V. and Melvin Van den Bark. *The American Thesaurus of Slang*. New York, 1953.

Brook, G.L. *A History of the English Language*. New York, 1964.

Bryant, Margaret A. *Modern English and Its Heritage*. New York, 1962.

Crystal, David. *The Cambridge Encyclopedia of Language*. New York, 1987.

Evans, Bergen and Cornelia Evans. *A Dictionary of Contemportary American Usage*. New York, 1957.

Farmer, J.S. and W.E. Henley. *Slang and Its Analogs*. Originally pub. 1910, New York, 1970.

Flexner, Stuart B. *I Hear America Talking*. New York, 1975.

———. *Listening to America*. New York, 1982.

Funk, Wilford. *Word Origins and Their Romantic Stories*. New York, 1978.

Gleason, H.A., Jr. *Linguistics and English Grammar*. New York, 1965.

Greenough, James B. and George Lyman Kitterage. *Words and Ways in American Speech*. New York, 1901.

Hook, J.N. *Family Names: How Our Surnames Came to America*. New York, 1982

Jesperson, Otto. *Growth and Structure of the English Language*, 9th ed. New York, 1961.

Jones, Charles. *A History of English Phonology*. London and New York, 1989.

Marchwardt, Albert H. *American English*. New York, 1958.

McArthur, Tom. *The Oxford Companion to the English Language*. New York, 1992.

Mencken, H.L. *The American Language*, 4th edition, abr. and ed. by Raven T. McDavid, Jr. New York, 1963.

Michaels, Leonard and Christopher Wicks. *The State of the Language*. Berkeley, 1980.

Myers, L.M. *The Roots of Modern English*. Boston, 1966.

Nist, John A. *A Structural History of English*. New York, 1966.

Partridge, Eric. *Shakespeare's Bawdry*. New York, 1958.

Potter, Simeon. *Our Language*. London, 1950.

Pyles, Thomas. *Words and Ways in American English*. New York, 1958.

——————. *The Origins and Development of the English Language*, 2nd ed. New York, 1971.

*Put-Downs and Other Formerly Unprintable Terms from Anglo-Saxon Times to the Present.* New York, 1989.

Schlauch, Margaret. *The English Language in Modern Times: Since 1400.* Warsaw, 1959.

Sergeantson, Mary S. *A History of Foreign Words in English.* London, 1935.

Sheard, J.A. *The Words of English.* New York, 1958.

Shipley, Joseph T. *In Praise of English: The Growth and Use of Language.* 1975.

Strang, Barbara. *A History of English.* New York, 1970.

Wentworth, Harold and Stuart B. Flexner. *Dictionary of Contemporary American Slang*, 2nd ed. New York, 1975.

Williams, Joseph M. *Origins of the English Language: A Social and Linguistic History.* New York, 1975.

****************************

*The Oxford English Dictionary.* Now available in the two volume compact edition complete with magnifying glass. Volume 3, the Supplement, is also available in a compact edition.

# INDEX